The Protestant Experience in Gary, Indiana, 1906–1975

The Protestant Experience in Gary, Indiana, 1906-1975: At Home in the City

JAMES W. LEWIS

The University of Tennessee Press / Knoxville

Library of Congress Cataloging-in-Publication Data

Lewis, James Welborn.
    The Protestant experience in Gary, Indiana. 1906–1975 : at home in
the city / James W. Lewis. — 1st ed.
        p.   cm.
    Includes bibliographical references and index.
    ISBN 0-87049-737-5 (cloth: alk. paper)
    1. First Presbyterian Church (Gary, Ind.) 2. City Methodist
Church (Gary, Ind.) 3. Protestants—Indiana—Gary—History.
4. Gary (Ind.)—Church history. 5. Gary (Ind.)—History.
I. Title.
BR560.G35L48   1992
285'.177299—dc20   91-24752
                                                                  CIP

*To my parents, W. T. and Marie Lewis,
and my wife, Marcia Lewis.*

Contents

Illustrations

Tables

Preface

This is living, breathing, sweating, drinking, cursing, laughing, singing Gary.
ARTHUR SHUMWAY, 1929

This is the story of two religious congregations in Gary, Indiana, from 1906 to 1975. On the face of it, it is not a subject to make one's blood race. But as journalist Arthur Shumway discovered of Gary's immigrant quarter in the 1920s, there is vitality and meaning in the life of a city that is worthy of study. Although Gary's mainstream Protestants probably did a little less sweating and perhaps less drinking and cursing than did the immigrants lauded by Shumway, their story too is worth the telling.

When I began this study a decade ago, I sought to answer one major question—how did mainstream Protestantism fare in the twentieth-century industrial city? Poorly, I assumed, since that was the consensus of most scholars of twentieth-century urban Protestantism. Unlike these previous scholars, however, I approached this question by studying two local congregations in the unambiguously urban-industrial setting of Gary, Indiana. As I worked through the extensive records of Gary's major Presbyterian and Methodist congregations, I discovered evidence of quite remarkable vitality until at least the early 1950s. Despite their subsequent decline, those two congregations were very much at home in the city—an important conclusion with implications for both urban historians and American religious historians.

American urban historians have, by and large, paid only cursory attention to the role of urban religious institutions. Although they acknowledge their presence, these historians rarely appreciate their profound contribution to American urban life. More rarely still do they examine closely the local texture of urban religious experience. But, if Gary is any indication,

America's urban citizens in the first half of the twentieth century regarded churches and synagogues as integral to American urban life. Moreover, as the following pages illustrate, Gary's Protestant congregations played a significant role in shaping life in the city.

This story also contributes to our understanding of American religious history in at least two ways. First, the experience of Gary's Protestants suggests that historians should take greater care in assessing the urban role of American Protestantism. Admittedly Protestantism's greatest strength remained outside the central cities, but its influence on America's cities, which was significant well into the twentieth century, merits increased scholarly attention. Second, the story of Gary suggests that the experience of local congregations is a rich, and largely ignored, resource for understanding American religious history.

In attempting to understand the role of Gary's religious congregations, it is necessary to place them against the backdrop of Gary's political as well as its social history. What follows, then, is in some ways a history of Gary, Indiana, as seen from the perspective of its religious congregations. But it is also a history of two congregations which attempts to take seriously their role as distinctively urban religious institutions. Beyond the several scholarly implications of this story lies its significance as a human drama, for Gary's Protestants were men and women striving to make sense of their lives in an exciting and challenging urban environment. Whatever else these Protestants did in Gary, they came to be, perhaps astonishingly, at home in the city.

I would like to express my appreciation to the many persons who provided ready access to research materials, including the reference librarians at both the Gary Public Library and the University of Chicago, Professor Ronald D. Cohen and Mr. Stephen McShane at the Calumet Regional Archives at Indiana University Northwest, Mr. David Horn and Mr. Wesley Wilson at the Archives of DePauw University and Indiana United Methodism, and the Reverends Roderic P. Frohman and Wendy Pratt at the First United Presbyterian Church in Gary.

Professor Martin Marty guided the University of Chicago dissertation on which this study is based and provided timely advice as teacher, adviser, colleague, and friend. Former Dean Franklin Gamwell encouraged me throughout the project, and Dr. Robert Lynn, formerly Senior Vice President for Religion at the Lilly Endowment, Inc., supported my interest in the history of American congregations in many ways. Professors Jerald Brauer and Arthur Mann read the original dissertation manuscript with a critical eye. I am also grateful for the perceptive suggestions for improvement from Professors Samuel Hill, Stan Lusby, and Peter Williams. I assume responsibility, of course, for errors or misjudgments that remain.

Finally, I wish to acknowledge my profound gratitude to those to whom this book is dedicated—my parents and my wife. The Reverend W. T. and Marie Lewis were my first and most influential teachers regarding the fundamental significance of religious faith in human experience and the vitality of local religious congregations. Marcia Lewis provided both a listening ear and unfailing encouragement throughout these years. Her love and support mean more than I can say, and, although she knows I have difficulty telling a debit from a credit, she should know that I am deeply and permanently in her debt.

CHAPTER ONE

Cities and Congregations

INTRODUCTION

In the early spring of 1906, three employees of the United States Steel Corporation drove a stake into a sand dune near the southern tip of Lake Michigan, thus marking what was to become the major intersection of the new town of Gary, Indiana.[1] By 1930 the infant settlement had grown to a young city of over a hundred thousand people and had spawned at least thirty schools and ninety-eight churches—all this in addition to boasting the largest steel mill the world had ever seen.[2]

Steel was undoubtedly the principal reason for Gary's existence. Concerned about both U.S. Steel's declining market share of the steel industry and its inadequate production facilities in the rapidly growing Chicago region, corporate officials decided in 1905 to build a massive new steel mill in the wetlands of northwest Indiana.[3] Their dream was to retain the dominance over the steel industry which U.S. Steel had enjoyed since incorporating in 1901, a dream dependent largely on the success of the strategically located new steel facility in Gary.

But Gary was much more than a steel mill. Once the corporation chose its isolated site in the dunes, it had to create a town near the mill, and Gary was born. Gary's first permanent residents quickly created the institutional infrastructure of a twentieth-century city—a municipal government, schools, housing, and business establishments.

They also established churches and synagogues, and alongside the dream of industrial dominance arose the dream of a Gary in which religious institutions undergirded municipal morality and respectability. To a remarkable extent both dreams were realized—for a time. U.S. Steel continued to dominate the American steel industry for decades, and its Gary plant was among its proudest achievements. Moreover, although outsiders often derided the city of Gary for its astounding number of saloons, many Garyites pointed instead to its vigorous religious congregations as evidence of growing urban maturity.

By the mid-1970s, however, both dreams had faded. The decline of the American steel industry in the face of automated foreign competition and systemic changes in the American economy spelled economic doom for the city in the dunes, and Gary itself became a national symbol of urban malaise. Many of its mainstream Protestant churches closed or moved to the suburbs.

But in Gary's first three or four decades, the ministers and rabbis of the larger congregations were significant public figures, and churches and synagogues were among Gary's most important social institutions. In important ways, Gary's religious institutions, including its mainstream Protestant churches, were an integral part of the city and thoroughly at home there. This claim, however, flies in the face of most scholarly accounts of American urban Protestantism in the early twentieth century, which have attributed to these years a pervasive Protestant distaste for the industrial city. Historians have maintained that Protestantism's rural roots nourished an anti-urban bias that hampered its ability to survive, or at least to thrive, in the twentieth-century city.

Admittedly American urban life had undergone radical change by the early twentieth century. Taken together, industrialization, immigration, and urbanization virtually created modern America. Formerly a predominantly agricultural and commercial country, the United States became an industrial giant. From a relatively homogeneous rural society emerged a pluralistic urban one. Although all these developments were underway by mid-nineteenth century, their acceleration in the last half of the century ingrained them forever on the American psyche. Like it or not (and many Americans did not), the United States by 1900 had become a pluralistic, urban industrial society.[4]

The transformation was a difficult one for many Americans, and it proved particularly troublesome for American Protestants, who had long exercised cultural hegemony over a relatively homogeneous, rural, agrarian society. But, in fact, the transformation did not immobilize them or drive them from the cities. Indeed at least some Protestant congregations sought to create in these new cities a distinctively urban Protestantism—a

Protestantism at home in the city. This, then, is the story of two such congregations in Gary, Indiana, and the relationship between these congregations and the city they called home.

CITIES

Protestant Ambivalence Toward the City

In 1630, aboard the ship *Arbella*, Governor John Winthrop of the Massachusetts Bay Colony wrote about the colonists' decision to move to New England and predicted that "wee shall be as a Citty upon a Hill, the eies of all people are uppon us." Winthrop's vivid metaphor assumed a life of its own in the American imagination and provided an enduring vision of a redeemed society that influenced many nineteenth-century American thinkers as they confronted the increasingly evident ills of an urban industrial society.[5]

Among these thinkers were those Protestant ministers and reformers who espoused what came to be known as the "social gospel." In both their analysis of urban problems and the methods they adopted to remedy them, these social activists resembled in many ways their more secular colleagues in the reform movement, both in this country and in Europe.[6] They shared with them as well a certain ambivalence toward the city. According to historian Andrew Lees, Europe's anti-urban critics frequently blamed the bad physical conditions of the cities—and even their physical ugliness—for the religious and moral decline and loss of social control to be found there. Pro-urban writers, on the other hand, concluded that the gains in individual liberty that urban life provided were worth the cost and that the cities themselves were, in fact, generating solutions to their own problems. Most European observers, Lees concluded, saw the city as "a complex mixture of both good and evil."[7] The same could be said of American observers as well.

This mixture of good and evil was apparent, for example, to such prominent Protestant spokespersons as Samuel Lane Loomis, Josiah Strong, Graham Taylor, Charles Stelzle, Paul Strayer, and Harlan Paul Douglass—all of whom were perhaps ambivalent but certainly not hostile toward the city.[8] In spite of the fact that they generally came from small-town backgrounds, as did many commentators on the city in the Progressive period, they did not hate the city. Of the six, only Taylor (Schenectady) and Stelzle (New York City) were born in cities. Strayer (Edesville, Maryland), Strong (Naperville, Illinois), Loomis (Littleton, Massachusetts), and Douglass (Osage, Iowa) were born in small towns.[9] They were, of course, painfully aware of its many social problems. But they also understood what Arthur Schlesinger called the "lure of the city," to which, after all, they themselves had succumbed. Samuel Lane Loomis, for example, described the city as a magnet that drew people to it irresistibly, citing Charles Lamb's observation on the appeal of London: "The wonder of these sights impels me into night walks about her crowded streets, and I often shed tears in the motley Strand from fullness of joy at so much life."[10]

Even Josiah Strong had mixed feelings. As general secretary of the Evangelical Alliance, Strong urged Protestants to save America's cities from the immigrant and Catholic invasion that threatened them. But his fervent rhetoric has often misled historians, who have concluded that Strong was fundamentally hostile to the city. Richard Hofstadter, for example, quotes both Strong's remark that "the first city was built by the first murderer, and crime and vice and wretchedness have festered in it ever since" and his citation from Shelley that "hell is a city much like London."[11] But in fact, Strong's view of the city was more nuanced than his rhetoric. Quoting his contemporary, Lyman Abbott, Strong clearly illustrated a fundamental ambivalence toward the city: ". . . on the one hand, the city stands for all that is evil—a city that is full of devils, foul and corrupting; and, on the other hand, the city stands for all that is noble, full of the glory of God, and shining with a clear and brilliant light. . . . It has been so in the past. It is so in the present."[12]

Sometimes this ambivalence was reflected in comparisons of the rural and city church. Many Protestants assumed, sometimes explicitly but usually implicitly, that Protestant churches were essentially rural institutions which were ill adapted to the city. A particularly flagrant example of this assumption is Carl Douglas Wells's 1934 study, *The Changing City Church*. Noting that "the Protestant church took its roots in American life when the vast majority of Americans lived in rural areas" (9), Wells claimed that the church's lack of success in the city resulted from the difficulty of "transferring a religious heritage from a rural to an urban environment" (7). Concluding with a flourish of sartorial imagery, he claimed (34) that ". . . religious institutions will succeed in the city only after they have been adapted to their new urban environment. The truths of religion are not changed in the process, but rather these truths are dressed up in urban clothes so they will be able to attract and serve the urban personality."[13]

But this assumption that Protestantism was essentially rural was often qualified to a far greater extent than recent scholars have acknowledged. Both Paul Strayer and Charles Stelzle, for example, explicitly denied that Protestantism was any healthier in the country than in the city.[14] They conceded that the city posed a serious challenge to Protestant Christianity, but it was a challenge which could be met successfully. In a similar vein, Harlan Paul Douglass acknowledged that Protestantism had suffered substantial losses in the city but also praised the marvelous ability of the church to adapt to urban conditions. In face of the fragmentation characteristic of modern urban life, Douglass proposed that religion had a more important integrative task than it had ever known before.[15]

Contemporary Protestant Historians and the City

Although not unaware of this Protestant ambivalence toward the city, scholars have tended to emphasize Protestant misfortunes in and complaints about the city. Despite the work of Strong, Stelzle, and others, they have thus reinforced the assumption that turn-of-the-century Protestants were basically antagonistic to the industrial city. Truman Douglass, for example, claims that "in almost direct proportion to the increasing importance of the city in American culture has been the withdrawal—both physical and spiritual—of the Protestant Church." Likewise sociologist William Petersen claims that "the Protestant ethos has long supported, and seems to continue to sustain, an anti-urban animus." Says Petersen, "the Protestant churches are rooted in rural America, linked to rural institutions, made up of rural-bred people."[16]

Although generally stated somewhat less baldly, this assumption also pervades the work of recent American religious historians. Robert Handy, for example, both reports it and reflects it when he observes both that "one of the reasons that city churches long have had difficulties is a stubborn tradition that religion is at home in the country but alien in the city, and that the patterns of the rural church are normative for the religious life. . . . Especially in the formative decades of the early nineteenth century, the churches found the atmosphere of rural America congenial, and were significantly involved in and influenced by the culture of the time with its agrarian individualistic motifs."[17] According to Handy, urban America was less congenial than rural America, and by the late nineteenth century the city was a "menace to be resisted and redirected into familiar Protestant patterns—this was the predominant understanding among Protestants at the turn of the century."[18] Sydney Ahlstrom agrees, seeing the Protestant rural bias as part of a more "fundamental difficulty of evaluating urban civilization itself and weighing its values in the light of the nation's agrarian past." He also notes that "the great reservoir of Protestantism lay in the middle-class churches of rural and smalltown America until long after 1920, when the census finally revealed that most Americans were city dwellers."[19] In discussing Josiah Strong, Martin Marty emphasizes the ethnic diversity of the cities, noting that "the new multitudes jammed into the cities, making these centers the most fearful jungles of the 'manyness' that threatened the Anglo-Saxon empire."[20] Finally Catherine Albanese, focusing on this manyness in American religion, observes that in the twentieth century "the increased urbanization of American culture caught many Protestants off guard and ill prepared. Protestantism had been a rural religion, and now it had to face an America whose future lay with the cities."[21] There is, then, a rather well-established consensus that Protestantism's rural identity hindered its ability to come to terms with urban America.[22]

But no matter how widely accepted it may be, this consensus is problematic for at least two reasons. First, the consensus seems to assume that Protestantism was unique in its rural bias, thus accounting for its comparative lack of success in the cities.[23] Without denying that nineteenth-century Protestants exhibited some rural bias (they probably did), they reflected a general cultural bias in so doing. Robert Cross, for example, has identified a similar inclination on the part of American Catholics, citing a quite remarkable panegyric by Bishop John Spaulding of Peoria: "Happy is the country child. With bare head and bare feet he wanders through wood and field . . . and drives the cattle home at milking-time; and all his dreams of peace and love gather around his mother and the home fireside. . . . Let his after lot be what it will, he has had at the outset twelve years of sweet liberty, and the dews of this fair dawn will keep still some freshness in his heart."[24] Such rural bias as there was, then, was not unique to Protestantism.

Second, the consensus confuses the descriptive and the normative. Acknowledging the descriptive conclusion that the dominant religious tradition in a predominantly agrarian culture found that culture congenial, the consensus then presumes that the religious tradition continued to accept that agrarian culture as normative, even in a new cultural situation. Maybe it did, and maybe it did not. But the situation is not as simple as the consensus claims. Indeed, as historian Herbert Gutman has noted, tradition itself often has been an important resource for a people confronting modernity. Similarly, Raymond Williams, in an important work on recent Indian and Pakistani immigrants to the United States, observes that many of them "are more religiously active and committed than before, with new identities formed in continuity with personal and group memory of the social and religious places they left, but requiring attention to new neighbors, new patterns of relationship, and adaptations of the beliefs and rituals to accommodate their new cultural situation."[25] It is quite conceivable, that is, that persons nurtured in the bosom of rural Protestantism might move into the city, adapting their faith successfully to a radically new cultural situation. That is, in fact, precisely what happened in Gary.

CONGREGATIONS

If scholars of American religious history have been ambivalent about cities they have also been inattentive to congregations. They have focused instead on denominational and broader cultural events such as the rise of the social gospel, the development of fundamentalism, and the debate over evolution.[26] Perhaps, as Martin Marty has suggested (citing Jacob Burckhardt), "the most important things do not get written because they are so important, so close to us, so taken for granted that we see no reason to remark upon them."[27] Or perhaps other religious phenomena (such as America's distinctive denominational pattern or its colorful theological warfare) or other promising historiographical approaches (such as social history, ethnic history, and women's history) have coopted the field.[28] Be that as it may, studies of the congregation in America have, since at least the 1930s, been dominated by amateur local historians on the one hand and social scientists, especially sociologists, on the other.[29] Histories of specific congregations, often brief accounts prepared by congregational members for church anniversaries and the like, typically are more chronicle than history.[30] Scholarly historical accounts of congregations are comparatively rare, and those that exist are not readily available.[31]

American religious history and Gary's religious history are, of course, more than the history of their religious congregations. But the history of congregations and their people can constitute what historian Jonathan Sarna calls the building blocks of a more comprehensive religious history.[32] A building block is not a building. But without the blocks the building remains a blueprint. To know Gary's religious history is at least to know its congregations.

In Gary, the importance of the public, civil function of religious congregations will be apparent in the pages that follow. In 1926, for example, Gary's forty-two thousand church members gathered into eighty-two congregations representing at least thirty-five denominations.[33] It was at least partly in Gary's religious congregations that moral and religious precepts brought from elsewhere—rural Indiana, Pennsylvania, Mississippi, Ireland, Transylvania, Mexico—were passed down from one generation to another. Moreover the congregations and their leaders played an important role in defining the city's moral order. When, for example, political vice and corruption were attacked, it was often Gary's religious leaders who led the charge. When the moral order faltered, as it did, for example, in Gary's persistent school segregation, it was Gary's congregations that had to shoulder some of the blame.

Not surprisingly, Gary's congregations also played a vital private role in the lives of Gary's citizens. From the top to the bottom of the social ladder, Gary's citizens participated in religious congregations to a significant degree.[34] Many basic family rites—baptisms, weddings, funerals, and so forth—were congregational rites. If one is to understand history "from the bottom up" one must understand the essential role of religious congregations at this private level.

If Gary's congregations played both private and public roles, they also mediated between the two.[35] Many Garyites were reared, married, worshipped, died in congregations. Like religious institutions everywhere, Gary's churches and synagogues provided their members a perspective on life and a source of meaning. But these same institutions also existed as social entities and helped their members situate themselves amidst Gary's diverse and confusing urban milieu. On the one hand, congregational lines were boundary lines, helping members identify themselves socially and ethnically over against members of other groups. To be a Serbian Orthodox was not to be a black Baptist, or a white Presbyterian, or a Jew, or even a Greek Orthodox. But on the other hand, congregations provided opportunities for service to other Gary residents and supported such efforts initiated elsewhere. They attempted to define what responsible and moral political participation might mean in the modern city, assisting their members to relate their private lives and religious sensibilities to the wider public arena of which they were a part. As Marty has recently observed, congregations themselves are a kind of public that helps members learn to function in the public realm.[36]

In the pages that follow, then, I argue that urban Protestant congregations, represented by Gary's First Presbyterian Church and City Methodist Church, played an important, active, and often overlooked role in America's cities until at least the middle of the twentieth century and that their subsequent failures in the city should not blind us to their earlier accomplishments there. In the words of my title, they were "at home in the city." But before we can understand these two congregations, it is essential to know something about Gary.

GARY

A Methodological Prologue

Gary, Indiana, is an especially appropriate test case for a reexamination of the scholarly consensus about turn-of-the-century American urban Protestantism. As scholars such as Liston Pope, Stephan Thernstrom, and Michael Frisch have suggested, larger theoretical issues are often best illuminated by in-depth studies of specific cities.[37] The danger of such detailed studies, of course, is that idiosyncrasy may be mistaken for normality, and Gary, admittedly, is not a perfectly representative American city.[38] But as historians Raymond Mohl and Neil Betten have claimed, "the history of Gary provides, in microcosm, a view of the rise and fall of the American industrial city."[39] Notwithstanding its relative youth, its unbalanced economy, and its precipitous decline, Gary is an almost ideal location in which to test the accepted stereotype about Protestant problems in American cities.

Established in 1906, Gary arose in the full light of day, insofar as American urbanization is concerned, and its early leaders were highly intentional about creating a city. Unlike Pittsburgh or Cleveland, for example, Gary had virtually no preindustrial history. In fact, despite several unsuccessful attempts to establish settlements there in the late nineteenth century, Gary exists principally because of the founding hand of U.S. Steel. It is the industrial city par excellence.

Moreover Gary has become a microcosm of the racial change and economic decline that have overwhelmed many "rust belt" cities in the United States. Its increasing African-American political power, culminating in the 1967 election of Mayor Richard Hatcher, also made it a political precursor of such other cities as Newark and Detroit. But political empowerment could not prevent either the economic downturn in the steel industry in the 1970s or the changing federal policies toward cities. Consequently, Gary remained a city of poverty, unemployment, crime, and physical deterioration—a national symbol of urban blight.[40]

Thus, as the Gary of the 1920s illustrates the young, prosperous industrial city, so the Gary of the 1970s reflects modern urban decay. A detailed study of Gary in both periods enables us to reassess the traditional wisdom about the Protestant plight in the industrial city.

Gary's Protestants

Discovery of either a Protestant avoidance of the new city of Gary or a failure to establish an effective presence there would confirm the historical consensus that turn-of-the-century Protestantism was no friend of the industrial city. But the facts were otherwise. In striking contrast to the stereotype, Gary's Protestants knew at first hand that the United States was becoming an urban society and were among its creators—proudly and self-consciously urban. They also knew that urbanization meant change, and they came to Gary in search of it. As urban men and women they appreciated both the church's contribution to urban change and its traditional, conserving role in the social order.

By the 1960s, however, Gary's Protestants, like their counterparts in other American cities, found that the nature and pace of change had outstripped their ability to adapt. But for fifty years in Gary, and almost one hundred years in the rest of the United States, Protestants engaged in a sometimes heroic effort, not to transplant a rural church to an urban setting, but to discern how to live as Protestant Christians in a rapidly changing urban world. There were failures aplenty, but they were not the failures, at least in Gary, of an anachronistic attempt to recreate the rural church in the big city.

In the end Gary's Protestants were victims, not of rural nostalgia or urban antipathy, but of rapid urban change and of social forces beyond their control. They were, however, not just victims. In their day, as we shall see, Gary's mainstream Protestants found in their churches a source of personal meaning for their lives. But they found as well a source of communal meaning, of civic conscience, of social reform. Their failure in later years to retain that sense of community does not mean that the original vision was mistaken. But it does suggest that their vision for urban America in the 1920s was not a vision for all time.

In a remarkable essay on "Religion in the City," British historian Hugh McLeod has observed that ". . . even where religious institutions are relatively uninfluential, there is still a need to show what systems of explaining the world, of giving purpose to individual life, of sanctifying obligation, of coping with suffering *have* been effective; which symbols of community, of the good life, or of something beyond the individual *have* evoked a response; how men have faced the death of others, or their own."[41] In contemporary Gary other institutions perform those tasks, but in Gary's early decades, active, mainstream Protestant congregations did so. In those years the significance of religion was apparent, and its influence was pervasive. I have not, it should be noted, chosen white, mainstream Protestant congregations because they were the most important or numerically dominant. Indeed Roman Catholic and Orthodox congregations may well have been more important to more people in Gary than their Protestant counterparts. But, despite their minority status, Gary's mainstream Protestant congregations were of distinctive public significance. They included on their rolls an inordinate percentage of Gary's leadership elite and were prominent institutional participants in Gary's public life. Moreover they provide an opportunity to reassess in a local setting the historical consensus about the rapid decline of urban mainstream Protestantism after World War I.[42]

First Presbyterian Church and City Methodist Church

Representing the heart of mainstream Protestantism, both First Presbyterian Church and City Methodist Church were major downtown congregations that ministered to Gary's social and economic elite. But they also sought, in different ways, to minister to the broader city as well. In general, the Presbyterians maintained a more traditional, evangelical stance over against the city, characteristic of an "Old First Church." Much of their energy was directed inward, to the needs of their own membership and the institutional maintenance of the congregation, even while they supported settlement houses and spoke out on selected social issues. By contrast, the Methodists, at least from 1916 to World War II, directed their energies outward, attending more explicitly to their vision for the whole city, even while they attended as well to their own institutional welfare and the needs of their membership. If the First Presbyterian Church exemplified "Old First Church," the City Methodist Church exemplified the "Social Gospel Cathedral."

Standard histories of early twentieth-century American religion frequently emphasize the role of the social gospel and tend to judge the social engagement of congregations by the extent to which they adopted social gospel strategies for urban ministry. Taking the social gospel as a measuring rod, these accounts typically focus on the role of liberal urban congregations.[43] On the other theological hand, George Marsden has written persuasively about the urban reform strategy of even the more conservative end of the evangelical spectrum, as figures like William Bell Riley and Dwight L. Moody sought to restore the social hegemony of their vision of evangelical Protestantism.[44] In fact, both evangelicalism and social gospel liberalism continued to inform mainstream urban Protestants.[45]

By evangelicalism, I refer to the broad consensus in nineteenth-century American Protestantism which emphasized the importance of an individual religious conversion experience. According to Sydney Ahlstrom's classic description, the main features of this evangelical Protestant establishment were "the infallibility of the Scriptures, the divinity of Christ, and man's duty to be converted from the ways of sin to a life guided by a pietistic code of morals." In recent years, of course, the term "evangelical" has come to refer almost exclusively to that group of theologically conservative Protestants who wish to distinguish themselves from both liberal mainstream Protestants on the one hand and fundamentalist Protestants on the other. Historian Harry Stout, however, has suggested that even the contemporary distinction between evangelical and liberal is sometimes misleading. "Denominationalism in America constitutes a great safety valve and unifying device . . . a ground for peaceable cohabitation amidst great debate. Lying beneath the shouting worlds of liberals and evangelicals is an unacknowledged hybrid Protestantism in which each borrows freely (if secretly) from the other in sincere attempts to satisfy the complete temporal and eternal demands of a gospel that neither side can fully accomplish alone." My findings in Gary tend to confirm Stout's hypothesis.

The history of the two congregations studied here confirms that mainstream Protestants in the first half of the twentieth century drew on both sides of their heritage—evangelicalism and social gospel liberalism—as they developed their own style of urban ministry. The mix varied from congregation to congregation and from one period to another. In Gary, First Presbyterian Church relied more heavily as a rule on the evangelical tradition, while City Methodist Church more often embraced the social gospel approach to the city. But in fact each congregation, to some extent, was both evangelical and social gospel. At City Methodist Church, the progressive William Grant Seaman insisted on the necessity of personal conversion, while at First Presbyterian Church the revivalistic Frederick Backemeyer also worked for urban political reform.

On the face of it, this is an obvious point. But it does fly in the face of two common misperceptions about mainstream Protestantism in the city. On the one hand is the assumption that evangelical piety was ill suited to the modern industrial city and undermined Protestant fortunes there. On the other hand is the notion that, although the social gospel inspired a noble Protestant attempt to deal with the city at the turn of the century, that attempt collapsed by the end of World War I. As we shall see in the following pages, the histories of Gary's First Presbyterian Church and City Methodist Church suggest that mainstream Protestant congregations attempted vigorously to respond to and shape their urban environment until well into the twentieth century. To a remarkable extent, they were at home in Gary—the city described in the next four chapters.

CHAPTER TWO

Gary, Indiana: Early Years

THREE IMAGES OF EARLY GARY

Perhaps because of Gary's unusually colorful past, it never forgot its early history. In retelling Gary's story, local historians frequently employed one of three vivid images to describe the city, images which served both descriptive and apologetic functions. One—a kind of biological image—personified Gary as initially a rapidly growing infant and later a boisterous adolescent. In 1927, for example, the *Gary Post-Tribune* praised Gary's growth "from a struggling infant cradled in industry's arms to a mighty giant in civic things in the short span of a score of years." This metaphor helped explain away Gary's unsavory reputation for vice and political corruption as little more than young Gary's period of "sowing wild oats" before a more responsible adulthood. Another image of Gary its historians frequently conjured up was that of a raw but exciting frontier town, an image that served a similar apologetic function. Like other frontier towns, Gary's initial roughness would surely give way to cultural sophistication and civic virtue, according to Gary's supporters.[1]

Gary's frontier was, of course, an industrial frontier, and the third persistent image one finds in histories of the city is an industrial one. Gary's urban boosters repeatedly praised its rapid development to a position of industrial prominence. For example, in a 1928 pamphlet, "Gary at a Glance," the Chamber of Commerce claimed that Gary's "unparalleled growth in twenty-two years to a city of 110,000 makes it one of the industrial wonders of the twentieth century."[2] The industrial image helped explain both Gary's large immigrant population and its accompanying social problems. But it also accounted for the close connection between the city of

Gary and the United States Steel Corporation and claimed for the new city a world-historical significance. Not content to live in the dominant industrial center of northwest Indiana, Gary's boosters hailed it as the future steel capital of the world. Indeed in 1926, the *Gary Post-Tribune* crowed that Gary "is the wonder city of the nation and destined to become the great industrial center of the universe."[3]

Brash adolescent, frontier outpost, steel town extraordinary—these self-images persisted throughout Gary's first half-century. Gary as the City of Steel was, of course, the dominant image as Gary left behind its adolescent and frontier past, underscoring the abiding importance of Judge Elbert Gary and the United States Steel Corporation.

U.S. STEEL AND GARY, INDIANA

Judge Gary and His City

Although he never lived in Gary, "the Judge" influenced its development profoundly in its first two decades. The son of devout Methodist parents, Elbert Gary earned a reputation for scrupulously honest business practices as chairman of U.S. Steel's Executive Committee. As chairman, he exercised immense influence in the management of U.S. Steel and played a critical role in its early public and governmental relations.[4] Compared to his peers Gary was, according to historian James Lane, "an enlightened innovator who championed cooperation, balance, frankness, mutual interest and goodwill." He helped encourage such reforms in the steel industry as a reduction of the seven-day work week and improvements in safety and workman's compensation. But he did so as much for business as for moral reasons. For example, while instructing U.S. Steel officials about employee welfare, Gary urged them to ". . . make the Steel Corporation a good place for them to work and live. Don't let the families go hungry or cold; give them playgrounds and parks and schools and churches, pure water to drink, every opportunity to keep clean, places of enjoyment, rest, and recreation; treating the whole thing as a business proposition . . . keeping the whole thing in your own hands, but nevertheless with due consideration to the rights and interests of all others who may be affected by your management."[5]

Whatever other sources informed his ethical position, Gary's staunch

Methodist convictions were significant. According to Tarbell, he was active in the Wheaton, Illinois, church and a member of the official board. Although he left the church after criticism by a minister on a matter of industrial relations, he remained generous to Methodist churches and organizations and renewed his Methodist membership toward the end of his life.[6] Brody noted that as "a Methodist and a moralist, he had a reputation of unshakable rectitude." But Lane observed that he could also be selective in his appropriation of the Christian tradition: "He quoted Scripture to support his labor politics but ignored the biblical injunction against working on the Sabbath." He also staunchly opposed organized labor and resisted the eight-hour day until forced to adopt it in 1923 by public opinion and presidential pressure from Warren G. Harding.[7] According to Lane, however, Gary's autocratic attitudes toward labor "sprang less from greed than from his naiveté about plant conditions and his aloofness from those at the bottom of the corporate ladder."[8]

Although the Judge never lived in Gary, he retained a paternalistic interest in the city which combined personal pride, a mixture of philanthropic impulses, and what he took to be sound business practices.[9] Recipients of his and U.S. Steel's "corporate liberalism," for example, included churches (white, black, and immigrant), the YMCA and YWCA, settlement houses, parks, and the library. Indeed according to historian Powell Moore, "hardly a church, hospital, welfare or civic organization in the city failed to receive a contribution from the steel company."[10] Distant though he was, Elbert Gary was a major influence in the city's first twenty years. But his principal importance to the city that bore his name was his connection with the corporation that first created and then, with varying degrees of success, dominated the town.

From before the city's birth until the present day, the history of Gary, Indiana, has been intertwined with that of the United States Steel Corporation. Like Gary itself, U.S. Steel was a twentieth-century creation. Although the steel industry grew dramatically in the last half of the nineteenth century, responding to the demand for steel for construction of railroads and cities, it was only in 1901 that the trend toward consolidation and economy in the industry climaxed in the organization of the United States Steel Corporation. In that year, J. P. Morgan bought out Andrew Carnegie's steel concerns, thus bringing under one corporate roof 213 previously independent manufacturing and transportation companies. Elbert Gary, long a proponent of an integrated steel operation in control of all phases of production from raw materials to finished products, was chosen by Morgan to be chairman of the Executive Committee of the new corporation. After a relatively brief power struggle with Carnegie's protégé, Charles Schwab, Gary became chairman of the board and chief executive officer.[11]

By 1905 Judge Gary and others in the corporation concluded that U.S. Steel's production facilities in the Chicago region were inadequate to meet the Midwest's rising demand for steel. The corporation's declining share of the market since 1901 further confirmed their conclusion. Although U.S. Steel had made 66.2 percent of the country's Bessemer and open hearth steel ingots in 1901, that percentage had fallen to 60.2 by 1905. Furthermore, U.S. Steel wanted to increase its capacity for open hearth production, which had been replacing the less efficient Bessemer process since 1900. Expansion of existing facilities at South Chicago was impossible, given the amount of land required for the large integrated plant envisioned by U.S. Steel leadership. The corporation did decide, however, that a new facility should be built in the Chicago region, which was roughly equidistant from the necessary raw materials (iron ore from Minnesota, limestone from Michigan, and coking coal from West Virginia and Kentucky), was served by inexpensive water transport, and was the transportation center for the Midwest steel market. So in 1905 Judge Gary instructed Armanis F. Knotts, a Hammond, Indiana, attorney, to examine several possible sites in the Chicago region. Knotts recommended a site in Indiana at the southern tip of Lake Michigan, east of Hammond. That he and his brother, Tom, later profited from Gary land sales should, at least, be noted in passing.[12]

Be that as it may, in July 1905 Knotts began to purchase large tracts of land in cash without identifying his client so as to keep the price from escalating.[13] Eventually U.S. Steel purchased some nine thousand acres, including more than seven miles of Lake Michigan shoreline, at a cost of $7.2 million.[14] Mainly an uninhabited tract of dunes wilderness, some of the land had been a hunting preserve for wealthy Chicagoans such as Potter Palmer and Marshall Field.[15] The site adjoined a few small settlements, later incorporated into Gary, such as Tolleston, Miller, Calumet, and Clark Station, and was crisscrossed by no fewer than seven railroad lines, which provided essential transportation through the dunes and marshes. According to Lane, for example, before the railroads the fifty-mile trip from Michigan City to Chicago took six days by horse team.[16]

On March 8, 1906, Ralph Rowley, Armanis and Thomas Knotts, and

The intersection of Fifth Avenue and Broadway (from the southeast corner looking toward the northwest) under construction, July 1, 1907. The Gary State Bank (headed by W. W. Gasser, a member of First Presbyterian Church) is in upper left-hand corner. Designed to be Gary's major intersection, Fifth Avenue was eighty feet wide and Broadway was one hundred feet wide. Courtesy of Calumet Regional Archives, Indiana University Northwest.

several other U.S. Steel employees first examined the site, although Rowley had already begun plans for the mill. Rowley returned on March 12 to survey the site officially, and by late April A. P. Melton began laying out streets on the standard grid plan favored by many urban real estate developers.[17] For the next several months preparation of the mill site, rather than the creation of a town, occupied work crews, initiating a pattern of profit over planning that characterized Gary's early history. This task required leveling dunes, filling in marshes, moving several railroad lines, and shifting the channel of the Grand Calumet River one thousand feet south. In all, some 12 million cubic yards of sand were moved—equivalent to the earth removal required for the construction of the Panama Canal. By any measure it was a gargantuan task.[18]

Attention then turned to the construction of the mills themselves and the preparation of an eight-hundred-acre townsite for what became known as the First Subdivision.[19] For almost its first three years Gary was little more than a construction camp, and its highly transient construction crews found accommodations, both summer and winter, in caves dug into the

Shacks along the river during the construction of Gary, March 15, 1907.
Courtesy of Calumet Regional Archives, Indiana University Northwest.

dunes, tents, tar-paper shacks, and occasionally structures of relative per-
manence such as the overcrowded boarding house known as McFadden's
Flats, where one could reserve a bed for one dollar a week.[20] Early photographs reveal a collection of tumble-down shacks strewn almost ran-
domly among the dunes, notwithstanding the grandiose attribution of
street names, such as Euclid Avenue, which have long since disappeared.
One observer in 1908 described Gary as "a combination of a vast world's
fair site in the course of construction, a mining camp, and a new boom
town gradually fading away and emerging a full grown modern city."[21]

The planning, what there was of it, and the construction of the First
Subdivision were the responsibility of the Gary Land Company, a subsidiary of U.S. Steel established in 1906 for the purpose. U.S. Steel's haphazard
approach to town planning was in marked contrast to its careful planning
of the steelmaking facilities which were designed "not only to be the
world's largest, but also the most modern, using the latest methods and
technology."[22] In fact, the extent to which a town entered into U.S. Steel's

planning for the Gary facility is unclear, although it was obvious that the thousands of workers would have to live somewhere nearby. But the fact that U.S. Steel failed to provide housing for even a substantial percentage of the total number of projected workers reflects the confusion. Did U.S. Steel intend to create a town under its control, or, as E. J. Buffington claimed in *Harper's Magazine,* merely to provide the essential conditions under which a town could develop on its own?[23]

Certainly no complete control, along the lines of that exerted in Pullman, Illinois, was envisioned. Indeed corporation officials repeatedly cited Pullman as the paternalistic model to be avoided. Mohl and Betten, for example, noted that, in contrast to Pullman, the Gary Land Company wanted "a community where workers owned their own homes and where local business and government functioned without excessive company interference."[24] But scholar after scholar has claimed, with varying degrees of success, that U.S. Steel attempted to exert considerable influence in the affairs of the city.[25] Moreover U.S. Steel was reluctant to relegate responsibility for the city to those real estate speculators and other entrepreneurial founding fathers who flocked to Gary from all over the Midwest. This was, it should be noted, the period in which Progressives throughout the country were attempting to regain control of their cities from the allegedly corrupt professional politicians. As Wiebe and Weinstein have shown, this Progressive mentality was reflected in the corporate liberalism of the day. For the upper-middle-class elite at U.S. Steel, some control of the largely immigrant population was considered essential for both moral and prudential reasons. As Edward Greer has observed, "the corporation wanted the political life of the community to be dominated by the respectable middle-class elements on which it could confidently rely."[26]

The case of liquor is a good example of the struggle for control. Prohibition, the darling reform movement of the Progressives, was acknowledged to be impossible in an industrial city, but strict liquor control was thought to be essential in order to insure a dependable workforce. Although plans actually called for four or five liquor-selling establishments in the First Subdivision, only two were actually provided—in the Binzenhof restaurant and the Hotel Gary. (The Binzenhof quickly became the center of Gary's social life and figured prominently in the early history of several Gary churches by providing room above the bar for services.) But this modest supply failed to meet the considerable demand, and by 1908, the immigrant section known as the Patch contained no fewer than eighty-seven saloons on Broadway alone, Gary's premier thoroughfare.[27] Town and mill disagreed early over saloons as they were to disagree subsequently over many things.

Town-Mill Conflict

In fact, the existence of a town-mill conflict was obvious even to early observers. As Graham R. Taylor noted in 1915, "At Gary one feels that friction and antagonism between townspeople and the industrial control are always just under the surface if not cropping out."[28] But there is considerable disagreement over its extent and its source. Several scholars have held U.S. Steel responsible for much of the conflict, insisting that the company attempted to control affairs in Gary—from electing politicians to thwarting town planning proposals. James Maloney concluded, for example, that by 1913 U.S. Steel virtually controlled Gary's political life. Quillen, on the other hand, claimed that quite early the corporation lost control over the town government and over the area south of the Wabash tracks.[29]

On occasion historians have echoed Henry B. Fuller's 1907 opinion that placing the mill so it would be surrounded on three sides by water indicated U.S. Steel's "premonition of trouble." But Fuller had in mind industrial unrest, not a town-mill conflict. Indeed he claimed that U.S. Steel was attempting to walk a thin line between Pullman paternalism and South Chicago chaos. "The new town is to be given the proper impetus under the best auspices, and then allowed to look largely after itself." That this policy would result in "two Garys" was already obvious to Fuller as it has been to later observers.[30] The existence of these two Garys, one for the American-born elite and the other for African Americans and foreigners, was to have profound and fateful implications for Gary's churches, as indeed for all its social institutions.

Moreover the existence of two Garys, separated by the Wabash tracks (the southern boundary of the First Subdivision near Ninth Avenue), confirmed that U.S. Steel could not control Gary, no matter what its intentions. Outside the First Subdivision, "the average man, in his compelling multitudinousness, is in control and checks the lofty plan of the original power."[31] If, that is, U.S. Steel intended to exercise complete control over

Gary, it was a botched job. It is, in fact, far more likely that the company's interventions in the town's affairs were driven more by profit than by urban policy.[32]

Indeed the demands of profit ruled on both sides of the Wabash tracks. If U.S. Steel failed to provide suitable housing for unskilled laborers because it was too expensive, private real estate developers provided minimal accommodations for them because it was so profitable. "In both parts of town, sound planning objectives were ignored and entrepreneurial values prevailed."[33] In this respect, Gary resembled many an earlier American city in failing to reconcile "profit with humanity."[34]

In its First Subdivision the Gary Land Company intended to provide only improved lots and easy financing rather than houses for rent or sale. But few lots were bought by workmen, and even fewer houses built. The need for housing grew. By the time Graham R. Taylor visited in 1909, U.S. Steel had abandoned its original plan and constructed 506 houses for employees, including fifty four-room frame houses designed for unskilled laborers.[35] But the tendency of the occupants of these fifty houses to take in boarders resulted in severe overcrowding and damage to the property, and this modest experiment in housing for laborers, dubbed "Hunkeyville," ended in 1911. The fifty houses were demolished, and their inhabitants found shelter in the infamous "Patch," the immigrant section south of the Wabash tracks characterized by overcrowding, wretched living conditions, and high profits for the owners.[36]

Very early, then, the First Subdivision became home to skilled labor, management, and other middle-class Gary citizens and to those institutions that served them. Broadway (running north and south) became the main commercial strip, not Fifth Avenue (running east and west) as mill officials had intended. Generally skilled laborers lived east of Broadway, and more affluent citizens lived west of Broadway, especially between Fifth and Ninth avenues. Also west of Broadway were the leading Protestant churches—Methodist, Presbyterian, Episcopal, Disciple, Congregational, and Baptist—as well as the leading English Roman Catholic Church and Jewish synagogues. Gary was thus a deeply divided city from a very early day. Furthermore the conflict between town and mill was only one among many conflicts and divisions.[37]

In both its diversity and its divisiveness, Gary was all too representative of American industrial cities at the turn of the century.[38] The massive new work force required by American industries had been recruited from cor-

630 Jackson, home of John Kirk, superintendent of the railroad yards at Gary Works, August 19, 1915. This kind of home was built in the First Subdivision for upper management. Courtesy of Calumet Regional Archives, Indiana University Northwest.

ners of Europe unknown to most Americans. In only a few years these new workers introduced a bewildering and frightening variety of customs, languages, and religions to urban America. The radical urban pluralism that resulted posed a major challenge to the dominant classes and social institutions, including both political and educational systems and the Protestant churches.[39]

SOCIAL AND ETHNIC DIVERSITY IN EARLY GARY

In his summary of Gary's history to 1918, Isaac Quillen observed that "Gary was approaching social maturity; a complex culture had arisen on the dunes, expressed in the wealth of institutions which had emerged to meet human needs, *but unity amidst diversity had not yet been achieved*" (emphasis added). He acknowledged the extraordinary physical accom-

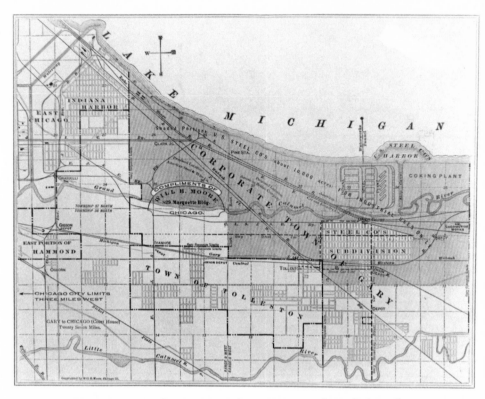

Map of Gary in 1906 showing original corporate town boundaries and neighboring towns. It also indicates the domination of the lake front by U.S. Steel facilities and the location of the First Subdivision and Gary's many railroad lines. The Wabash tracks running east and west marked the northern boundary of "The Patch." The Town of Tolleston was annexed in 1910. Courtesy of Calumet Regional Archives, Indiana University Northwest.

plishment of creating a city of 55,378 in less than fifteen years, a feat celebrated enthusiastically in the popular press of the day.[40] But he also emphasized both the social accomplishments and the social failures of Gary's early residents as they attempted to create an urban society as well as a physical city. By early 1911, for example, Gary boasted no fewer than fourteen churches alongside forty other social organizations.[41] But this impressive social infrastructure did not enable early Garyites to wrest a civic unity from the fundamental socioeconomic, ethnic, and political diversity that characterized their city.

Diversity was apparent from the first. As noted above, the U.S. Steel Corporation laid out the mills and the city during the spring of 1906, and construction began almost immediately, at first on the mill site but shortly thereafter on the First Subdivision. The early work crews were a mixed lot, including African Americans and representatives of at least two dozen European ethnic groups.[42] Social, racial, and ethnic diversity was endemic in Gary, as in many northern industrial cities in the early twentieth century, confronting them all with the problem, as Arthur Mann has put it, of "the one and the many."[43]

This extraordinary diversity was largely a result of the waves of foreign migration to American shores from 1840 to 1920. The rate and source of this immigration varied dramatically over that period, but in retrospect 1880 was something of a watershed year. Prior to 1880 fewer than one-third of the immigrants from the 1820–1920 era had arrived. But between 1880 and 1920, almost 6 million persons per decade entered the United States, with almost 8 million arriving in the 1900–1909 decade alone. The national origin of the immigrants also shifted markedly after 1880. Prior to that year 85 percent of the immigrants had come from the British Isles, Germany, Canada, and the Scandinavian countries. But by 1896, more than half of all immigrants in the United States had come from Italy, Russia, and the Austro-Hungarian Empire.[44]

As varied as their origin was their destination. Ports of arrival, especially New York, continued to draw a disproportionate number, and the presence of earlier immigrants in a city drew still others.[45] Changing demands for labor had an important influence as well. Whereas many of the earlier immigrants moved to rural areas, by the turn of the century most new immigrants moved to the areas of rapid manufacturing growth, mainly the cities of the northeastern and north central states, such as Gary. Consequently by the last quarter of the nineteenth century, immigrants and their

Table 1. Population of Gary, Indianapolis, Pittsburgh, and Youngstown, 1910–1940

	1910	1920	1930	1940
Gary				
Native Whites of Native	4,480	16,519	33,635	——
Parents*	26.6%	29.8%	33.5%	[73,976]
Native Whites of	3,681	17,065	26,012	[66.2%]
Foreign/Mixed Parents	21.9%	30.8%	25.9%	
Foreign-Born Whites	8,242	16,460	19,345	17,270
	49.1%	29.7%	19.3%	15.5%
Blacks	383	5,299	17,922	20,394
	2.3%	9.6%	17.8%	18.0%
Other Races+	16	35	3,512	79
	.09%	.06%	3.5%	.07%
Total Population	16,802	55,378	100,426	111,719
Indianapolis				
Native Whites of Native	150,593	219,297	265,349	——
Parents*	64.5%	69.8%	72.9%	[325,200]
Native Whites of	41,420	43,156	40,975	[89.3%]
Foreign/Mixed Parents	17.7%	13.7%	11.3%	
Foreign-Born-Whites	19,767	16,958	13,740	10,555
	8.5%	5.4%	3.8%	2.9%
Blacks	21,816	34,678	43,967	51,142
	9.3%	11.0%	12.1%	13.2%
Other Races+	54	105	130	75
	.02%	.03%	.04%	.02%
Total Population	233,650	314,194	364,161	386,972
Pittsburgh				
Native Whites of Native	176,089	216,530	272,182	——
Parents*	32.9%	36.8%	40.6%	[524,630]

Table 1. continued

	1910	1920	1930	1940
Native Whites of	191,483	213,465	233,063	[78.1%]
Foreign/Mixed Parents	35.9%	36.3%	34.8%	
Foreign-Born Whites	140,436	120,266	109,072	84,606
	26.3%	20.4%	16.3%	12.6%
Blacks	25,623	37,725	54,983	62,216
	4.8%	6.4%	8.2%	9.3%
Other Races +	274	357	517	207
	.05%	.06%	.08%	.03%
Total Population	533,905	588,343	669,817	671,659
Youngstown				
Native Whites of Native	25,595	46,459	62,605	——
Parents*	32.4%	35.1%	36.8%	[126,385]
Native Whites of	26,654	45,302	59,565	[75.4%]
Foreign/Mixed Parents	33.7%	34.2%	35.0%	
Foreign-Born Whites	24,860	33,834	32,938	26,671
	31.4%	25.6%	19.4%	15.9%
Blacks	1,936	6,662	14,552	14,615
	2.4%	5.0%	8.6%	8.7%
Other Races +	21	101	342	49
	.03%	.08%	.2%	.03%
Total Population	79,066	132,358	170,002	167,720

Sources: Bureau of the Census, *Thirteenth Census of the United States, 1910: Population,* 2:430, 568, 574, 609; *Fourteenth Census of the United States, 1920, Population,* 3:297, 307, 785, 867; *Fifteenth Census of the United States: 1930, Population,* 3:494, 689, 715, 716; *Sixteenth Census of the United States: 1940, Population,* 2:Part 2, pages 806, 809; Part 5, pp. 737, 740; Part 6, pp. 217, 220, 813, 816; Part 14, pp. 9, 153.

*Figures in brackets for 1940 include all native whites, regardless of parentage; the 1940 census did not distinguish native whites by parentage.

+Mexicans were classified with "Other Races" in 1930 and with whites in 1940. The category "Other Races" was used in 1930 and 1940. In 1910 the comparable category was "Chinese and Japanese;" in 1920, it was "Indian, Chinese, Japanese, and all others."

American-born children constituted two-thirds of the urban population in America's industrial cities. Moreover they were, in language, culture, and religion, alien to the native population and represented, as historians Glaab and Brown have noted, "a fundamental challenge to traditional American values." Social diversity had become an urban problem.[46]

Gary was a microcosm of urban America's ethnic and racial diversity, a fact noted by commentators from its earliest days. It also represented the range of American responses to this diversity. By November 1908, according to Graham R. Taylor, Gary's population of 10,246 included representatives of no fewer than twenty-four nationalities and was over 60 percent foreign. Although Gary's early business community included a few immigrants, the vast majority of the foreign born came to Gary to work in the mills. Prejudice against them appeared almost at once. John Mumford, for example, described them in 1908 as "the human product of the Balkan States, brutal, unlettered, in some cases little better than a cave dweller."[47] Fortunately, as we shall see in the next chapter, fear and prejudice were not the only response of Gary's native residents to the strangers in their midst.

Several characteristics of this immigration, summarized in Table 1, illustrate vividly the nature of Gary's ethnic diversity. First, the immigrants in Gary's first decade were principally from Southern and Eastern Europe, the so-called "new immigration."[48] Gary's immigrants, like those in similar industrial cities at the turn of the century, were thus profoundly alien to the native white population in language, culture, and religion.

Second, they and their children constituted what was to many a frightening percentage of the population. The foreign-born and their children ("foreign-born white" and "native white–foreign or mixed parentage") constituted over 60 percent of the population in Gary, Pittsburgh, and Youngstown—all northern industrial steel towns. In Gary these groups made up fully 71 percent of the population in 1910. By contrast, Indianapolis, a city with little heavy industry, numbered just over 26 percent of its population in that category in 1910. The percentage of foreign-born and their children did decline in subsequent years, but it remained high in all three steel towns. In Gary it was 60.5 percent in 1920 and 45.2 percent in 1930. Although the percentage of "native white–native parentage" increased, it did so only slowly in Gary—26.6 percent in 1910, 29.8 percent in 1920, and 33.5 percent in 1930. Native whites of native parents, that is, remained a minority for at least Gary's first twenty-five years. Significantly, many of Gary's mainstream Protestants came from precisely this group.

Third, as the number of eastern and southern European immigrants declined after the Immigration Act of 1924, the black percentage of Gary's population increased even more rapidly than in comparable industrial cities. In fact, African Americans had been coming to Gary in increasing numbers since at least World War I and numbered 9.6 percent of its population in 1920 and 17.8 percent by 1930. By comparison African Americans in Pittsburgh, Youngstown, and Indianapolis in 1930 numbered 8.2 percent, 8.6 percent, and 12.1 percent, respectively. Although black population growth slowed during the depression years, it accelerated again during and after World War II. By 1950, African Americans accounted for 29 percent of Gary's population, increasing to 39 percent in 1960, 53 percent in 1970, and 71 percent in 1980. Like the eastern European immigrants before them, Gary's black residents encountered systematic prejudice from Gary's native white population. But they continued to experience it long after the former immigrants had become part of the white majority.[49] Diversity in Gary, then, was a permanent condition, and Gary's native-born whites constituted a minority virtually from the beginning. Consequently its mainstream, white Protestants ministered in and to an urban environment in which their own population base remained small.[50]

LIFE IN EARLY GARY

Gary's population was thus divided from its very early days. Moreover, Gary's social divisions were reenforced by physical ones. With surprising speed, the First Subdivision arose as an orderly, eight-hundred-acre community of apartments and single-family homes for managers and skilled workers. Streets were wide, and utility lines were buried in alleys. Tons of imported Illinois topsoil enabled lawns to thrive where dunes had been. A wide variety of commercial establishments arose, principally along Broadway, Washington, and Fifth avenues, and churches dotted the area.[51]

South of the Wabash tracks was another Gary, a Gary in which the greed of the speculator replaced the dominance of the Steel Company, in which an unregulated mélange of motley buildings arose instead of spacious single-family homes, in which a babble of languages replaced the monotony of midwestern English. Once U.S. Steel relinquished the goal of providing housing for unskilled labor, Gary's immigrant population and its few African Americans sought housing south of the Wabash tracks in the area that became known as "the Patch," a term commonly used in steel and mining towns for such areas. In Gary it originally referred to a four-block-square area south of the Wabash tracks from 9th Avenue to 14th Avenue and from Broadway west to Madison. Later newly drained land increased the size of the Patch, and it became known as the Central District.[52] By whatever name, its housing stock, provided by speculative real estate interests, was less than ideal, and reformers regularly condemned its overcrowding, crime, and saloons.[53]

It was, however, no less urban and no less lively for its disorder. Indeed Arthur Shumway, an astute observer two decades later, found it to be much the most vital part of Gary: "This is living, breathing, sweating, drinking, cursing, laughing, singing Gary. This is the old world. Streets are narrow. . . . stores bear exotic names and advertisements; cafes have distinct national airs. . . . coffee houses, those rendezvous of the Balkans, shelter gossiping, card-playing men who read papers with the L's and P's crazily inverted; churches even bear Byzantine domes. . . . mothers sing to dark babies strange, alien lullabies, remembered from European hearth sides— all this is Gary's real charm."[54] The Patch, that is, grim as it was in many respects, was home to much of Gary's immigrant and African-American community. It provided not only housing but a nursery for a myriad of social institutions from the oft-mentioned saloons to businesses, newspapers, and the large and influential black and immigrant churches. As we shall see, it provided as well an important political base for Gary politicians from Tom Knotts to Barney Clayton in the 1930s and, to some extent, George Chacharis and Richard Hatcher in the 1950s, 1960s, and 1970s.[55]

The five to six thousand construction workers who built the mills and First Subdivision of Gary remain to us a nameless mass, and many of them moved on when the job was done. In fact, Quillen cited an estimate "that during the first year, Gary's population changed almost completely every three months."[56] By contrast, we know a great deal about Gary's early elite.

Ora Wildermuth, for example, who became a prominent attorney and businessman, was born in Star City, Indiana. His German ancestors had come to America before the Revolutionary War, moving first to Pennsylvania and later to Ohio and Indiana. After graduating from Indiana University School of Law in 1906, he went to Gary on August 2, 1906. As he later recounted, he tried with no particular success to find someone in the bustle of construction who knew what was going on. According to Wildermuth, "each fellow knew what his job was. . . . but I just could not find anybody that had any notion of the general scheme of things." After working for two months as a dishwasher with a construction company, Wildermuth became Gary's first practicing attorney and schoolteacher, working and living in a tar-paper shack on Broadway across the street from the schoolhouse. After teaching for one year, he moved full time into the practice of law and served from 1910 to 1913 as Gary's first city judge. As one of Gary's leading citizens, he played a prominent role in founding a variety of organizations, including the First Congregational Church in 1907 and the public library in 1908.[57]

These subsequent Gary leaders were almost invariably white males of American birth. Many of them came to Gary as young men with little in their pockets and with few "contacts." In their own eyes at least they recapitulated the frontier success of an earlier generation of self-made Americans, and pride in their accomplishments (not altogether unjustified) followed them to the end of their days.[58]

Though comparatively few, women also came to Gary in its early days. Few construction workers, American or immigrant, brought families with them for their brief stay. But a number of professional men, including future mayors Tom Knotts and William Hodges, brought their wives and families during the first months of construction. Other women, single and married, followed. Many of these women had family responsibilities while others ran fledgling businesses or taught in Gary's pioneer schools. Fondly remembered ice-cream socials, conversations at the ice house, early church experiences, and effective political activity (the lack of the vote notwithstanding) suggest the important role these women played in the development of a rudimentary cultural life in Gary.[59]

This early cultural life required education for the children, and in September 1906 Gary's first citizens hired Ora Wildermuth and R. R. Quillen as the town's first teachers. One resident later recalled that "there was a question among us as to whether it was worth while to try to start a public school or not as most of the families were still living in tents and we didn't know whether we would be able to live that way through the winter or not. However, we at last decided to have a school. . . . The seats in the school were only benches but at once that school became the community center."[60] School opened on October 2, and thirty-five pupils gathered in the one-story building at 4th and Broadway. By the end of that school year, four teachers were instructing 123 students, and William Wirt, the superintendent of schools at Bluffton, Indiana, had been hired as the Gary superintendent beginning in July 1907. Wirt responded to the persistent fiscal crisis and the ethnic diversity of the Gary schools with an innovative educational system which made the Gary schools world famous.[61] But not even an innovative educational system was able to snatch unity from the jaws of Gary's fundamental diversity.

Gary's first two years, to men and women alike, were difficult times of temporary housing, unpaved streets, omnipresent sand, and persistent violence and disorder. But by the end of 1907 the First Subdivision provided adequate housing, principally for managers and skilled labor. By February 1909 steel making had begun, and by 1911 the basic construction of the mills was complete. Some twelve thousand people called Gary home and trod the fifteen miles of paved streets. Several churches, representing ten denominations, held services. Finally a rudimentary school system and municipal government were in place, both of which reflected the extraordinary ethnic and social diversity of the new steel city.[62] Diversity, not unity, was the order of the day, and it remained to be seen how Gary's social institutions would respond to the challenge.

CHAPTER THREE

Diversity in Gary: A Historical and Political Survey, 1906–1975

POLITICS AND DIVERSITY: 1906–1919

In Gary, the response to the challenge of diversity was swift and impressive. As in other American industrial cities, politicians attempted to capitalize on the rapidly growing number of potential new voters, while others established settlement houses, under both secular and religious auspices, to address the social needs of an immigrant population. In addition, under the leadership of William A. Wirt, Gary school officials implemented an innovative new educational plan designed for just such an industrial context.[1] Finally, several of Gary's Protestant churches attempted to minister to these new Americans in a variety of ways. None of these efforts, political, social, educational, or religious, successfully came to terms with Gary's fundamental diversity. But they represented in their day significant attempts to do so. In this chapter, Gary's political response to ethnic and racial diversity takes center stage. Although less important in subsequent chapters, Gary's political history will remain an important backdrop against which to view Gary's social, educational, and religious responses to the challenge of the industrial city.

Politics

Oddly enough, diversity proved to be an indispensable precondition for Gary's political independence. Gary's early politicians quickly realized that elections could be won with little support from middle-class voters in the corporation's First Subdivision, so long as they could count on the Patch and the greater Southside. Diversity, in fact, was an ally of the politicians who, after all, sought victory, not unity. Their search for political control led to bitter, and sometimes bloody, political contests. One local wit, W. A. Woodruff, penned the following verse about the 1909 election, for example:

> Now father dons his shirt of mail
> His cuirass and his greaves,
> While mother dear, all wan and pale,
> Clings to him ere he leaves
> The house, his rifle in his hand,
> Two pistols in his coat,
> A bowie knife between his teeth—
> For father's going to vote.[2]

Such political battles reflected not only the central conflict between mill and town, but other divisions such as that between the white, middle-class Northside and the black and immigrant Southside.[3]

Political conflict even lay behind Gary's legal incorporation as a town, a process that proceeded quite independently of U.S. Steel. As noted above, it is unclear when or if U.S. Steel intended to incorporate Gary as a town. But its early citizens, led by Thomas Knotts, took matters into their own hands.[4] According to Quillen, Knotts initiated Gary's incorporation after learning in June 1906 that nearby Tolleston intended to annex much of the land south of the Wabash tracks, land not owned by the steel company. Partly to protect his own real estate interests in that section, Knotts acted quickly. Fourteen of the 19 eligible voters among the 334 official inhabitants of the area signed a petition asking the commissioners of Lake County to incorporate Gary as a town. The commissioners called an election for July 14 at which 37 of 38 voters favored incorporation, and they officially incorporated Gary on July 17, 1906.[5]

An election of town officers (one trustee from each of the three wards, a town clerk, and a treasurer) was scheduled for July 28. But, as Quillen observed, in actuality "the most important issue to be decided was the extent to which the municipal government was to be dominated by officials of the Corporation." The results represented a setback for the corporation. Knotts won election along with Willard Caldwell and John Sears; they were regarded as representatives of the town, the mill, and the older settlers, respectively. But Louis A. Bryan and C. Oliver Holmes defeated a mill-backed candidate for the offices of treasurer and clerk. In referring to this election almost three years later, the president of U.S. Steel's Indiana Steel Company, E. J. Buffington, rather grumpily claimed that the voters "had no conception whatever of community interests or needs, and little idea of the fitness for office of candidates posing for election." But Quillen's more charitable assessment was that in the election "the townspeople early asserted their political independence from the mill and won." "Democracy," he concluded, "was functioning."[6]

The conflict, however, continued the next year over the awarding of a trolley franchise. Although the water, gas, and electric power franchises had been awarded to a U.S. Steel subsidiary, the trolley franchise was far more controversial. As Quillen noted, "the key to expansion was transportation," and in early Gary the key to real estate profits was expansion. Thus much was at stake when the board of trustees voted two to one on July 6, 1907, to award the trolley franchise to Frank N. Gavit, a friend of Thomas Knotts, rather than to U.S. Steel's Gary and Hammond Traction Company. That controversial decision enriched several Gary real estate men by steering Gary's expansion south along Broadway rather than east and west along Fifth Avenue. The decision also insured that that southward growth would be virtually uncontrolled with respect to lot size, building standards, and municipal services.[7]

As Gary's population grew, its legal status changed. In October 1909, Gary became a city of the fifth class, and an election of a mayor and council members from the city's five wards was scheduled for November 2, 1909. Gary's first mayoral election proved to be one of its bitterest, in which, in Quillen's words, "the issues of corporation control of Gary, vice and politics, the voting of foreigners, the use of force, and the struggle of real estate interests were brought blatantly into the open." Thomas Knotts, despite concerted opposition from the steel corporation, won the election, but by only 71 votes out of 3,778 votes cast. He was to be Gary's last Democratic mayor until 1934.[8]

It was during Knotts's term as mayor that Gary flirted with prohibition, one of the more bizarre incidents in Gary's early political history. Indiana's Local Option Law permitted county commissioners to deny liquor license renewals for a period of two years if a majority of a town's voters at the last election petitioned for such action. The population numbered almost 10,000 by 1908, but since the previous election (1906) had involved only

384 voters, the petition required only 193 signatures. Instigated by a number of civic and religious leaders, including Methodist minister George Deuel and Methodist layman and town politician C. Oliver Holmes, and supported by a number of women, a prohibition petition in 1908 gathered 229 signatures. Despite legal attempts to overturn the action, Gary was legally dry from April 1, 1909, to May 1, 1910. Although Knotts, first as trustee and later as mayor, opposed the prohibition experiment, he promised to enforce the law. But in fact he consistently assessed arrested tavern owners a fine equal to the cost of a saloon license and suspended their jail sentences. When the experiment ended May 1, 1910, there was a rush to enter the tavern business, and the city soon had over two hundred saloons, more than one for each one hundred inhabitants. The only significant result of the incident, according to historian Powell Moore, was "an intensification of the strife between the mayor and his critics."[9] This strife continued throughout Knotts's term in office. On fourteen different occasions charges were brought against him, on none of which he was ever brought to trial. Despite the charges, in fact, Knotts enjoyed an enthusiastic following, particularly on the immigrant Southside. He was, said Quillen, "a politician in a rough town and in a rough age, and his rugged honesty and sincere desire to further the welfare of Gary was generally recognized."[10]

But the anti-Knotts forces prevailed in 1913 with the election of Roswell O. Johnson. Elected mayor in 1913, 1921, and 1929, Johnson was convicted in 1923 of violating the Volstead Act (which enforced Prohibition) and served seven months in prison before being paroled in 1925. But in 1913 he enjoyed strong support from U.S. Steel. According to James Lane, "mill officials sought clerical allies for him by assuming the mortgages of a number of churches" and exercised considerable influence during Johnson's first administration. But Johnson developed his own independent constituency on the immigrant Southside and became associated in the minds of many with Gary's reputation for vice. In 1917, he was defeated by lawyer William F. Hodges, a reform candidate who ran with the backing of U.S. Steel.[11]

War

Gary's early political history, then, was far more complex than just a two-sided conflict between town and mill. U.S. Steel was certainly a major force in Gary, but on at least several crucial occasions in Gary's first decade, the corporation was bested by Gary town leaders and real estate promoters. In addition to these two camps, Gary's large, fragmented immigrant community was a force to be reckoned with by both mill and town leaders. As was the case in so many other U.S. cities in the first decades of the twentieth century, unity was an elusive goal, and World War I, in addition to bringing prosperity to Gary's maturing steel industry, provided still another barrier to its realization. Wartime prosperity came hard on the heels of Gary's "worst depression up to that time." As war spread in Europe the demand for steel increased, and the Gary Works increased its labor force 27 percent between 1916 and 1918. Gary's population in turn doubled from approximately 30,000 in 1914 to 60,000 by war's end, including a dramatic growth in Gary's black population.[12]

This heterogeneity was a source of concern to Gary's native white elite. When war came they formed several organizations devoted to winning the war, a task they claimed required unanimity on the part of the Gary population. A number of Gary's leading church members participated in some of these organizations, such as the Four Minute Men and Fourteen Minute Women, and church groups supported Red Cross efforts to provide bandages and clothing for the war effort.[13]

More xenophobic organizations such as the Loyalty League and the Wrecking Crew engaged in activities that sometimes included threats and harassment of those suspected of disloyalty. Enthusiasts even inquired about the number of people attending German language churches in Gary. This suspicion of disloyalty, according to Quillen, was totally unwarranted. Quoting Tom Cannon, one of Gary's leaders during these years, Quillen notes that "for the first time in its history Gary became a real community of men and women having something in common."[14]

But this unity was short lived. Although Gary's laboring men and women were for the most part patriotic during the war, at war's end they felt that they had not received their fair share of wartime prosperity."[15] Thus the uneasy unity that existed in Gary during the war came apart in its aftermath, and Gary shared in the national wave of Red Scare and labor unrest, one result of which was the response to the famous Steel Strike of 1919.[16]

Strike

The Great Steel Strike of 1919 was a major national event, and Gary was at its very center. The union organizing campaign began in Gary, and the strike first broke there. This was not, however, the first attempt to organize

American steel workers. In fact, the Amalgamated Association of Iron, Steel, and Tin Workers had begun attempts to do so in 1876. Although U.S. Steel and its chairman, Elbert Gary, were known for their antipathy to organized labor, their announcement of an open-shop policy on June 1, 1909, surprised the union, and the ineffective strike that followed was its death knell. By 1910 the steel industry, according to labor historian David Brody, was "effectively unorganized from the ore to the finished product."[17] Furthermore Brody claimed that, in the decade prior to the strike, the steel industry had achieved a pattern of labor stability in the mill towns based on differential treatment of skilled and unskilled workers, a pattern evident in Gary, Indiana. Skilled, native workers enjoyed home ownership, stock ownership plans, and the promise of promotion, whereas unskilled, immigrant workers held jobs at low pay with little chance of promotion.[18] In Gary and other mill towns U.S. Steel generously supported churches, hospitals, and other institutions, and its officers were active in municipal affairs. As a result, clergymen and other town leaders rarely spoke out against the company, and, according to Brody, the mill towns themselves became a "stabilizing influence on the labor status quo."[19]

Nevertheless, the actual working conditions in the mills, combined with U.S. Steel's open-shop declaration of June 1909, inspired continued union efforts to organize the steel workers. As the Interchurch World Movement's influential report later documented, most steel workers were terribly underpaid, despite toiling in hazardous conditions twelve hours a day, seven days a week. Only in 1919, according to Quillen, did a common laborer at U.S. Steel earn the minimum amount necessary to support a family of five—this on an eighty-four-hour work week. These conditions, combined with the intransigence of Judge Gary and the increased self-confidence of labor occasioned by the war, prepared the ground for a nationwide movement, and on September 10, 1919, labor's national committee to organize the steel industry voted to strike on September 22, beginning in the Calumet Region.[20]

The strike was clearly a grassroots campaign for a living wage, an end to the twelve-hour day and seven-day work week, and recognition of the union. Far from evidence of radicalism, it was, according to Brody, ". . . an effort by labor unions under conservative leadership to win recognition. The campaign had followed strictly trade union procedure, and there was hardly a word open to radical interpretation." But, as he observed, "the misfortune of the steel strike was its coincidence with the crest of the Red

Scare."[21] Fear of Bolshevism had prevailed in Gary well before the strike and clearly contributed to widespread hostility to the strike among Gary's business and professional elite. Tom Cannon, for example, claimed "that the organization of foreign steel workers and activities of Soviet propagandists were being conducted simultaneously and it became apparent that the union organization leaders were active sympathizers and many of them pronounced advocates of Bolshevism." Many of Gary's elite even participated in a vigilante disruption of a labor parade on May 4, 1919, a day that became known as Gary's Red Sunday. As the strike neared, the Corporation mounted a public-relations campaign that included a donation to the city of some lake-front property for a park and a series of full-page advertisements in the newspapers. On September 13, an alleged one thousand Gary men revived the wartime Loyal American League. On the day the League began to run newspaper advertisements criticizing the strike, the corporation ceased its ads.[22]

The strike began impressively for the union on September 22, 1919. But gradually U.S. Steel drove a wedge between its skilled and unskilled workers, and many of the former returned to work. After a strike-related "riot" on October 4, Mayor Hodges called in the state militia. Then, on October 6, he requested the aid of federal troops, and martial law was declared in Gary. Over the next several weeks, skilled workers returned to the mills in large numbers, and many unskilled workers left Gary altogether. By November, it was increasingly clear that the strike was lost. On January 8, 1920, the strike ended officially, leaving behind defeat for the union and a bitter legacy for Gary of violence and lawlessness, hostility between native and immigrant, and cynicism. As Lane put it, "At the dawn of the 1920s, Gary had lost its innocence and some of its illusions of grandeur."[23]

PROSPERITY AND DIVERSITY: 1920–1929

Prosperity

In a celebrated 1929 article in *The American Parade,* former *Gary Post-Tribune* reporter Arthur Shumway simultaneously summarized and satirized Gary with telling effect:

Mention the magic name, Gary, anywhere but in that boisterous young city and immediately your hearers shudder and draw drab mental pictures of desolate sand flats, smoke-belching steel mills, sweaty "Hunkies," squalid shacks, sun-cracked streets, unbelievable heaps of dirty golden dollars and one great, awesomely intricate School, the whole alternately sweltering and freezing under a pall of black smoke. Your hearers will be right, and they will be wrong. Gary, whatever else, is a paradox. It is busy; it is dull. It is modern; it is backward. It is clean; it is filthy. It is rich; it is poor. It has beautiful homes; it has sordid hovels. It is a typical overgrown American mill-town; it is a unique new city of the old world. It has a past, but it has no traditions. It has a feeble glow of culture, yet the darkness of prehistoric ignorance. In a word, it has everything, and at the same time has nothing.[24]

Bombastic rhetoric aside, it is difficult to improve upon Shumway's description of the contradictory reality that was Gary. On the one hand was Gary's undeniably spectacular growth and prosperity. On the other hand was the glaring evidence of Gary's persistent problems—significant pockets of population isolated from the general prosperity and a troubling political connivance with or toleration of lawlessness, bigotry, and vice.

Oddly enough the prosperous decade of the twenties began with economic hard times in Gary. In 1920 mill operations declined to 29 percent of capacity, and the city's attempt to help five thousand unemployed workers created a million-dollar budget deficit. By 1922, however, the economy had improved, and by 1923 the mills were operating at full capacity. The adoption of the eight-hour day in 1923 improved relations with labor, and, Judge Gary's misgivings notwithstanding, company profits remained high.[25]

Acknowledging that "as the steel mills go so goes Gary," the *Post-Tribune* proudly printed articles concerning the industry's record-breaking production levels and rosy prospects, concluding that "there is every reason to believe that the Gary steel industries will continue to lead the prosperity parade." Indeed for the remainder of the decade, the steel industry did just that, giving rise to a period of population growth, building boom, and rampant boosterism.[26]

That Gary's population grew rapidly from its 1920 level of 55,378 is indisputable; by just how much it grew, however, was hotly disputed. Whereas some estimated Gary's 1927 population at 100,000, the chamber of commerce defended an "estimated, boasted and often fought-about total population of 110,000." As the *Post-Tribune*, which defended the 110,000 figure, put it, "all 'average population' estimates have been set at defiance by Gary which grows according to its own rules."[27] But, whatever the precise figure, the direction was clear.

As evidence of its prosperity and civic maturity in the 1920s Gary boosters pointed as well to its building boom. For example, the Gary chamber of commerce claimed for 1927 "a construction record of 2,857 projects totaling $15,016,529, exclusive of $15,000,000 of industrial construction." Nor was building limited to one sector of the economy. It included public works projects, industrial construction, major civic and church buildings, and housing. But even the building boom was not without its darker side. A passing interest in city planning in 1920 encouraged Mayor Hodges to appoint a civic service commission. But its recommendations, opposed by the corporation, the railroads, and the realtors, were generally ignored. Furthermore, Gary's rapid population growth outstripped its building boom, and low-income residents remained in substandard housing.[28]

Boosterism

The building boom, the burgeoning steel industry, and the accompanying population growth fueled the already bright flames of boosterism in Gary. From its earliest days Gary shared fully in the booster tradition that has characterized American urbanization. By the mid-1920s, it was in full flower, leading Arthur Shumway to claim that "no American city, lest it be Los Angeles or Miami, is so completely cursed by boosterism. To borrow a handy figure, Gary is one who lies in the gutter and looks at the stars." For example, a 1928 pamphlet published by the chamber of commerce claimed: "Gary occupies a position unique in the history of American cities. Founded in 1906, its unparalleled growth in twenty-two years to a city of 110,000 makes it one of the industrial wonders of the twentieth century. Gary, however, is not merely a material city of brick and mortar, commerce and industry. Here is found the highest type of American citizenship, united in the determination to develop and maintain in and for Gary that priceless possession: civic character."[29]

But, overblown as it was, the booster rhetoric suggested at least a tacit acknowledgment that civic maturity required more than economic prosperity and the pursuit of private gain. It required attention to the public realm as well. In fact Gary's boosters claimed that Gary was unusually responsive to the greater good of the community. "It contains the highest type of citizenship, banded together in civic, business and religious organizations to promote the industrial, commercial, and social and spiritual welfare of the community. Here, indolence and private self-interest are displaced by aggressiveness and public interest in their larger aspects."[30]

"Citizenship, banded together"—in Gary, as in other communities in the twenties, joining organizations was an epidemic. Gary, according to the chamber of commerce, boasted "over 500 social, charitable, civic, fraternal, patriotic, professional, religious, and commercial organizations." Prominent among these were service clubs like Rotary and Kiwanis and commercial organizations like the Gary Commercial Club and the Gary Chamber of Commerce. But important as well were the more philanthropic organizations such as the YMCA, settlement houses, and hospitals.[31] Though one should not take all their claims at face value, the claim of service to the wider community was, in fact, an integral part of the booster rhetoric in Gary.

In many ways, then, Gary was booming in the twenties, but it was not a boom shared by everyone. Many African-American and Mexican-American residents south of the Wabash tracks continued to occupy substandard housing, often in close proximity to each other and to earlier European immigrants. As their numbers increased, they were subject to discriminatory law enforcement practices and found job security and advancement in the mills to be elusive goals. The prosperity of the twenties clearly had its limits in Gary.[32]

Vice and Violence

Apparently unlimited, however, was the growth of vice and lawlessness. As noted above, some observers accounted for Gary's early lawlessness and vice by referring to its frontier character or its municipal adolescence. But by the 1920s, Gary's leaders claimed to have achieved civic maturity—a claim that appeared hollow in the face of Gary's national reputation for vice and lawlessness. In fact the relationship of Gary's populace to vice and crime was not altogether clear. On the one hand, as we shall see below, vice was regularly deplored by church leaders and other reformers. But others among the populace (and perhaps some of the reformers themselves) appeared to have a thirst for it literally (in the form of Prohibition-era brew) or metaphorically (in the form of the extensive, sensational news coverage of crime, gangland activity, and corruption). Gary was both appalled and titillated by its seamier side.

It was a complex seamy side including individual crime, organized crime, systemic violence, and political corruption. Of the first two, suffice it to say that Gary's residents appeared no less inclined to rob and murder each other than did residents of other American cities nor were they less disposed to support with their patronage the various activities of organized crime, including prostitution, gambling, and illegal liquor. The results of both were reported in the paper with something like shudders of delight.

But more frightening in the long run was the evidence of systemic violence and political corruption in Gary in the 1920s. Perhaps the two most striking examples of systemic violence in this era were the influence of the Ku Klux Klan and the Emerson School Strike. As Kenneth Jackson has observed, the resurgence of the Klan in the 1920s, although widespread in several urban areas of the country, was especially strong in Indiana. Established in Gary in 1921, the Klan's initial appeal was anticommunist and anti-Catholic and, in a bizarre sense, reformist.[33] Indeed it helped Floyd Williams win the 1925 Republican mayoral primary, thus defeating the R. O. Johnson administration, which had been supported by Catholics and immigrants and had been implicated in Gary's vice trade.[34] But the Klan was opposed by many groups in Gary, including several religious leaders, and after a 1925 scandal discredited the Klan in Indiana, it quickly lost influence in Gary. As James Lane observed, however, the fact that the Klan influenced even briefly Gary's political life "demonstrated the degree of division in Gary's body politic."[35]

The Emerson School Strike of 1927 provided still further evidence of that division. The Gary schools, for all their achievements, failed to take the initiative in the integration of Gary's black and white citizens. Indeed Betten and Mohl claimed that the schools were one of the major tools used by Northside whites to introduce racism into Gary by the mid-1920s. From as early as 1908 through 1947, Gary schools practiced "a complicated system of partial segregation" with almost totally segregated elementary schools and at least one segregated high school, Emerson, which was the school for the Northside middle and upper classes. But serious overcrowding at a black school in 1927 led to the transfer of eighteen African-American students to Emerson. On September 26, 1927, six hundred white students walked out in protest, precipitating a five-day strike which ended with the capitulation of the school authorities and a decision to build Roosevelt High School as a segregated black school. The strike succeeded, according to Lane, "because civic leaders were not committed to integration and too willingly bowed to the vigilante actions of a small pressure group." Even in the schools, lawlessness appeared to have its reward.[36]

But it was perhaps in the political arena, sometimes in the mayor's office itself, that the pervasiveness of vice and corruption in Gary was most evident. Indeed the real political story in Gary in the 1920s, however, was R. O. Johnson (1914–18, 1922–25, 1930–34), described by Richard Meister as "the most colorful character in Gary's history." Johnson was first elected mayor in 1913, defeating Thomas Knotts's bid for reelection. By the end of his first term, according to Quillen, public discontent over the extent of vice in Gary made Johnson an "embarrassment to the city and the Corporation," and he was roundly attacked by members of the clergy and other reform-minded groups and individuals. He lost the 1917 election by a wide margin to William Hodges, one of Gary's earliest residents and a prominent attorney. Hodges (1918–22) was a conservative mayor who had the ill fortune to serve during the Steel Strike of 1919. Although criticized for his subservience to the Corporation and his conservative attitude toward labor, his administration was to all appearances free of the taint of corruption that characterized the remainder of the decade.[37]

Despite renewed accusations of his connection with vice in Gary, Johnson again won the Republican nomination and the election for mayor in 1921, demonstrating the strength of his Southside political organization. His second term, however, was even stormier than his first, and within six months of taking office Johnson was defending himself before a grand jury on charges that he was cooperating with the vice trade in Gary.[38]

A fascinating letter to Mayor Johnson from W. A. Forbis, his chief of police, illustrates vividly the nature of the vice trade in Gary during the twenties. Dated April 22, 1922 (and discovered by the author, improbably enough, in the church records of the First Presbyterian Church in Gary), the letter reported raids and other police action against fifteen establishments allegedly involved in illegal liquor sales, gambling, and prostitution. Although clustered on Gary's Southside, at least one of the establishments, the Wabash Inn, catered to Northsiders as well. Despite their proprietors' insistence that they ran soft drink parlors and other legitimate businesses, Forbis knew that illegal activities flourished there. But he complained to Mayor Johnson that the use of informants was complicated both by the proprietors' suspicions and by the fact that many of the places catered to a foreign-speaking clientele.

The Metropolitan Hotel at 1550 Jefferson Street, for example, had been raided numerous times, in response to 213 citizen complaints. "In this place they have one or two Chamber Maids and do the work, we know they are Prostitutes, but to get evidence and prosecute is another question. In fact in most cases they are to wise for our hired stools" [*sic*]. Forbis also observed that a coffee house on Washington Street, which had generated at least eighty-eight complaints, was difficult to investigate because it was "a place where Greeks congregate and it is next to impossible to secure a Greek stool." Given the facts that Johnson was coming increasingly under fire during these months and that the letter surfaced in church records, Johnson perhaps had the letter written as a defense of his administration's record with respect to law enforcement. But in any case, the letter confirms there was much law enforcement to be done.[39]

In January 1923 Mayor Johnson was arrested for Prohibition violations along with sixty-one others, including a number of city and county officials. Convicted in 1923 and sentenced to eighteen months in prison, he remained in office until March 1925 while unsuccessfully pursuing his case in the courts.[40] Public outrage over Gary's reputation as a wide-open vice town led to a reformist campaign calling for a city manager form of government. But in a special election in June 1923, the referendum, which was perceived on the immigrant Southside as a Northside power grab, was defeated 7,390 to 2,970.[41]

Incredibly Johnson's career revived after his 1929 pardon by President Coolidge, and he won election for a third term in 1929, giving him the dubious privilege of presiding over Gary during the onslaught of the Depression. He also endured an onslaught from Northside Protestant pastors. For example, Frederick Backemeyer, pastor of the First Presbyterian Church, criticized Johnson openly in a 1932 sermon entitled, "What's the Matter with Gary?" But despite such public criticism, he "remained the toast of the Southside until the depression caused most working-class voters to vote Democratic," a shift in voter preference that cost Johnson the primaries in 1934 and 1938. He died in 1939.[42]

As Arthur Shumway observed, Gary in the 1920s was a most contradictory city, a city of boom and booster, but also of poverty and disunity. His withering attack in *The American Parade* caused a sensation in Gary, and the *Post-Tribune* invited Rabbi Garry August, one of Gary's most respected figures, to respond to it. Rather than denying the truth of Shumway's accusations, he asserted that ". . . whatever has been written about Gary differs in no essential respect from what can be calmly and truthfully written of any community in wide America. . . . Gary is America. Every American city is Gary writ large or small."[43]

Echoing August's assessment, Isaac Quillen ended his extraordinary account of Gary's first two decades by observing that: "In 1929 Gary stood on the threshold of its greatest crisis, the depression of the thirties, a divided community, and like American culture generally, it was politically, economically, and spiritually unprepared for the ordeals to come." Quillen's summary is an apt one, not just for Gary in the 1920s but for much of its next fifty years as well. If it is true, as Garry August claimed, that "every American city is Gary writ large or small," then Gary's experience in the 1920s illustrates certain fundamental realities of American urban life in this century—realities of persistent diversity rather than unity, of poverty coexisting with wealth, of reform coexisting with corruption, of optimism coexisting with despair.[44] Although these realities have appeared somewhat differently in Gary in the past half-century, they have remained recognizable.

FROM DIVERSITY TO BLACK POWER: 1930–1975

As in the rest of the United States, the dominant reality of the 1930s in Gary was the Great Depression. As economic activity, including steel production and construction, dropped sharply, unemployment rose, pushing Gary's relief capacities to the breaking point and beyond. Housing starts, for example, fell to a third of their level in the 1920s, and, according to Greer, "the physical plant of the city began an aging process which has continued to the present day." Unemployment was generally high in Gary and particularly severe among African Americans and Mexicans, until the unionization of the steel industry in 1937.[45] Suffering was widespread, and sometimes the mood turned ugly as in the 1932 campaign to deport some fifteen hundred Mexicans in order to reduce the welfare rolls. Despite heroic efforts by settlement houses and other local organizations, only the massive intervention of the New Deal was able to meet the challenge of human need on anything like an adequate scale. According to Lane, by 1938 "New Deal agencies had pumped 35 million dollars into Lake County, about half of which went to Gary."[46]

The failure of many local businesses and all but one of Gary's fifteen banks contributed to the city's woes as did the plight of both the municipal government and the school system. Between 1929 and 1935, for example, "retail sales, the expression of mass purchasing power, declined by 40 percent." As tax delinquencies soared to nearly 50 percent, the city government and the school system found themselves in deep financial trouble. Only tax payments by U.S. Steel, which paid 35 percent of all local taxes, kept them in operation.[47]

Churches also suffered from the depression, especially the large, Northside Protestant churches which had incurred heavy indebtedness during the previous decade's building binge. But hardship notwithstanding, churches continued their services, and Meister even detected "greater understanding between the faiths and greater charity," as the multiracial Gary Council of Churches replaced the white Gary Ministerial Association.[48]

Even Gary's boosters suffered. Most of the luncheon clubs suspended their activities for a time in the thirties, and no city directory was published from 1932 to 1934. In contrast to the 1920s, Gary's population growth slowed to a trickle, its population increasing from 100,426 to 111,719 during the decade of the thirties.[49]

Politically the 1930s saw both a swing to the Democrats and a continuation of political corruption in Gary. In 1934, for example, Lee (Barney) Clayton became Gary's first Democratic mayor since Tom Knotts, enjoying the support of labor and at least 30 percent of black voters. He won despite the killing in his home in July 1934 of a beer salesman, probably as a result of a gang war. The margin was a narrow one however—268 votes out of approximately 31,000 votes cast. His victory, according to Meister, "marked the change in political leadership in Gary from the upper middle class Republican Westside to the working class, Democratic Eastside and Glen Park."[50] But Clayton's flagrant toleration of vice in Gary precipitated still another Northside reform movement. Consequently in 1938, despite the Roosevelt landslide, Gary's voters elected their last Republican mayor, Ernst L. Schaible. Commenting on Gary's electoral swings, Meister noted that "Gary could not decide if it wished a reformer for a mayor or a man of the people who would probably take a little more from the people than just their votes."[51]

Less sudden than the switch of political parties, but equally important to the future of Gary, was the profound change in the relationship between Gary and U.S. Steel. Under the first generation of U.S. Steel leadership, the corporation had wielded substantial influence on Gary. In addition to Judge Gary himself, the local corporate leaders, especially William Gleason and H. S. Norton, took an abiding interest in Gary and held positions of political and commercial leadership from 1906 and 1907 until the 1930s. Mohl and Betten, critical of their activity, described them as "a paternalistic pair who sought to shape and control the growing steel city. They kept things under control for several decades, breaking the steel-workers union in 1919, working closely with Republican politicians, and manipulating the programs and policies of Gary's newspapers, schools, churches, and settlement houses." William Gleason, who died in 1936, was connected with the steel industry virtually all his life. He came to Gary in 1906 to oversee the construction of the mills and was superintendent of the Gary Works from 1907 to 1935, running it, according to James Lane, "like a feudal lord." Actively involved in the civic affairs of Gary, he served as head of the park board for many years. Although a devout Catholic, he adamantly opposed integration in Gary, including integration of the parks.[52]

H. S. Norton came to Gary in 1907 and served as the president of the Gary Land Company from 1907 to 1938. Because of two years in the Illinois National Guard, he was known as "Captain Norton" by all except William Gleason, with whom he had a decades-long rivalry. Norton was, if possible, even more active than Gleason in civic affairs. He helped found the Gary Commercial Club and Gary Country Club and served on numerous boards of trustees, including those of the YMCA, YWCA, Red Cross, and Stewart Settlement House. A devout Episcopalian, he was senior warden for many years at Christ Church in Gary. He was, according to Lane, "Gary's preeminent civic leader."[53]

But the financial and personal paternalism represented by Gleason and Norton was rejected by the new generation of steel leadership in the 1930s, and "after 1937 the corporation maintained a sense of aloofness to the internal affairs of Gary."[54] One evidence of this change was the rotation of upper level management among the corporation's facilities around the country. Whereas Gleason served as general superintendent for twenty-eight years, for example, his three successors served between two and nine years each and took a far less prominent role in civic affairs than had the powerful Gleason. As Meister noted, this change in corporate philosophy brought an end to the conflict between town and mill, but "with the disappearance of paternalism came the problem of the absentee landlord," and "Gary suffered because the corporation failed to take any further interest in its development and growth."[55]

Thus by the end of the thirties Gary had managed to solve some of its problems, such as the town-mill conflict and the conflict between native white and immigrant Europeans. But the fundamental problems of disunity, racism, poverty, and corruption remained a challenge, even as the economic effects of the Depression came to an end with the onset of World War II.[56] As during World War I, war provided an ephemeral unity for the community, and a dramatic but temporary improvement in the employment picture. Once again African Americans, Mexicans, and women were welcome in the labor-starved mills. But many of these gains disappeared with the end of the war.[57]

Racism, however, did not disappear, and within a month of the war's end, a major school strike at the Froebel High School lasted for almost two months. A number of important organizations, including the Anselm Forum, the Race Relations Committee of the chamber of commerce, and the CIO opposed the strike. The Anselm Forum even arranged for popular young singer, Frank Sinatra, to give a benefit concert in Gary in order to express opposition to the strike. The strike ended in defeat in November 1945. In 1947, school integration was implemented in other Gary schools, but "Gary's ghettoized housing patterns drastically limited its practical consequences."[58]

James Lane has called the post–World War II period "the anxious decade" in Gary's history, a decade that included a Red Scare, renewed labor unrest (five steel strikes between 1946 and 1959), a crime wave, and continuing concern over political corruption.[59] After the murder of a much-loved teacher in 1949, for example, two thousand women formed the Women's Citizens Committee in opposition to crime and vice in Gary. Although the organization had only a limited success in stamping out vice and crime in Gary, its well-publicized campaign to do so actually contributed to Gary's national image in the 1950s as a wide open town. Some critics claimed that what the WCC really disliked was immigrant participation in Gary politics.[60] But their efforts were no more effectual against immigrant politicians than against criminals.

In fact, the major political figure in Gary in the 1950s and early 1960s was a Greek immigrant, George Chacharis. His political organization, which dated from the 1930s, combined immigrants and African Americans in a power base that controlled the mayor's office from the early 1950s until late 1962 when Chacharis was convicted of income tax evasion.[61]

The postwar period was also a time of suburbanization, white flight, and black power. Although Gary's black population rose rapidly from 1919 to 1929, it remained virtually stable during the 1930s. In 1930, Gary's African Americans constituted 17.8 percent of the population and in 1940 only 18 percent. But in the postwar period, many of Gary's whites began to move to the suburbs, while blacks continued to move to Gary. The result was a sharp increase in the black percentage of the Gary population—29 percent in 1950, 39 percent in 1960, 53 percent in 1970, and 71 percent in 1980.[62] Despite some efforts to improve race relations in the 1950s and early 1960s, Gary's African Americans remained second-class citizens until the 1960s. Housing patterns and white flight sustained de facto school segregation, and systematic racial discrimination in the steel industry kept black workers in the lower-paying segments of the labor force. Such conditions contributed to the rise of the civil rights movement, a national force which in Gary resulted in the rapid rise to power of Richard Hatcher.[63]

Hatcher, a native of Michigan City, came to Gary in 1959 after graduating from Valparaiso Law School. As Lane summarized: "Aided by the political demise of George Chacharis, the recent black migration into Gary, and the support of a small but significant number of white liberals, he became within eight years Gary's first black mayor," with the aid of 96 percent of the black vote and 12 percent of the white vote in the 1967 election.[64] In the late 1960s, he was extremely successful in bringing federal and foundation money into Gary. He was less successful, however, in solving some of Gary's fundamental and intractable problems such as white flight, crime, the collapse of the downtown economy, and the demise of the steel industry. Nonetheless, Hatcher was reelected in 1971, 1975, 1979, and 1983.[65] As Greer noted, "the collapse of Gary as a viable urban environment took place consequent to larger tendencies in the political economy which are beyond the power of local government to control." Nor was Gary's situation unique. Marshall Frady noted that from the moment Hatcher assumed office, "Gary became a kind of crucible, an image of the American travail." And Lane suggested that Hatcher's "tribulations reflected the general plight of American cities."[66]

Despite these massive problems, Hatcher, according to Frady, managed to effect some changes in Gary both physically and socially and "kept alive the dream of progress . . . that had sustained Gary in the past." Concluded Lane in 1976: "The city was probably less polluted, better governed, less a pawn of U.S. Steel, and more responsive to the needs of black people than at any point in its history."[67] But notwithstanding Lane's optimistic assessment, Gary became in the 1970s a national symbol of urban malaise and decline, not a symbol of urban rebirth.

In Gary's first six decades the political realm was a major arena in which rival politicians capitalized on differences between immigrants, African Americans, town, and mill in their search for power. But the political response to Gary's diversity was not the only one. Other major public institutions, including settlement houses, schools, and churches, saw Gary's disunity as a serious problem and worked in a variety of ways to counter its effects. Although their own motives for doing so were mixed, their responses to Gary's diversity complement the standard picture provided by the often self-serving political response. Their responses also provide important clues about their vision for Gary and for the urban public order in the country. In the following chapters, then, we turn to Gary's settlement houses, its schools, and, especially, its Protestant congregations.

CHAPTER FOUR

Dealing with Diversity: Gary's Social History

In 1921, William Grant Seaman, an astute Methodist pastor concerned about Gary's immigrants, observed that although "the name of God is taken in vain in 43 different languages and dialects . . . his praises are sung in only 16 languages in Gary." His remark documents Gary's striking social diversity but also suggests that, at least to Gary's mainstream Protestants, social diversity was perceived more as a challenge than an asset.[1]

Other Garyites, however, saw it as an opportunity to be seized. Politicians attempted to organize Gary's new citizens for their own political purposes, and many entrepreneurs, both the more and less legitimate, saw the immigrants as an opportunity for personal gain. The *Gary Evening Post* deplored this treatment of the immigrants at the hands of ". . . a crowd of jackals hovering around the foreigners seeking whom they may devour. Under the guise of friendship these foul beasts seek their prey and in a place like Gary many of these poor fellows have no real friends to lead them."[2] This early prejudice against the Eastern European "Hunky" gave way in the 1920s and 1930s to even stronger animosity directed at African Americans and Mexican immigrants. According to Mohl and Betten, "racism penetrated every aspect of the city's life."[3]

But manipulation, prejudice, and racism were not the only responses to Gary's diversity. Indeed a whole cluster of institutions represented a more praiseworthy attitude toward the city's new arrivals. Through the establishment of such important institutions as settlement houses, the Gary schools, and the weekday church schools, some of Gary's citizens sought to deal in more responsible ways with the challenges of urban America.

SETTLEMENT HOUSES

Gary's settlement houses were part of a broad response in England and America to the problems of the modern industrial city. Although some were secular institutions, many settlement houses began under religious auspices and constituted one of the social gospel's principal strategies in the cities, often as part of so-called institutional churches.[4]

Some critics have dismissed the settlement houses as outposts of bourgeois social control and Anglo-Saxon Protestant cultural imperialism. Focusing on the issue of "Americanization" and the metaphor of the melting pot, they have charged that much of the American settlement house movement ignored or undervalued immigrant cultures in the interest of a homogenized, American culture—homogenized along generally white, Protestant, conservative lines.[5]

As with many stereotypes, there is some truth here. The melting pot was an important metaphor, and Americanization was often the goal in early twentieth-century American cities. For example, in a series of articles on various immigrant groups, the *Gary Daily Tribune* referred to the Greeks as "a rather malleable foreign substance easily absorbed and readily made a substantial part of the great American commonwealth" and to the Hungarians as "efficient workmen and excellent material for incorporation into the great melting pot."[6] But the stereotype fails to explain the multiplicity of motives that inspired American settlement house workers, motives which, if sometimes mixed with cultural imperialism or fear of the immigrant, often included genuinely religious and benevolent intentions as well. As Lois Banner has observed, settlement workers "had little conscious desire to control society or to resurrect an older social order in which clerical wisdom was supreme." To the contrary, they made important contributions to American society and to the cause of genuine social reform.[7]

Happily Gary is a marvelous laboratory for examining the settlement house movement in all its complexity.[8] In fact the establishment of settlement houses, usually by religious groups, was one of the earliest responses to the new community's social problems. For example, the Presbyterian Neighborhood House, dedicated to meeting "the physical, mental, spiritual, and social needs of the community," opened its doors in May 1909, just three months after steel production began in Gary. At first working principally with Gary's European immigrant groups, it worked with blacks

Neighborhood House was founded by Indiana Presbyterians in 1909 and moved into this building at 1525 Washington in 1910. In the doorway is the director, the Reverend B. M. Baligrodski. Courtesy of Calumet Regional Archives, Indiana University Northwest.

as well by the 1920s.[9] Five years later, Methodists established the Campbell Friendship House. Both settlements owed their existence to the initiative of women—Kate and Jane Williams for the Presbyterians and Abbie J. Campbell for the Methodists.[10] The Roman Catholics established their Judge Gary–Bishop Alerding Settlement House in 1917 with, as was often the case, generous assistance from U.S. Steel. Finally the Methodists established the John Stewart Memorial Settlement House in 1921, specifically to meet the needs of Gary's African-American community.[11]

These religious settlements included religious activities along with "typical settlement activities" and have consequently been tarred with the assimilationist brush, not altogether undeservingly. As Mohl and Betten put it, "In their pervasive paternalism, in their continual efforts at immigrant assimilation, and in their implicit denial of the worth of old world cultures in the new world environment, Gary's Protestant settlements became active and rigorous forces for Americanization."[12]

But that critique is only one side of the story. In her excellent dissertation on the settlement house movement in Gary and Indianapolis, Ruth

Crocker acknowledges the force of the cultural imperialism and social control critique. Indeed she explicitly describes the Protestant Home Missions movement, which gave rise to many settlement houses, as "a domestic equivalent to imperialism abroad."[13] But she persuasively contends that the role of the settlements cannot be understood adequately without an appreciation of the distinctively religious motivations behind them and the important role they played in immigrant communities, especially in the lives of women and children. In fact, she claims that in spite of the attempts of the settlement leaders to keep the movement secular, "those who were prepared to leave comfortable lives and live as brothers and sisters to the poor usually did so out of religious motives."[14]

Such was the case, she found, at Gary's Campbell Friendship House, which functioned clearly both as "an agency of Americanization" and as a mission outpost against sin.[15] Similarly Gary's Neighborhood House, "founded in 1909 by Presbyterian churchwomen in order to speed up the Americanization of Gary's immigrant wives and mothers," was also both settlement and mission, and its target group was immigrant women and children.[16] The end was not to prepare women for work in the labor force, but "to fit them as American homemakers," and the means included popular classes in such topics as cooking, sewing, and nutrition.[17] In such efforts, "the Protestant settlement houses attempted to provide what Gary lacked—the influence of religion and women, stable influences to turn wild young men into family men, drifters into regular disciplined workers, foreign women into American wives and mothers."[18]

In fact, the Gary settlement houses were major providers of social services to Gary's needy both in Gary's early years and later, particularly during the Depression. The *Post-Tribune,* for example, reported that in 1934 alone Neighborhood House activities drew 97,340 clients and those of Friendship House 81,200. As for Stewart House, the Reverend Frank S. Delaney reported that 300 to 700 people per day passed through its doors from 1930 to 1935. As Crocker notes: "For people who had no alternative, the weekly health clinic was better than no clinic at all. The settlement playground, however dilapidated, was an alternative to dirty and dangerous streets. The settlement dance, even though closely chaperoned, had a middle-class aura that appealed to the upwardly mobile." Moreover the settlements, more so than many other organizations in Gary, adapted to the increased presence of African Americans among Gary's needy. As Balanoff observed, "In some ways the settlement houses kept up the older

Neighborhood House moved to these larger quarters at 1700 Adams in 1912. This picture, probably taken on May 8, 1917, shows the director, the Reverend Ralph Cummins, and Grace Mary Warmington, the coordinator of charity work and nursery, on the left. (They later married.) The settlement offered Sunday services as well as typical settlement house activities, and the sign board on the building notes the following activities for May 8, 1917: "9:30 Sunday School (Picture Taken); 10:45 Choir Practice; 12:30 Italian Service; 6:30 Christian Endeavor and Earnest Workers; 7:30 Evening Service (Subject: 'Are You Ready?')." The sign at the rear of the building reads: "Baths 20 cents." Courtesy of Calumet Regional Archives, Indiana University Northwest.

Stewart House Better Baby Club in the 1930s. On the far right is the Reverend
Frank S. Delaney. Courtesy of Calumet Regional Archives, Indiana University
Northwest.

traditions of the neighborhood by maintaining integrated facilities while
public facilities were being increasingly segregated."[19]

In addition to the four settlements mentioned, additional assistance was
provided to Gary's needy by the Salvation Army, U.S. Steel's W. P. Gleason
Welfare Center, and by the International Institute. If the religious settlements strove for Christianity, Americanization, and assimilation, the International Institute stood for nonsectarian cultural pluralism.[20] In addition
to providing typical settlement house services, the institute, many of whose
social workers were themselves immigrants, assisted immigrants in their
dealings with various government bureaucracies and served as an advocate
for the rights of immigrant groups in Gary. For example, the International
Institute opposed the involuntary repatriation of Mexicans from Gary in
the 1930s. Moreover, it worked to counter American nativist prejudice in
the 1920s and 1930s, in the latter decade sponsoring "Know Your City

Tours" in Gary.[21] But despite the work of its settlement houses, Gary remained a city more divided by its diversity than united by it.[22]

GARY SCHOOLS

In his 1929 satire, Arthur Shumway parodied even the celebrated Gary school system. Although outsiders considered it "a great Utopian university, dominating a raw city and metamorphosing raw youngsters of ignorant laborers into juvenile savants," Shumway described it as a "system of utilizing teachers, pupils and equipment the greatest number of hours a day . . . at the least possible expense." If he intended to antagonize his former home town, he could have chosen no better target. The schools were to many Gary residents, as well as to several outside observers, the city's greatest claim to fame. Graham R. Taylor, for example, praised the schools in 1915 as "the city's greatest civic achievement," and on a visit two years earlier, Jacob Riis had had nothing but praise for them. According to historian Powell Moore, the Gary schools were "one of the most original and thoroughly constructive attempts at educational reorganization in the history of American education." To Richard Meister, they were "the soul of the community."[23]

To an extraordinary degree, the Gary schools were the creation of one man, William A. Wirt, superintendent of schools from 1907 to his death in 1938.[24] Upon coming to Gary in July 1907, Wirt faced two major problems—too many pupils and not enough money. Like everything else in Gary, school enrollment grew at a formidable rate in Gary's early years. From 35 students in 1906, the enrollment in Gary's schools grew to 492 by the fall of 1907, 1,100 by 1908, and 4,188 by 1912. By 1927 the number of students had climbed to over 17,000, second in the state only to Indianapolis, and by 1934 the public schools served over 21,000 students. Moreover, Gary faced a perennial revenue shortage in the early years.[25]

Wirt's response came to be known as the "platoon system," although he preferred the term "work-study-play system." The system divided each school's student body into two groups which, although they used the same desks, athletic facilities, playgrounds, and so forth, never used them at the same time.[26] Ideally a school plant on the Wirt system could house a student body twice as large as a traditional school plant. A basic tenet of the Wirt system was that the schools should provide not only traditional educational subjects, but also manual/vocational training and extensive sports and supervised play activities. In order to accommodate this enlarged schedule and to maximize the use of the physical facilities, the school day and the school year were lengthened considerably. According to Wirt, the Gary school day included "three hours for study, three hours for work and constructive play and two hours for voluntary sport," compared to a five-hour school day in a traditional school. In addition the facilities were utilized at night for Wirt's ambitious programs in adult education.[27]

But a longer school day and school year were not just practical necessities. They also reflected Wirt's fundamental assumption that the nature of the twentieth-century city and its population required a different kind of educational system.[28] The new urban environment was both challenging and threatening because of the deplorable physical conditions in many of America's cities and, more fundamentally, because of the failure there of the church and the home to discharge their traditional functions.

Wirt's rationale for the work-study-play schools was in some sense deeply anti-urban. Like many others among Gary's first generation of leaders, Wirt grew up on a farm and maintained throughout his career that "cities have never been good place for the rearing of children." Indeed Wirt claimed that the moral well-being of the city depended on constant migration from the country. Unfortunately, said Wirt, "since only the stronger men and women are drawn from the country to the city," the rural population itself is replenished by the weaker half of the population left behind. As for the stronger half who moved to the city, they "do not reproduce themselves for the next generation in boys and girls of as good a type because the city is not a fit place for the rearing of children." In fact, in the city both individuals and institutions were problematic. According to Cohen and Mohl, Wirt concluded that "schools would have to supply the virtues of country life missing in the city because the traditional bastions of morality and control—family, church, work—had declined in importance."[29] According to Wirt, small-town children were familiar with the world of productive work as well as the world of nature, leaving the small-town school only the responsibility to teach formal educational skills. This integrated style of life provided these children with the "four fundamental requirements for success in life: good health, intelligence, reliability, and industry." By contrast, modern city life impeded the sort of character building that occurred in the country, leaving to the school the responsibility for tasks formerly shared by the home, church, and school.[30] If the city school met its responsibility, however, both the children and the entire city would benefit. As Wirt promised in a 1916 speech, . . . we are going to get a pure life for our children in the cities just as we have pure water for our homes and good transportation and good sidewalks. And just as soon as you get wholesome environment, you don't need to worry about what kind of men and women the children are going to become."[31]

In Wirt's view, the traditional schools of his day gave ample cause for worry, subjecting the child as they did for two and one-half hours a day to "every device perfected for keeping children rigid and quiet in fixed school seats." "Modern schools," Wirt said, "are not designed for the activities of children, but for the suppression of their activities." By contrast, the "school of the street," where children spend most of their time, has been a most efficient school "for developing the vicious tendencies of children." Echoing his mentor, John Dewey, Wirt observed that "the child himself is the greatest factor in the learning process," and the function of the school is to provide the proper conditions in which that self-education can occur.[32]

For Wirt, these proper conditions included both adequate facilities and sufficient time in order to undo the damage done by life on the streets. Thus in Gary "the schools try to appropriate the street and alley time of the child by providing opportunities for work and play as well as opportunities for study." Wirt's position was not, however, simply a version of the proverb about idle hands and the devil's playground. Instead, although he did in fact cite the proverb, he believed firmly that the child involved in a complete program of work, play, and sports was more likely to succeed in the more strictly academic subjects. "Not only will the wholesome work and play be a substitute for the demoralizing activities of the street and alley, but planned in connection with the study school they will motivate and give new vitality to the child's study hours."[33]

Wirt was quick to acknowledge that his comprehensive plan represented nothing less than the creation of an alternate world for children "within the adult world of the city." In fact, he compared the simultaneous use of facilities in the Gary schools with such shared urban facilities as art galleries, symphony orchestras, and water systems. Said Wirt, "We try to give the children not a playground, not a shop, not a study room, but a life."[34]

If the schools provided a world for children they also provided a "clubhouse" for adults. In fact one of the characteristic features of the Gary schools during the Wirt years was a large night school program for adults, the enrollment in which "occasionally surpassed the regular student body,"

according to Lane. Many of these adults were, of course, immigrants seeking to learn English.[35]

In Gary, Wirt's system did not long outlive him. He had had to fight
during the Depression to save what some regarded as unnecessary frills in
the school system, and he occasionally faced resistance from teachers,
African Americans, and immigrants. In addition, he made himself look
foolish during the Depression years with a celebrated but ill-advised attack
on President Franklin Roosevelt and the New Deal. After Wirt's death in
1938 his successor kept the system going for a few more years. But in 1942
a critical Purdue University study led to the end of the work-study-play
system in the Gary schools.[36]

Although celebrated, Wirt's schools were not, and are not, beyond criticism. Critics have charged that immigrant children were frequently steered
toward vocational education rather than toward a college preparatory
course and that the schools were devoted to Americanization of the immigrant and the maintenance of the status quo, including racially segregated
schools.[37] Acknowledging the truth, or partial truth, of many of these
charges, Cohen and Mohl observed that ". . . for Wirt, the Gary schools
served elitist purposes—Americanizing immigrant children and adults,
molding docile workers and citizens, manipulating students for the purposes of an orderly society."[38] In their *Steel City,* Mohl and Betten concluded in a similar vein that ". . . despite all the innovations of the platoon
school system, Wirt had simply brought a new level of efficiency to the
notion of the school as an instrument of socialization—socialization in
the norms of a Protestant, rural America fast disappearing before the
onslaught of industrialization, urbanization, and immigration."[39]

But Cohen and Mohl also acknowledged the quite extraordinary contributions of the schools to Gary and gave Wirt full credit for his central role.
Moreover they suggested that Wirt's schools reflected clearly the "paradox" of Progressive views of education in America. On the one hand the
schools strove relentlessly for efficiency and social control. On the other
hand, they attempted to provide a stimulating, child-centered educational
environment in which the abilities and capacities of the individual child
could be nourished. As Cohen has said, ". . . at their worst, the Gary
schools were places where bored, frightened students were endlessly
herded from room to playground to auditorium; at their best they were
free, exciting, creative environments, assisting and enriching the lives of
rich and poor, black and white, native and immigrant children."[40] As for

Wirt, H. S. Norton, the aristocratic head of the Gary Land Company, said in 1926 that Wirt was one who "while radical was not visionary, while a revolutionist was practical, and while a dreamer of great dreams yet withal was a hard-headed business man."[41] Norton could give no greater praise.

WEEKDAY CHURCH SCHOOLS

The weekday church schools were one of the major ways in which Gary's Protestants cooperated to shape the life of their city, striving to impress Protestant moral values upon a community that was not predominantly Protestant. In doing so, they also cooperated with Gary's business community and school officials. Moreover the Gary example inspired communities throughout the country to adopt "released time" and "dismissed time" programs of religious education during the school day, programs that generated considerable controversy and, eventually, significant Supreme Court rulings in 1948 and 1952.[42] According to students of the movement, William Bower and Percy Hayward, "weekday religious education as it is known today had its beginning in Gary, Indiana."[43]

Plans for the church schools were discussed by William Wirt in an address to the Gary Ministerial Association on October 21, 1913.[44] But they resulted not so much from Wirt's initiative as from his adoption of a suggestion made by religious leaders. Methodist pastor Joseph M. Avann, in particular, claimed credit for the idea of Protestant weekday church schools, observing that the idea "did not originate with the school men, it originated with the church men. The men of the church saw an opportunity and they grasped it." Avann approached Wirt with the idea of weekday church schools after learning that "Jewish children spent a part of the day in the public schools and a part in the synagogue, where they received religious instruction." Wirt, who was a member of Avann's First Methodist Church, assured him of the feasibility of such an arrangement for the Protestant churches and later "explained before the Pastors' Union how such church schools could be adjusted to the Gary school system."[45] Wirt offered to excuse children during the public school day for religious instruction in the churches, provided that the teachers were sufficiently qualified.[46]

According to Seaman and Abernethy, the Presbyterian and Episcopal ministers and the Reform rabbi provided initial instruction in 1913. By the fall of 1914, religious instruction had expanded to nine Protestant church-es, Neighborhood House, and the Reform Jewish synagogue. The plan was decentralized, and each institution provided instruction for its own chil-dren, hired its own teachers, and provided its own curriculum.[47] Financial difficulties closed several of the centers in the first two years, however, and the erratic geographical distribution of the churches meant that provision of weekday religious education across the school system was uneven.[48]

In good Progressive fashion, the friends of religious education in Gary adopted a centralized, cooperative plan in 1917, placing the religious schools under a Board of Religious Education, which included representa-tives from each participating church. The board was to provide centralized funding, hire a faculty, and provide a uniform curriculum.[49] In the fall of 1917, five churches, including First Presbyterian and City Methodist, and Neighborhood House opened three centers with three teachers serving eight hundred pupils. The next year, three more churches joined, and the program more than doubled in size with six teachers in seven centers serving over two thousand children.[50] Over the next decade the enrollment grew steadily, reaching 3,100 in 1919, 4,200 in 1923, and 4,800 in 1929, while the centers varied from eight to ten and the faculty size fluctuated, numbering as many as fourteen (full and part time) in 1922 and 1923. By 1920, "every English-speaking, white Protestant Church in Gary, except the Episcopal Church, which has a school of its own" was cooperating in the program.[51] Mary Abernethy, who came to Gary in 1914 with the original church schools, served as the superintendent of the weekday church schools from 1917 until her resignation during troubled times in 1930.[52]

The Board of Religious Education provided centers (usually a room in a church building) as near as possible to the public schools. Once or twice weekly, children with parental permission were released from school dur-ing their play or sports period to attend religious classes.[53] The Board of Religious Education claimed that the principle of separation of church and state required that the classes be held outside the school buildings, but it also insisted that the classes occur during the school day, not as an extracur-ricular activity. This ambiguous arrangement almost at once raised ques-tions about the separation of church and state, although Arlo Brown claimed that "the indictments against the Gary plan, charging it with fostering sectarian influences within the public school system, do not seem to be well founded." Wirt's correspondence concerning the plan also reflected such criticism. In a letter to Joseph Barondess, for example, Wirt insisted that religious instruction was not integral to the work-study-play schools but was merely one among several activities, such as music lessons, which occurred during the expanded school day and which were "purely a matter for parents and for religious institutions to manage." In a letter of June 19, 1916, to Paul Blakely, editor of *America,* Wirt insisted that "in no instance is religious instruction permitted in the school building and by school teachers." Financial exigency in 1930 overcame principle, however, and Wirt helped develop a plan by which church school classes met in school buildings for four-week sessions, four days a week. The Board of Religious Education still controlled faculty and curricular matters, but the Wirt plan eliminated the necessity of maintaining accommodations separate from the schools.[54]

During the two hourly class sessions students used a curriculum based on Methodist materials and adapted by the Gary church school teachers. Although their major goal was instruction in the Bible, the church school materials also addressed "vocational information, citizenship, personal problems," and so forth. In addition to biblical knowledge, the undeniably Protestant goals of the Board of Religious Education included bringing "each pupil into personal relationship with God," developing "Christian character," and inspiring service to God and others.[55]

In practice, they emphasized biblical knowledge and character development more than conversion. Mary Abernethy, for example, described the different approaches to the various grade levels as follows: "In the first grade the children are told that God is the Father of everyone and are shown how their relation corresponds to their relation to their own mothers and fathers and to the policeman on the corner." In the fifth and sixth grades, "Christian citizenship in the larger life of the community is developed," and in seventh and eighth grades, teachers "show their pupils that there is no conflict between science and religion." In a 1923 letter to supporters, she cited student contributions to relief funds for Japan and the Near East as evidence "that the Church School is trying to teach good citizenship, neighborliness, and world friendship as well as to give instruction in the Bible, in morals and right conduct." Writing in the *Gary Post-Tribune* (January 21, 1924) she insisted that the church school was thoroughly nondenominational and that no creeds were taught but that every thing was done "to help the boys and girls to grow into the finest type of dependable Christian citizens." The church schools did, however, keep records of the religious affiliation or preference of the students and forwarded the names of unchurched students to local pastors.[56]

Weekday church school leaders acknowledged the difficulty of adequately assessing the accomplishments of their schools other than to cite attendance figures. But they did report, with a certain glee, that when a contingent of visiting theological students attempted to keep up with a group of Gary's fifth and sixth graders in finding biblical passages, "they were left hopelessly behind." In general they reported, however, on examples of behavioral change as evidence of their success. One boy, for example, confessed that "before me and me brudder [*sic*] went to Church School, we used to fight. Now if we happen to bump into each other, we say 'Excuse me.' " Another child localized the lesson about the blind man at the Pool of Siloam, telling how "Jesus put sand on the blind man's eyes and told him to wash in a saloon," and still another identified Paradise as "things you play with in a game." One enterprising young scholar even reported, "I asked God for help in arithmetic and He gave it to me." Evidently the leaders maintained a sense of humor over their pupils' selective appropriation of Christian teaching. On the efficacy of prayer, for example, Seaman and Abernethy recounted the following tale: "A tousled headed, collarless, lanky boy raised his hand,— 'There was a feller at school that was always pickin' on me, I told him to quit but he wouldn't. He started in again yesterday and when he wouldn't quit I asked God to help me and I cleaned him up.' "[57]

As with the Gary schools themselves, the community church schools took pride in their work with immigrant children, a work in which Americanization was a clearly articulated goal. In 1920, for example, no fewer than thirty-one nationalities were identified among the 3,300 students. Said one Gary resident: "As an agency for Americanization of the best sort, nothing can equal the Church Schools of Gary."[58] Inasmuch as Protestant leaders realized that their opportunities to reach these children through their normal church programs were slim, the weekday church schools were an important form of mission outreach. According to Cohen and Mohl, however, they were not particularly popular with immigrant children and were poorly supported by foreign parents.[59]

Financial support of the schools was a persistent concern and one of the factors that led to the centralization of the schools in 1917. In that first year of cooperative effort the Church Schools operated on a budget of $6,000, which increased to $9,000 in the second year and to approximately

$11,000 in the third. By the end of the twenties the schools required approximately $19,000 annually.[60] During the prosperous twenties the church schools raised such sums from several sources, including local congregations, denominations, corporations, parents, and private donors. Businesses were solicited for support on the grounds that they would "reap the benefits in more reliable, trustworthy employees."[61] U.S. Steel was particularly generous and for a while in the twenties contributed $4,000 annually. But denominational giving declined in the mid-twenties, and the Depression cut corporate, congregational, and individual giving. By 1934, the church schools were resigned to a budget of only $1,300.[62]

Somehow the church schools managed to survive the Depression decade into the early 1940s. But in its March 1948 *McCollum* decision, the Supreme Court ruled that released time programs for religious education were unconstitutional. In June 1948 the Gary school board reluctantly "ruled that because of the court decision there could be neither religious use of school property nor released time for religious instruction during school hours." As Cohen summarized it, "a thirty-year era had come to a sudden end."[63]

In the total history of the Gary schools, of course, the experiment in weekday religious education was a minor footnote. But for the Protestant churches in Gary, including First Presbyterian and City Methodist churches, it was extremely important for at least four reasons. First, it represented one among several ways in which they attempted to address Gary's diversity by ministering to the immigrant and, to a lesser extent, the African-American population. They realized their standard church programs attracted comparatively few immigrants, but the church schools provided one outlet for their desire to minister to this mission field in their own backyard.[64] Second, the church schools constituted one important avenue for interdenominational cooperation. Hardly a truly ecumenical endeavor, the church schools at least saw Protestants working together.

Third, they illustrate the extent to which Gary's Protestants cooperated with other groups in the community. Although they were an explicitly religious undertaking, the leaders of the church schools relied on businesses and other community groups for support of their endeavor to raise the moral tone of this raw industrial city.[65] Gary churches, in turn, quite actively cooperated with and contributed to other community organizations.

Finally, the weekday church schools provide a window through which to examine the Protestant view of what life in the city should be. That this view echoed middle-class standards of behavior and the economic status quo should not be surprising. The church schools, as indeed the Gary schools themselves, did not advocate radical change in society. They praised instead a set of largely personal attributes that they thought would contribute to greater orderliness in their unruly city. The list of virtues is unsurprising—honesty, fairness, truthfulness, civility. When it came to their view of urban society, Gary Protestants preferred character formation to revolution or radical social change. They firmly believed, as well, that religious institutions had a unique contribution to make to character formation in the modern city. As Seaman and Abernethy observed, "The highest welfare of the state is possible only by its possessing such a citizenship as religious training alone can give."[66]

Furthermore, they claimed that their example should be adopted by other parts of the country, reflecting a common feeling in Gary that all the world was watching. In 1918, William Grant Seaman, president of the Board of Religious Education, said, "This 'Gary Idea' seems destined to spread, and this fact gives strong support to the conviction we expressed in seeking financial aid, that we were blazing a trail that might be followed generally thruout [*sic*] America." By 1924, Mary Abernethy claimed that "over 1000 cities in America" were following Gary's example and warned that "if Gary fails, no one can predict the result."[67] That the weekday church schools did eventually fail does not deny the significance of this Protestant attempt to mold urban life in Gary, Indiana.

As the example of the weekday church schools vividly illustrates, the line separating Gary's churches and its other social institutions was very thin indeed. In fact, Gary's mainstream Protestant churches continued to act as integral partners in the broad institutional life of the city until well after World War II. Despite its numerical minority status, the Protestant mainstream, acting through both individuals and institutions, continued to exert an enormous influence in Gary, Indiana. Chapters 6 and 7 will trace that influence in some detail by looking closely at First Presbyterian Church and City Methodist Church. The next chapter, by contrast, sketches the broader Gary religious landscape of which those two congregations were a central part.

CHAPTER FIVE

Faith and Diversity: Gary's Religious Landscape

The weekday church schools, the Gary schools, and the settlement houses were three of the social institutions within which Gary's Protestants worked alongside other elements of the community in response to the city's diversity. But in addition to these cooperative efforts, there was in Gary a pervasive and active Protestant presence. If, as I have claimed, Gary's Protestants were at home in their city, then this distinctive Protestant presence represented their way of being at home there.[1]

But this Protestant presence presupposed two other factors. On the one hand, it assumed the existence of a rich fabric of religious commitments at the local, congregational level. As noted in chapter 1, Americans have generally expressed their religious sensibilities through local congregations, which, as James Wind observes, hold "a strategic location at the boundary of the public and private spheres of modern life" and serve as "nurseries which form people for public life." Although the concept of congregations as "mediating structures" between public and private has, in recent years, defined the nature of that boundary relationship, Martin Marty has recently proposed that the congregation is itself a kind of public and indeed "the meeting where public life begins." This notion of the congregation as a public is particularly suggestive with reference to the Protestant presence in Gary. But whatever the exact relationship between public and private in congregations, it is clear that religious congregations have served, as Marty observed in *The Public Church,* as "a way station between the encompassing world and the private individual, between the church catholic and faith in solitude."[2] The following two chapters portray in some detail the richness and complexity of this congregational achievement in two particularly influential Protestant congregations in Gary.

But in addition to its specific congregational context, Gary's Protestant presence was part of the steel city's broader religious landscape which also included prominent Roman Catholic, Orthodox, African-American, and Jewish congregations. Although Gary's Protestants constituted a minority of its religious population, it was a substantial and influential minority that was especially important in Gary's first three decades. Never monolithic, the Protestant presence entailed a basically cordial tension between Protestant congregations as they both cooperated and competed—a tension between frontier ecumenism on the one hand and a persistent denominationalism on the other.

WHITE PROTESTANT CONGREGATIONS

The first six or seven years of Gary's religious history constituted a period of frontier ecumenism. Remarkably similar accounts from the various Protestant churches of their first few years in Gary document the magnitude of the task they faced in creating from nothing an entire religious superstructure in the brand-new city. A summary of the Episcopalian experience, for example, reveals the difficulties ". . . of building a church without money and making a congregation without church people, of watching debts compound themselves, while clergy came and went. Looking back over the record we can appreciate that it was all part of the task of building a city quickly, that as it was with the parish, so it was with other organizations and institutions."[3] But the common difficulties they faced seemed to engender among these transplanted Protestants a spirit of frontier ecumenism alongside their inherited denominational rivalries.

Frontier Ecumenism and Persistent Denominationalism

This frontier ecumenism began in the summer of 1906, concurrent with the first construction activity. Twenty-five years later, Ella Knotts, wife of Gary's first mayor, recalled that John Sears, one of Gary's first trustees and a Congregationalist, and another man held Sunday services in front of her house in May 1906, with only Mrs. Knotts and her baby in attendance. The congregation was a little larger by the following week, however, and thus began union services in Gary.[4]

Later that summer, a union Sunday School began with C. Oliver Holmes, later a prominent banker and Methodist layman, as superintendent. They met under the trees in good weather and later in the new town jail and the schoolhouse, and people attended "without regard to denomination."[5]

Within a year, however, these early ecumenical efforts gave way to virtually simultaneous attempts to establish congregations with clear denominational identities—Congregationalist, Episcopal, and Christian Church (Disciples of Christ). The Congregationalists were first on the ground, their work apparently developing from the union Sunday School. According to Ora Wildermuth's recollections twenty years later, "Somebody conceived the idea that it was not sufficient to have Sunday School, that we ought to have some church connected with this thing." Consequently a committee sent to Chicago to secure a preacher arranged for Arthur J. Sullens, a Congregationalist minister, to preach the following Sunday. Although Wildermuth confessed to some confusion about the date, he claimed these preaching services began in the winter of 1906– 1907.[6]

That first winter, ". . . the congregation was made up of not Congregationalists so much as everybody. . . . There were Presbyterians, Baptists, Methodists, all kinds and creeds of people, but we all met together. This man did not preach doctrine, but he preached Christianity, and we all listened to it, and we all enjoyed it." According to another eyewitness, Sullens "was a bright, wide-awake young man with a cheery, happy personality that attracted many to his services.[7] On June 28, 1907, the congregation was formally organized as a Congregational church, and trustees were elected.[8] Their covenant on that day bespoke a vision common to many of Gary's early congregations: "We agree to co-operate in every way in our power to make this church a blessing to the community." Since the congregation included persons from several denominations, including some Roman Catholics, the covenant served as "an agreement as to things that everybody could assent to."[9] Frontier ecumenism was still alive.

At first the Congregationalists had no building—a difficulty faced by all new churches in Gary, since "buildings were preempted by business and industry as fast as they were put up." Twenty years later, M. L. Maxon recalled Reverend Sullens's ingenuity in 1907 in finding a newly constructed building that had a roof but was still vacant and claiming it for church services for at least one week. Often "he could not tell until about Saturday where church would be the following Sunday."[10] Consequently they held services in the Broadway Theater, then successively in rooms above the Binzenhof Saloon and in several stores before completing Gary's first permanent Protestant church building in February 1909 at Sixth Avenue and Madison Street. According to the *Northern Indianan*, "the location is central and convenient to the best residence section in Gary."[11]

The summer of 1907 also saw the beginning of Episcopalian work in Gary as the Reverend L. W. Applegate commuted from nearby Valparaiso, serving both communities for several months. Aware of other instances of rapid urban growth, Applegate "recognized quickly the opportunity for religious work which Gary would present and as a veteran mission worker was ready to realize it for the church." As one of his successors noted, however, his efforts were complicated by the lack of suitable space, since "the Roman Catholics had the only hall; the Congregationalists had the only theater; the Presbyterians had the Sunday use of a storeroom; and Father Applegate remained a curbstone person."[12]

But thanks to the efforts of Episcopalian H. S. Norton and others, Applegate enlisted the assistance of U.S. Steel, and a temporary building at Fifth Avenue and Adams Street was opened on December 15, 1907—the first building constructed in Gary specifically for religious purposes. The accomplishment was celebrated by the bishop of the diocese who quipped: "For once in the history of the universe the Episcopal Church is promptly on the ground and in Christ Church we have the first church building in the new city of Gary."[13] The "civic importance of the occasion was recognized by the attendance of the Commercial Club," Gary's principal organization of civic leaders, headed, not incidentally, by H. S. Norton, the head of the Gary Land Company. Because Applegate "thought of the Church's ministry as something for the entire community," he made the facility available to many other groups in Gary, including other churches. John Mumford wrote in 1908: "God is worshipped in more tongues and more rituals at this humble shrine, it is safe to say, than in any other church in the country, and it is hard to resist the notion that if this were only a microcosm of the earth's religions the Devil would shortly be out of work."[14] By the time Applegate resigned in 1911, Christ Church had approximately 150 communicants and, by the end of the year, a new church building at Sixth and

Temporary building for Christ Church Episcopal in Gary. On the front of the
photograph is the following notation: "Episcopal Church, 1st Church in Gary,
Ind. 1st Service Dec. 15, '07. Photo Jan 5, '08." The first building in Gary built
explicitly for religious purposes, it was used by several religious groups before
the Episcopalians completed their permanent building in December 1911.
Courtesy of Calumet Regional Archives, Indiana University Northwest.

Adams. The next nine years saw a succession of four rectors, at least two of
whom resigned in the face of "indiscretions." The last of these, Wilbur
Dean Elliott, came to Gary at the beginning of 1917, and was rector during
the 1919 steel strike. Many in the congregation, which included several
U.S. Steel executives such as H. S. Norton and A. P. Melton, strongly
sympathized with the corporation in the strike. Nonetheless, the young
rector defended from the pulpit "the right of the men to organize." Surprisingly, according to James Foster's account of Christ Church, "no attempt
was made to put any pressure on the rector." Pressure or no, however,
Foster acknowledges that Elliott suffered in the situation "and doubtless
driven by a sense of frustration became so careless of his personal conduct
that in June, 1920, his resignation was asked for and promptly given."[15]

Foster himself succeeded Elliott as rector and served in that post into the
mid-1940s. His years saw an initial period of rapid membership growth
and a building program before the beginning of the Depression in 1930.
Financial conditions were so bad that the congregation defaulted on its
mortgage and until 1937 had to fend off threats from creditors to foreclose

before finally raising and borrowing sufficient funds to save the building.[16] Throughout its history, Christ Church was blessed with a number of members, according to Foster, who "combined leadership in the community, ability in their work, and zeal for the Church." Although it never became as large as City Methodist Church or First Presbyterian Church, it exercised significant influence in the community.[17]

After a tent meeting in July 1908, the First Church of Christ (later the Central Christian Church) was organized with fifteen charter members.[18] Under the leadership of the Reverend H. H. Clark, the tiny church struggled through a year without a permanent home and with few members and funds. At the end of the year, the pastor was not retained, and services lapsed for approximately another year. According to O. F. Jordan, the church's difficulties included the youth, poverty, and mobility of its members. The minister may also have been part of the problem. Although Jordan described Clark as "an enterprising young evangelist," others described him as "frail physically, a dreamer and visionary . . . not fitted for this environment."[19]

In the summer of 1910 the work resumed and, under the two-year pastorate of Nelson and Martha Stout Trimble, both of whom were ordained ministers, a temporary building was constructed at Seventh and Jefferson. According to the *Gary Tribune,* Trimble, who had come from the Metropolitan Church of Christ in Chicago, advocated an "institutional church" plan for Central, and "one of the suggested propositions for the new building is a business block to contain a chapel and apartments in which to hold lectures, social functions, etc." The social gospel thus made an early appearance in Gary. The congregation did build a two-story frame building with two rental apartments on the second floor, but the apartments were soon converted to Bible school use.[20] The church membership grew to two hundred by 1913, growth that continued under Central's two most prominent ministers, O. E. Tomes (1918–28) and Monroe G. Schuster (1928–41). By 1938, the membership numbered 750. During Tomes's pastorate, the congregation replaced its temporary frame structure with an attractive brick building which became a prototype for Disciples of Christ churches around the country.[21]

Although it never in fact became a full-blown "institutional church," Central Christian was quite active in the community. In particular it played a leading role in the weekday church schools, and it sponsored for two decades the Community Vespers program. As for the weekday church schools, the Reverend S. W. Nay (1912–16) quickly responded to William Wirt's invitation in October 1913, and the denomination's American Christian Missionary Society sent the Reverend Myron Settle to Gary to help launch the schools in 1914. Myron Settle became a national leader in the weekday church school movement, directing the Department of Vacation and Weekday Church Schools from 1928 to 1931. Throughout the schools' history, Central Christian Church supported them financially and in other ways. Schuster, for example, chaired the curriculum committee in 1940.[22]

Schuster also helped initiate what proved to be a twenty-year series of Community Vespers. Although sponsored by Central Christian Church, the Sunday evening programs were "non-sectarian, non-partisan, free of racial prejudices and draw attendance from the entire community." The Vespers brought in major speakers from outside Gary to address contemporary problems and were "as important to the City of Gary and vicinity as the Sunday Evening Club meetings are to Chicago."[23]

The period of frontier ecumenism did not extend beyond 1916, by which time the first generation of Gary churches had been established. But three important conclusions may be drawn from mainstream Protestantism's first ten years in Gary. First, the pioneer years represented a tradition of sharing and cooperation. Since denominational allegiances were tenuous at first, some Roman Catholics attended Congregational services, several churches used the temporary Episcopal chapel, and the prominent Catholic family of W. P. Gleason held a tea to raise money for elms for the Presbyterian church grounds.[24]

Second, there was among Gary citizens a widely shared appreciation of the value of religious institutions to Gary. Among other things, the new congregations fulfilled an important social function. They were among those nascent organizations in which Gary pioneers "came to know and co-operate with each other—in those settings the social organization and the spirit of the community took form." One woman, for example, described a 1907 church visit as follows: "we went to the Congregational church in the Moe theater near 7th and Broadway that Sunday and met many fine people."[25]

But the churches were more than social organizations. Almost from the beginning there was broad agreement in the community that churches played a central, active role in the new city, and the churches themselves explicitly expressed their commitment to work for the welfare of the community. As the Congregationalists put it in 1907: "We agree to cooperate in every way in our power to make this church a blessing to the community."[26]

The community responded positively. In December 1908, shortly before the cornerstone ceremonies of the Congregational and Presbyterian congregations, the *Gary Daily Tribune* editorialized on the place of churches in Gary. Noting that ten different denominations had already purchased land, the *Tribune* concluded that "in the way of churches the Magic City of Steel will be supplied as few places ever have been in years of their early history." Moreover it applauded the optimism of the churches, noting that current building projects provided for generous future growth. Finally the editorial writer connected church and city: "There is much more to cities than mills and industries. No part is more important than that of church life." Two years later the *Tribune,* employing wildly mixed metaphors, made much the same point about the importance of Gary's churches: "They are the great leavening power for good; the gigantic filters that purify and sweeten the rapid influx of a heterogeneous population. Manufacture, trade, thrift, labor occupy the days and nights of the busy people of Gary, but the churches, the messengers of God, see to it that the banner of righteousness and devotion is every [*sic*] kept floating on the stiff lake breezes."[27]

Third, despite the common commitment of the churches to their community, even Gary's first ten years revealed a persistent allegiance to denominationalism among Gary's mainstream Protestants. Despite early ecumenical cooperation, each congregation expressed delight when it completed its formal organization and, especially, when it constructed a building—the Episcopalians in 1907 and 1911, the Congregationalists in 1909, and the Disciples in 1911.[28] Cooperation among Protestant churches did continue, but it was cooperation among well-established, autonomous congregations, rather unlike the brief period of frontier ecumenism.

Later Years: A Survey

During the twenties, as Quillen observed, these Protestant congregations shared with other Gary institutions a "worship of bigness," characterized by ambitious plans and grandiose building programs. For example, a year-end report in the *Gary Post-Tribune* on church life in 1926 stressed Gary's "endeavor to express religion through beautiful architecture" and noted that "growth in church membership has kept pace with building during the last months."[29]

The twenties was among Gary's most exciting decades insofar as the Protestant churches are concerned, and it was certainly a central period in the history of First Presbyterian and City Methodist churches. But their prosperity during the twenties left the Protestant churches unprepared for the austerity they, along with the rest of Gary, faced in the Depression years. According to Meister many of them were hobbled by large building debts incurred in the twenties. Consequently mission efforts often suffered as the churches literally fought for their survival. Christ Church, for example, from 1932 to 1937, "was under constant threat of losing the church property and of constant pressure to pay when there was no money to pay."[30]

Recovery was a slow process, but there was some improvement by the mid-1930s. For example, although acknowledging that there had been "little outward evidence of church growth" in 1934, the *Post-Tribune* pointed to signs of continuing spiritual vitality and observed that at least "the majority of congregations were out of the 'red' in their financial budgets at the beginning of the new year."[31] But only after the steel industry, and consequently Gary's payroll, rebounded at the beginning of World War II did Gary's churches return to normal.

During the 1940s and 1950s Gary's Protestant churches reflected several national Protestant trends.[32] Membership and church budgets grew. Churches founded missions in suburban areas, missions that often outstripped the parent church in a few years. Although some Protestants began to discuss "urban problems" in the late 1950s, there was little sense of urban crisis until the 1960s and 1970s in Gary. In those two decades Gary's Protestant churches, like "inner city" Protestant churches elsewhere, saw much of their white population base flee to the suburbs, leaving Gary a largely African-American city. The accounts to follow of First Presbyterian Church and City Methodist Church will illustrate this later mainstream Protestant history, but for now I return to the period of Gary's frontier ecumenism.

Gary's first ten years did not belong just to white Protestants. Black Protestants, Roman Catholics, Orthodox Christians, and Jews were quick to establish their own houses of worship in Gary's formative years. Although they functioned in many respects as did the Protestant churches, they ministered in a distinctive and important way to their constituents, many of whom were among the more marginal members of Gary's frontier society.

AFRICAN-AMERICAN CONGREGATIONS

As in many another U.S. city, "the church was the first, the strongest, and the most all-encompassing of the institutions to develop among Negroes." As early as 1907, Gary's small African-American community held its first worship service.[33] Within two years the First Baptist Church (1908) and the First African Methodist Episcopal Church (1909) were founded, and both of them grew to be large and influential in the black community.[34] By 1917 several other black congregations were at work, including St. Paul's Baptist Church (1916) and Trinity Methodist Episcopal Church (1917). Meister estimated that by the 1930s, in fact, half of Gary's 20,804 Protestants were members of one of Gary's forty-three African-American congregations.[35]

Like their white counterparts, several of these major churches were served by influential ministers during long pastorates: Charles E. Hawkins at First Baptist (1913–44), Frank S. Delaney at Trinity Methodist Episcopal Church (1920–39), and William F. Lovelace at St. Paul's Baptist Church (1926–41).[36] Generally these black ministers espoused middle class values and, like many of their white colleagues, they were sometimes accused of undue subservience to U.S. Steel.[37] But they also established an active welfare tradition, a tradition that became particularly important immediately after World War I, with the establishment of the John Stewart Memorial Settlement House in 1921, and on through the Depression.[38]

Gary's black churches also evidenced a remarkable spirit of cooperation, both with white churches and organizations and with each other. Thus in the 1920s, a Gary Interracial Council, half white and half black, met periodically to discuss the race issue. White cooperation and financial support were eagerly sought by some black organizations. For example, the board of directors of Stewart House in the mid-1920s constituted a virtual honor roll of white Gary and included members from City Methodist Church, Central Christian Church, First Congregational Church, and Christ Church Episcopal.[39]

Black ministers met with each other prior to 1910 to discuss an anti-vice campaign and during times of crisis in the African-American community such as the Emerson School Strike in 1927. In 1926 they formed the Interdenominational Ministerial Alliance, inasmuch as the Gary Ministerial Alliance was all white. Balanoff claimed, in fact, that these frequent meetings "on every possible occasion bound the Black church leaders of all denominations together in a larger Black religious community more tightly integrated than its counterpart in the white community and more active and influential in civic affairs."[40] Be that as it may, these congregations were immensely important to Gary's African-American community.

ETHNIC CONGREGATIONS

Equally important to their communities were Gary's various ethnic congregations, especially the Roman Catholic and Orthodox.[41] As Mohl and Betten have argued persuasively, Gary's immigrant churches both served to defend the traditional culture of their parishioners and to ease their gradual adjustment to American life. In this dual capacity they also helped to strengthen relationships between the immigrant adult generation and their American-born children, softening the impact of the Americanization programs in the public schools.[42] There were, of course, significant differences among the various immigrant groups in their attitudes toward religion. Whereas the Polish-American parish was "simply the old primary community, reorganized and concentrated," Gary's Mexicans, Spaniards, and Italians often retained their traditional anticlericalism and regarded the church with suspicion.[43]

As was the case with Gary's churches generally, many immigrant congregations received assistance from U.S. Steel in their early days. One priest later claimed that ". . . the Corporation hoped that these parishes would stabilize the work force by tying the immigrant to Gary and by giving the immigrant a place to maintain his culture. With an established neighborhood for each nationality, the Corporation believed that other immigrants would follow, thus providing an inexhaustible supply of unskilled labor for the mills."[44] Whether or not the contributions from U.S. Steel were that effective, the immigrant churches founded in Gary's earliest years thrived quickly. Within six years of its founding, then, Gary boasted Roman Catholic parishes for both the Poles (St. Hedwig's, 1908) and the Slovaks (Holy Trinity, 1911), as well as Serbian Orthodox (St. Sava's, 1910), Russian Orthodox (St. Mary's, 1911), and Greek Orthodox (SS

Constantine and Helen, 1912) congregations.[45] By 1936, Gary had fifteen Roman Catholic parishes, only six of which were English speaking, along with its four Eastern Orthodox bodies. Their total membership was 28,082, well over half of Gary's total reported church membership of 51,381.[46] Although their influence centered on the particular ethnic group in question, they cooperated to an extent with other religious groups in Gary. The Orthodox churches, for example, were quite active in the Gary Council of Churches from the late 1930s.[47]

Gary also had two large Jewish congregations. Temple Beth-El was founded in May 1910, and in October that year Temple Israel was organized. By 1920 they numbered some 2,200 members.[48] Temple Israel was particularly important in Gary's history due partly to its scholarly, flamboyant rabbi, Garry August, who served the congregation from 1926 to 1951 and remained in Gary until his death in 1985 at the age of ninety-one.[49] Frequently compared to H. L. Mencken, August was witty, learned, and sometimes acerbic. Described by Arthur Shumway as "head, shoulders, waist and knees above the Gary clergy . . . in liberalism, tolerance, breadth and depth of learning, originality, personality, and courage," he was a popular and active Gary lecturer, a novelist, and an audiophile. During the 1930s, he wrote book reviews for the *Post-Tribune*, served on the library board, and was the first president of the Gary symphony.[50] August, in sum, was among Gary's most prominent and influential religious leaders.

Gary's religious landscape in the twenties and thirties was thus a richly varied one, with its nearly one hundred congregations for Jews, Roman Catholics, Orthodox Christians, and both black and white Protestants. But such complexity was, in fact, characteristic of northern industrial cities. As Kevin Christiano concluded in his statistical study of religion in American cities, "diversity is the hallmark of religion in America." That was certainly the case in Gary.[51]

RELIGIOUS MEMBERSHIP IN GARY

As summarized in table 1, Gary remained ethnically and racially diverse, even as its population grew from 16,802 in 1910 to 55,378 in 1920 and 100,426 in 1930. Native whites of native parentage made up only 26.6 percent of Gary's population in 1910, 29.8 percent in 1920, and 33.5

percent in 1930. Moreover as the percentage of first-generation immigrants ("foreign-born whites" in the census parlance) declined (from 49.1 percent in 1910, to 29.7 percent in 1920, and 19.3 percent in 1930), the percentage of Gary's black residents increased (from 2.3 percent in 1910, to 9.6 percent in 1920, and 17.8 percent in 1930). That is to say, although the nature of its diversity changed in its first three decades, Gary remained an ethnically and racially diverse community, a diversity reflected in its religious landscape as well.

As table 2 indicates, Gary's citizens, for all their lawless reputation, identified themselves as church members to a marked degree. Even in 1936, 51 percent of the population belonged to a religious body, although the sharp decline from 1926, when 76 percent belonged to such groups, is striking.[52] In addition, table 2 confirms that Gary was an overwhelmingly Roman Catholic city—47 percent of its church members in 1926 and 42 percent in 1936 were Catholics. But the Jewish presence in Gary was also notable, with approximately as many Jews as Presbyterians. The mainstream Protestant groups held their own during the twenties, but their net growth was extremely slow. Presbyterians added only 138 members, and white Methodists added only 616, although the native white population of the city grew by over 26,000 from 1920 to 1930.[53]

In sum, members of the mainstream Protestant denominations, including Presbyterian, Methodist, Disciples of Christ, Baptist, Episcopal, Lutheran, and Congregationalist of all races were a minority, even among that portion of the Gary population that belonged to some religious organization. In 1926 these mainstream Protestants totaled 16,281 (38.5 percent of the total church membership); in 1936 they totaled 18,639 (36.2 percent of the total church membership).[54] Nevertheless that minority loomed large in Gary's religious and civic life, including, as it did, large numbers of Gary's socioeconomically elite citizens. For all their size and importance, the Roman Catholic and Orthodox groups remained largely ethnic enclaves. The white Protestants, on the other hand, were thoroughly integrated into the public life of Gary and were in fact major shapers of that public life. Notwithstanding the dramatic decline in church membership during the twenties, Gary Protestants remained among the most important players on the municipal scene.

If I am correct about the importance of the Protestant presence in Gary, the portraits in the following chapters of First Presbyterian Church and

Table 2. Religious Membership in Gary, 1926–1936

Denomination	1926	1936	Percent Change
Baptist	6,750	6,360	−5.8%
Congregational	245	370	+51.0%
Disciples	863	915	+6.0%
Episcopal	819	665	−18.8%
Lutheran	2,200	3,377	+53.5%
Methodist	3,569	4,579	+28.3%
Orthodox	2,234	6,405	+186.7%
Presbyterian	2,235	2,373	+6.2%
Roman Catholic	20,063	21,677	+8.0%
Jewish	2,200	2,450	+11.4%
Other groups	1,067	2,210	+107.1%
Total Membership	42,245	51,381	+21.6%

Source: Bureau of the Census, *Religious Bodies:1926*, 1:426, and *Religious Bodies:1936*, 1:527.

Note: Many of Gary's black Protestants belonged to black Methodist and Baptist churches. In 1926, the Baptist groups included only 486 Northern (white) Baptists and 6,264 Negro Baptists. In 1936, the Baptist membership included 80 Northern Baptists, 1,032 members of the General Association of Regular Baptist Churches, and 5,248 Negro Baptists. In 1926, the Methodist figures included the following groups: 1,921 from the Methodist Episcopal Church; 9 from the Free Methodist Church; 761 from the African Methodist Episcopal Church; 155 from the African Methodist Episcopal Zion Church; and 723 from the Colored Methodist Episcopal Church. (The latter three were black denominations.) In 1936, the Methodists included 2,517 from the Methodist Episcopal Church, 29 from the Free Methodist Church, 906 from the African Methodist Episcopal Church, 232 from the African Methodist Episcopal Zion Church, and 895 from the Colored Methodist Episcopal Church.

City Methodist Church should illustrate that presence in detail at the congregational level and should confirm Protestantism's significant contribution to Gary's wider public life. But before moving to these specific congregations, some tentative conclusions are in order in light of the preceding summary of Gary history and brief survey of its religious landscape.

PROTESTANT PRESENCE

Criticism

First the Protestant presence, important or no, was not without its critics, from at least three directions. First, the Gary churches—white, black, and immigrant—came under fire consistently for what some regarded as an unseemly subservience to U.S. Steel. As noted above, U.S. Steel contributed regularly and generously to organizations in Gary until the mid-1930s. As the *Calumet Region Historical Guide* put it in 1939, "There is scarcely a church, hospital, fraternal or civic organization in Gary that has not received a contribution from the United States Steel Corporation." Descriptions of this process are often artlessly straightforward. For example, when Christ Church Episcopal was facing the need for building expansion in the early 1920s, "at the suggestion of some well-placed friends an appeal for assistance was addressed to the steel corporation and the corporation responded with a check for $40,000." By 1923, according to H. S. Norton, U.S. Steel had given more than $250,000 in cash to Gary churches alone, and this figure did not include the huge gift to City Methodist Church in the mid-1920s.[55] These critics claimed that U.S. Steel, aware of the importance of the church, was attempting to purchase the loyalty or at least the acquiescence of the churches. As one historian put it: "Many of the churches in Gary were trying to preach a social gospel and to make the church serve the needs of the industrial worker, but most of them, at the same time, remained financially dependent on United States Steel and consequently served its interests when a conflict developed."[56]

Black and immigrant churches also were criticized. Meister, for example, cited a Catholic priest's claim that U.S. Steel's benevolence to immigrant churches intended to stabilize immigrant neighborhoods and consequently to provide an unlimited work force. Greer cited a black minister who put it even more bluntly: "What has happened is that the churches have become subsidiaries of the steel corporation and that the ministers dare not get up and say anything against the company."[57] Likewise L. H. Caldwell, a black attorney, charged during the 1919 steel strike that "the local churches and ministers instead of working for humanity and preaching Christianity are directly and evidently working for the interests of the steel mills."[58]

By and large the charge is a just one, and there is only limited evidence of ministerial opposition to the corporation. But, as noted above, in the 1919 steel strike the rector at Christ Church, the church attended by H. S. Norton, A. P. Melton, and other U.S. Steel officials, defended from the pulpit the right of the workers to organize, and Balanoff pointed to at least two pro-union black pastors of major churches in the 1930s. Moreover, as Quillen suggested, the churches were not so much intentionally subservient to the corporation as they were in an ambiguous position with respect to it, a position "which few of its ministers probably admitted even to themselves."[59] But whatever their exact relationship, it is clear that Gary churches did not represent a radical critique of the place of U.S. Steel in the community.

A second and even more complex criticism of the churches' presence in Gary arises from their stance in the area of race relations. As we shall see below, Gary Protestants did respond to racial concerns in the 1920s, 1930s, and 1940s, and there were some successes. But there were many failures as well. Until the late 1940s Gary schools were, by and large, racially segregated, a practice that does not appear to have been criticized by the churches until the 1940s. According to Mohl and Betten, "Gary's religious life was segregated, too, since white Protestant and Catholic churches admitted no blacks."[60] Although black ministers were active in the Gary Council of Churches, organized in 1938, the ministers of Gary retained separate ministerial associations until late in the 1940s.[61] As we shall see, the Protestant churches were not silent about race, but neither were they radical advocates of progressive racial policies despite the growth of segregation in Gary prior to World War II.[62]

A third, more general critique of Gary's Protestant churches and ministers is that they consistently supported the white, middle-class, status quo. Admittedly Gary's Protestants were not radical advocates of social change. Although some, such as William Ward Ayer and Robert Ketcham of Central Baptist Church, were extremely conservative, most were more moderate.[63] But radicals they were not, and when a genuinely radical minister visited Gary, such as the defrocked Episcopal bishop William M. Brown, it was regarded as a newsworthy event.[64] Some ministers, Rabbi Garry August acknowledged, "are not men of strong determination who will utter truths in the face of opposition." Several years later during the Depression, August was more strident in his condemnation of the clergy: "Churches should not lull men into a state of bovine contentment. Churchmen should be criers in the market places and crossroads. But we became Babbitts too."[65]

To say that Gary's Protestant churches and ministers failed to advocate radical social change is to say that they were in this respect typical of American urban Protestantism. But it is not to say that they were hostile to the modern city or either unaware of or unresponsive to its needs. To the contrary, as Quillen noted of the 1920s, "many of Gary's churches developed well-balanced programs to meet the varied spiritual needs of the city."[66] Their impact may have been modest, but it was important.

Protestant Presence: Individual

The Protestant presence in Gary, that is, made a difference to this industrial city, although it clearly did not transform it. This pervasive presence manifested itself both individually and institutionally. By individual presence I mean to suggest that the mainline Protestant churches influenced Gary through their individual members. Such influence is impossible to document unambiguously, inasmuch as human motivation is such a complex matter. How can one tell, for example, if H. S. Norton made a decision because he was an Episcopalian, or a steel official, or something else altogether? Clearly one cannot. But the history of Gary is replete with clues that religious faith and church membership were often, not always, extremely significant to many of Gary's leaders.

On the simplest level is the undeniable fact that a large percentage of Gary's leaders claimed a religious affiliation. Meister, for example, noted that in a series of biographical sketches prepared in 1937 and 1943, 93 of the 111 "civic leaders" included claimed a religious affiliation. This 84 percent figure is well above the 51 percent of Gary's 1936 population which claimed religious affiliation. Of these ninety-three "twenty-four considered themselves Presbyterians, twenty-one Roman Catholics, nineteen Methodists and ten Episcopalians." Although, according to Meister, Gary's leaders had no established church, "the moral leadership for the community as a whole came from the larger Northside Protestant congregations, the Methodist City Church, Christ Episcopal Church, and the First Presbyterian Church."[67]

The figures bear him out. Of his ninety-three leaders who were church members, twenty-four (26 percent) were Presbyterians, although Presbyterians accounted for only 4.6 percent of Gary church members in 1936. Methodists constituted 20 percent of the leaders but only 9 percent of church members, and Episcopalians made up 11 percent of the leadership group but only 1.3 percent of total church members. By contrast, Catholic leaders constituted fully 42 percent of the city's church membership in 1936. Furthermore Meister claimed that "Gary was fortunate to have educated, outspoken clergymen leading these congregations" who were widely respected in the community.[68]

Granted then that many of Gary's elite belonged to Gary's Protestant churches, what difference, if any, did church membership make? Here statistics must give way to more impressionistic evidence. For example, it is undeniably true that several of Gary's major leaders gave immense amounts of time and energy to church affairs as well as to civic affairs. H. S. Norton is a good example. Aristocratic and sometimes autocratic, Norton was often accused of trying to run Gary on his own. As head of the Gary Land Company from 1907 to 1938, he wielded immense influence in Gary's formative decades and was known as the "Father of Gary." He served on many boards in Gary, including those of Stewart Settlement House, and was a powerful voice in Gary's commercial and political life. But Norton was also active in Christ Episcopal Church, where he served on the vestry, along with his U.S. Steel colleague, A. P. Melton, from 1908 to 1918. Another of his vestry colleagues, Harry Hall, was a builder and insurance agent, who served as senior warden of Christ Church for twenty-three years. Hall illustrates as well the wide-ranging activities of many of these men. In addition to church and business responsibilities, Hall was involved, sometimes in leadership positions, with the chamber of commerce, YMCA, Rotary Club, Gary Country Club, and Masonic Lodge.[69]

Each of the major Protestant congregations counted at least some of these leaders. The First Congregational Church had Ora Wildermuth, a lawyer and judge, and William F. Hodges, who was mayor of Gary and later a state senator. The Methodists had C. O. Holmes, a banker and state senator. Central Christian Church had Charles D. Lutz, a superintendent of schools after Wirt, Judge C. V. Ridgely, and pharmacist Edgar A. Ridgely.[70]

Less well known than Norton and some of the others, Edgar A. Ridgely illustrates perhaps even more clearly the Protestant presence at the individual level. When he died in January 1935, Ridgely had been a Gary druggist for twenty-six years. Over seven hundred persons attended his funeral at Central Christian Church, including many of Gary's leading citizens. H. S. Norton described Ridgely as one of those "who gave so much, not only of their means but of their time and energy, to the economic, social and cultural upbuilding of the community." The *Post-Tribune* noted that he had been an active member of Central Christian Church for over twenty years, praised him editorially as "the type of man communities depend on," and reported his funeral on the first page. His pastor, Monroe Schuster, eulogized him as "quiet, unassuming, self-effacing . . . an invaluable servant to our church and our community."[71] Clearly religious commitments were widely regarded, even in the public press, as a significant part of an individual's life that informed his or her civic life as well.

A Special Case: The Anselm Forum

The example of Reuben Olson and the Anselm Forum bridges Protestantism's "individual" presence and its "institutional" one. In 1932, Olson, a Norwegian-American Lutheran and foreman at U.S. Steel, and seven other young laymen began meeting regularly to discuss issues in human relations. From their meetings developed the Anselm Forum, named for the eleventh-century Archbishop of Canterbury who, according to Olson "urged men to forget hatred and work for peace." They sought "to bring reason, tolerance and intelligence to all problems, issues and associations in life; to put into action some of the truths proclaimed by our various religions and by democracy."[72] In a city known for its ethnic and racial animosities, the popularity of the Forum during the Depression decade was remarkable. By 1940, its membership of 100 represented five different races, forty-four nationalities, and forty religious faiths. By 1949, although its membership had increased to 150, there was still a long waiting list of others wanting to join.[73]

Although the Anselm Forum was not a religious group as such, religion was perhaps its major motivating force. But religious creeds apparently counted for little compared to religious action. As one member put it, "It's easy to be tolerant, you know, but we want men who are really strong in their religious feeling and who are willing to *do* something about it."[74]

The Forum's overall goal was to realize "brotherhood, the universal brotherhood of all mankind." In its pursuit the Forum intentionally sought diversity in its membership. For example, it sought out a black member and readily welcomed a Christian Scientist and a Moselm, even though each addition resulted in the departure of some other member in protest. The Forum even initiated an interracial family camp in 1946. As we have seen, Gary remained an extremely diverse community in the 1930s and 1940s— a diversity which threatened many in the steel city. But the Anselm Forum affirmed this diversity and perhaps embodied it more completely and intentionally than any other group in Gary. For example, the Forum set up thirteen five-man panels which led public discussions on a variety of issues throughout Gary and elsewhere in the state. As Margaret Frakes observed, although only one of the panels was devoted to discussing brotherhood, each of them embodied it "by having on its roster a Negro, a Jew, a Catholic and a member of a Protestant or Orthodox congregation." In addition to its panel discussions the Anselm Forum assembled a library of two hundred books and eight films on brotherhood which it made available to people in Gary and beyond, held open meetings on issues of current interest, and sponsored a radio program. In addition, the Forum often took public stands on social issues, such as the 1945 Froebel School Strike. But Frakes claimed that "despite the influence Anselmites have come to exert on the community as a group, it is probably the routine, everyday impact they make as individuals that counts most."[75]

One result of this individual influence was to take the message of brotherhood back into the churches from which the members had come. Claimed one member: "We have found here a way to put what religion teaches into action, and we have gone back into our churches to act as 'exciters' there." At least two members served as president of the Gary Council of Churches; Reuben Olson, in fact, was its first president in 1938. In addition, "many of the members have been or are church school superintendents; others are vestrymen, elders or other parish officers. Anselm, they say, makes them better churchmen."[76] Like the influence of the churches themselves, the influence of the Anselm Forum was both institutional and individual. Although a clearer example than most, the Anselm Forum illustrates at least one of the ways in which individuals in Gary expressed their religious convictions.

Protestant Presence: Institutional

The Protestant presence was also expressed institutionally in Gary as the churches themselves acted, sometimes singly and sometimes cooperatively, to influence the character of civic life in Gary. Four zones of Protestant presence will illustrate: social service and Americanization, race relations, the struggle against immorality and political corruption, evangelism and church extension.

From almost the beginning Gary's Protestants sought to provide social services to immigrant groups and later to blacks. The Presbyterians, for example, established their Neighborhood House as early as 1909, and the Methodists followed suit with Friendship House in 1914 and Stewart House in 1921. Unlike many another settlement house elsewhere in the country, Balanoff observed, both Neighborhood House and Friendship House extended their services to blacks as the black population began to rise in the 1920s and 1930s, thus "maintaining integrated facilities while public facilities were being increasingly segregated."[77] As noted in chapter 4, a principal goal of these church-sponsored settlement houses was the assimilation or Americanization as well as the conversion of the immigrant groups, but that does not deny that genuinely religious and altruistic motives were at work as well.

Similar mixed motives of social service and Americanization lay behind the weekday church schools. The original intent of the experiment in 1914 appears to have been the religious education of each church's children. But by the time the churches jointly formed the Board of Religious Education in 1917, the goal of the church schools had broadened to include an outreach to the unchurched. If the unchurched were immigrants, Americanization efforts were included as well. Gary's weekday church schools gained national attention, and stories appeared "about the new city that was interested in making character as well as rolling steel."[78] Both the settlement houses and the community church schools illustrate that in the area of social services and Americanization Gary's Protestants attempted to shape the life of their city.

A second important zone of institutional Protestant presence in Gary was the area of race relations. Although the Protestant record, by our standards, was not a distinguished one, the churches took several steps that should not be overlooked. In 1919, a year of race riots in nearby Chicago, the Calumet Church Federation sponsored a study of Gary's black population which identified three small ghetto areas and recommended certain corrective actions.[79] Later in the 1920s an interracial commission of black and white church members met to discuss racial issues. In 1926 its members included, among others, black pastor Charles Hawkins, white Congregationalist pastor W. C. Lyon, white Methodist layman C. O. Holmes, black social worker Thyra Edwards, and Buel Horn. Horn, a white Methodist minister and settlement house worker, chaired a subcommittee on housing and living conditions which derailed city plans to raze ninety-six tenement dwellings and thus prevented the displacement of their residents in the middle of the winter.[80] In 1924, William Grant Seaman, pastor of City Methodist Church, joined with four other ministers and the NAACP in an unsuccessful effort to prevent the showing of the racist film *Birth of a Nation*.[81] Churches cooperated in interracial church services and initiated others on their own. On February 13, 1927, for example, Gary churches planned an interracial Sunday evening service, in conjunction with Abraham Lincoln's birthday, that featured addresses by Seaman as well as black pastors Charles Hawkins and Frank Delaney. Attended by over eight hundred, despite bad weather, the service, according to Seaman, "should be a significant step toward guaranteeing that our community will not be cursed with the race riots and other unfortunate race relations that are all too common." The very next week Gary held its third annual "Better Understanding Day" to promote good will among people of various races and creeds.[82]

Black and white ministers occasionally met on an ad hoc basis to discuss particular problems, such as the Froebel School Strike in 1945. On that occasion the ministers discussed a resolution affirming that "the Christian ideal of brotherhood and equality must be the common approach of our entire community and its public institutions."[83] African-American churches and ministers participated prominently in the activities of the Gary Council of Churches in the 1940s, including the Gary Council of Church Women.[84] In 1940 these activities included a series of Fireside Forums—interracial, interreligious discussion meetings held in private homes, which gained national attention. According to the *Post-Tribune* the forums were "winning fame for Gary as a city where tolerance and prejudice are being overcome."[85] In 1946, the Council of Churches praised the board of education for adopting an interracial policy ending official segregation in the public schools.[86] These activities do not, however, represent a well-established, consistent advocacy of racial equality by Gary's white Protestant churches. But although their record on race was a mixed one, they periodically advocated better understanding between the races, thereby signaling a Protestant presence in the area of race relations.

A third zone of Protestant presence was as part of the protracted struggle against immorality and political corruption in Gary. Both individually and cooperatively Protestant churches played their role of community conscience in a variety of ways. The brief local experiment with prohibition in 1909 was largely an accomplishment of the Protestant churches and foreshadowed a sustained commitment, by at least portions of the Protestant community, to the cause of prohibition.[87] The more conservative Protestant groups inveighed, often in revival meetings, against all manner of individual vices and sins, and the *Post-Tribune* carried regular and sometimes lengthy accounts of their sermons. In October 1926, for example, it reported on Nazarene evangelist Forman Lincicome and his sermon on "A Lot in Sodom," in which he gave "advice to young girls on selecting the man they should marry, with occasional allusions to jazz, movies, card playing, dancing, questionable magazines, cigarets and drinking."[88] But even more mainline Protestants also participated in moral crusades of one kind and another. In 1934, for example, Protestant and Catholic leaders cooperated in a boycott of "motion pictures of an immoral and salacious nature." As for live entertainment, the Gary Ministerial Association, including the ministers from City Methodist, First Presbyterian, First Congregational, and Central Christian churches, sent a resolution to the city council protesting the promotion of endurance contests in Gary, such as walkathons, skatathons, and kissathons![89]

But they did not limit their targets to personal vices and dubious fads. Indeed, to a perhaps surprising degree, the Protestant pulpits of Gary turned their attention to Gary's political situation, condemning political corruption and even taking stands for and against particular candidates. For example, several Protestant leaders attacked mayors R. O. Johnson and Barney Clayton for their toleration of vice in Gary in the 1920s and 1930s; the Women's Citizens Committee mounted a campaign in the early 1950s against Mayor Peter Mandich; and the Lake County Churchmen for Good Government protested lax law enforcement in Gary and worked for specific reform candidates as late as 1962.[90] Protestants were thus active throughout Gary's history in a variety of campaigns against immorality and political corruption.

Finally, Gary's Protestants made their presence felt in efforts on behalf of evangelism and church extension. Given the traditional emphasis on conversion in American evangelicalism, this fact is hardly surprising. But it is instructive to observe in Gary the variety of ways in which Protestant churches attempted to discharge these traditional obligations. Some of the more conservative churches continued the tradition of annual evangelistic campaigns, but this approach was not always to the liking of the more liberal ministers and their congregations. As we shall see in the next two chapters, Joseph Avann and Frederick Backemeyer, of First Methodist Church and First Presbyterian Church, respectively, advocated revivals. But other mainline ministers, including William Grant Seaman and Frederick Walton of the same two churches, were less enthusiastic about traditional evangelistic services. In 1922, the Northwest Indiana Conference of the Methodist Church cautioned against "superficial emotionalism" and discouraged "the importing of professional evangelists . . . to do in an inferior way the work that should be done and can be done much better by the pastor." In Gary, the revivalistic tradition appears to have withered away in the 1920s and 1930s.[91]

Whatever else they were, the various cooperative church services in the city were one form of church extension. Monroe Schuster recalled that, in addition to the community church schools, the churches "worked together in union Thanksgiving and Lenten services as well as union Summer Vespers, every year, on the YMCA lawn downtown. . . . Our Ministerial Association, even that far back, provided weekly radio programs." These events, faithfully reported in the *Post-Tribune*, imparted a certain liturgical regularity to Gary's civil religious year and provided at least faint echoes of the frontier ecumenism of Gary's early years.[92]

But Protestant church leaders also sought, both individually and collectively, to preach to the unconverted and to add members to their church rolls. In so doing they revealed not only their enduring if changing commitment to the Protestant evangelical tradition but also their perception of their role in the urban community. Two major cooperative campaigns within a six-month period in 1926–27 are illustrative. The first was a city-wide church membership drive sponsored by the Gary Ministerial Association in October and November of 1926. Two months later, many of the same churches participated in the chamber of commerce's Civic Week, a quite extraordinary few days of "municipal evangelism" and 1920s boosterism.

Called by the president of the Ministerial Association "the most comprehensive campaign to increase religious attention ever attempted in Gary," the back-to-church campaign united eighteen Protestant churches in an attempt to increase Protestant church attendance by 20 percent. The campaign included a house-to-house religious census in October, ten days of noon-time Bible recitations by H. H. Halley of Chicago, a simultaneous delivery on October 24 in all eighteen churches of a common sermon on "The Place of the Church in the Community," and two weeks of personal evangelism led by H. R. DeBra, a Methodist minister, and involving some two hundred laymen from the churches.[93]

The results are somewhat unclear. The house-to-house visitors encountered several excuses for neglecting church membership, including uncertainty as to the length of one's stay in Gary, working on Sunday, and fatigue. DeBra reported a gain of 510 church members; the *Post-Tribune* reported elsewhere that "more than 200 new members were added to church rolls."[94] But it is clear that the leaders of the campaign regarded personal evangelism as an important part of the churches' mission both to the unchurched individuals and to the community as a whole. Said O. E. Tomes of Central Christian Church, "It is the spirit of every true American to do his part in developing those institutions upon which rests the safety of our country."[95] Prominent among those institutions were the churches.

The Civic Week campaign of February 1927 resembled nothing so much as a city-wide revival, although it was basically a chamber of commerce membership drive. Preceded by two weeks of newspaper publicity, the campaign was described in a *Post-Tribune* editorial as "a period of municipal evangelization, a week during which the gospel of community service will be preached from press, pulpit, rostrum and school . . . a municipal revival." The visiting "evangelist" was Dan Weigle, a civic booster from St. Paul, Minnesota. In speeches at First Presbyterian Church and at a combined meeting of the Rotary, Kiwanis, Optimist, and Lions clubs, Weigle called for "an integration of religion, education, and business" and claimed that "religion is the factor which keeps towns alive." He also identified the four "keystones" of the community as "the church, the school, the home, and the chamber of commerce."[96]

The campaign began on Sunday, February 6, with special sermons in Gary churches, including First Presbyterian and City Methodist churches. The chamber claimed that the cooperation of pastors was essential to the success of Civic Week, and several of them complied with sermons on "The City," "The Challenge of the City," and "Civic Righteousness." But the centerpiece of the drive was a personal visitation campaign in which 163 men sought to increase the membership of the chamber of commerce from six hundred to one thousand. Among those visitors were several prominent laymen from Gary Protestant churches, including Herschel Davis, E. A. Ridgely, and William Wirt. Although falling short of its goal, the campaign was a modest success, adding 303 new members to the chamber.[97]

That the Civic Week program of February 6, 1927, was followed on February 13 by Inter-Racial Sunday and on February 20 by Better Understanding Day illustrates the pervasive and complex Protestant presence in Gary. Although a minority of the community, Gary Protestants regarded themselves, and were regarded by others, as distinctively responsible for the welfare of the urban community.

The last few pages have suggested in general terms ways in which some of these congregations attempted to fulfil their responsibility in Gary's first few decades. But if I am to make the case that Gary's Protestants were "at home in the city" during these years, it is necessary to examine in greater detail the pattern of the Protestant presence in Gary. It is impractical to produce an "ecclesiastical biography" of each congregation in Gary. But a closer look at two of Gary's principal downtown congregations, First Presbyterian Church and City Methodist Church, will enhance the more general account of Protestantism provided in this chapter by bringing to bear the distinctive perspective of congregational history.

It should also give some names and faces to the inquiry, as we meet Frederick Walton, Frederick W. Backemeyer, William Grant Seaman, William Clark, and others. They are largely forgotten today, even in Gary. But fifty and sixty years ago, they were central players in Gary, Indiana, and in some cases were known well beyond its borders. Their stories and the stories of the congregations they served illustrate eloquently the nature of urban Protestantism prior to World War II.

CHAPTER SIX

"Old First Church": First Presbyterian Church and Traditional Protestantism in Gary

INTRODUCTION

Gary's social history confirms that the collective Protestant influence on the city, through such institutions as settlement houses and weekday church schools, was considerable. But an adequate understanding of the experience of urban Protestants requires careful attention not only to the city-wide Protestant presence but to the congregational level as well. Unfortunately, aside from relatively brief treatment in the standard scholarly accounts of Gary, professional historians have paid little attention to Gary's Protestant congregations. Nonetheless a retrieval of their experience in Gary and their contributions to the city's civic life can inform in significant ways our understanding not only of Gary's social and religious history but of how mainstream Protestant congregations fared in the twentieth-century industrial city.

No two congregations, of course, can adequately represent the rich complexity of American Protestantism. But First Presbyterian Church and City Methodist Church do represent two major tributaries of the Protestant mainstream.[1] Presbyterian and Congregationalist congregations were the earliest and most important representatives of the Calvinist, Reformed tradition in American Protestantism. Methodism, originally a revitalization movement within Anglicanism, was a champion of revivalism and one of the major success stories on the American frontier. By the late nineteenth century, Presbyterians and Methodists were two of the most important Protestant groups in the United States.[2] Although particularly significant within liberal Protestantism, each contained major conservative elements as well. In effect, they represented a theological cross-section of American Protestantism.[3]

In Gary, First Presbyterian Church and City Methodist Church were the major representatives of these two denominations. In addition they embodied two different emphases within mainstream Protestantism—the rather traditional, evangelical stance of First Presbyterian and the more progressive, social gospel orientation of City Methodist. But despite these differences, the actual experiences of the two congregations were remarkably similar. Both Presbyterians and Methodists founded congregations out of a sense of urgency, motivated at least partly by the conviction that Protestant churches were essential to any civilized community. In a day when the civility of Gary was in doubt, the appearance of Presbyterian and Methodist congregations augured well for the new city. Eventually of course a congregation required a building, and the appearance of church buildings on the landscape was a welcome sign. For the congregations a building was also an assertion of denominational pride, an embodiment of basic symbols of the faith, a realization of sacred space, and at least a suggestion (much more in the Methodist case) of the church's envisioned role in the city.[4] In addition to the congregations themselves and their buildings, the ministerial leadership of the churches was important to both the churches and the city. In Gary's formative decades, the ministers of the leading churches were prominent public figures, and their ministry had broad public implications.

Consequently, in the accounts to follow of First Presbyterian Church and City Methodist Church, these three common themes—congregational formation, building programs, and ministerial leadership—will occupy center stage, illustrating both the attitude of these congregations toward their city and the ways they functioned within it.[5] At times during, for example, the pastorate of William Grant Seaman at City Methodist Church, this attitude to the city was clearly articulated. But more often we will have to examine how these Protestants actually lived in their urban community in order to determine what they thought about the city and their relationship to it.

As we will see, Gary's Protestant congregations filled at least two distinct roles in their city. On the one hand, they functioned as what we might call subcommunities within the broader urban community. As historian Thomas Bender has argued, community in the modern city must be sought not at the level of the entire city but at the level of the city's many subcommunities. Citing Louis Wirth's famous 1938 essay, "Urbanism as a Way of Life," Bender agrees that the modern city precludes the traditional, homogeneous community. But this decline of traditional community does not eliminate the possibility of a vital public life in the modern city. Says Bender: "A sense of commonweal, rather than community, provides the essential foundation for a vigorous and effective political life . . . based upon shared public ideals, rather than upon acquaintance or affection."[6]

Like other voluntary associations, these congregations struggled for survival, recruited and served members in a variety of ways, and sought to differentiate themselves from other like organizations. This need to differentiate, for example, helps to explain the rapid emergence of denominational loyalties in the midst of the city's frontier ecumenism. Denominational loyalties were, among other things, subcommunity loyalties.[7] The congregations also facilitated the creation of other organizations, such as Bible classes and various clubs, which functioned as still another layer of subcommunities and which were of extraordinary importance to many of Gary's Protestants. Gary's Protestant congregations themselves, then, functioned as subcommunities and fostered still others in the midst of the modern city.

On the other hand, Gary's Protestants also played a broader public role in the community, a role that was more problematic for urban Protestants than rural ones. Whereas their subcommunal function in the cities resembled that of rural Protestants, the public presence of Protestantism in the modern city was quite different. Clearly Protestants did not dominate the pluralistic, industrial city as they had dominated the more homogeneous, rural America. But neither did they turn inward or withdraw to the periphery of urban life. As the accounts of First Presbyterian Church and, especially, City Methodist Church will show, their public role continued to be important for both the congregations and the city at least until the early 1950s. By virtue of their public significance in Gary, the churches felt they had a right and even a duty to speak out on issues of public importance, especially questions of morality. Admittedly they did not do so with equal fervor on all such issues, and their choice of issues (for example, prohibition and Sunday baseball) might seem to the modern observer idiosyncratic or bizarre. But the very confidence with which they spoke manifests their acknowledged public role. The Protestant role was thus both subcommunal and public, but the relative importance of one role or the other varied substantially from congregation to congregation.

First Presbyterian Church, for example, represented a more traditional Protestant presence in Gary and was more likely to emphasize the subcommunal role, directing much of its energy toward the concerns of its members and its own institutional well-being. But in the process, it also recognized its public role and responded in significant ways to the city of which it was a part. City Methodist Church, by contrast, emphasized for much of its history its public role and its outreach to the city, while at the same time fulfilling its subcommunal responsibilities to its own members. In their own ways, then, both congregations attempted to influence their city by virtue of a prominent public presence from 1906 to approximately 1950. During those years, in good times and bad, these congregations saw themselves as integral participants in the wider life of their community. They were, in a word, at home. But the rapid changes that engulfed Gary in the 1950s and 1960s undercut their own self-image and altered dramatically their role in the city they called home.

THE WALTON YEARS

Congregational Origins

Out of the historical haze surrounding the origins of First Presbyterian Church, one date stands out clearly. On October 18, 1908, in the Broadway Theater, the Reverend Frederick E. Walton held a communion service, ordained two elders and a deacon, and accepted twenty-nine charter members into the First Presbyterian Church.[8]

Presbyterian beginnings in Gary, however, were far less precise than this first service would suggest and were part and parcel of early Gary's frontier ecumenism. But, unclear as it may be, this early history provides a vivid and fascinating account of just how difficult it was to establish a Protestant congregation in the new steel city. It also illustrates a denomination's desire both to help a local congregation and to control it, the importance of local leadership, and the idiosyncratic effect of clerical ambition.

Gary's first official Presbyterian presence was inaugurated by the arrival of M. A. Stewart, "a Presbyterian Sunday School missionary" sent to Gary in July 1906. Stewart began his work "among a hodgepodge mass of people of various nationalities who had for their homes temporary shacks, tents, and dugouts and utterly without religious privileges; no religious work having been undertaken by any denomination." Another Presbyterian Sunday school worker, I. M. Houser, first visited Gary in October 1906 and became heavily involved in the establishment of Presbyterian work in Gary. According to Houser, "A union sunday school was organized and had its first meeting under an oak tree near the present corner of Broadway and Third Avenue." This was almost certainly the union Sunday school described in the previous chapter. According to Houser, it "had a checkered experience due to the lack of workers and a place of meeting and was closed on that account when winter came."[9] Stewart then began a ministry to the construction workers in a construction camp euphemistically referred to as the Falkenau Inn. But the Presbyterian Sunday school work moved in October 1906 to Tolleston (an older settlement to the west which Gary annexed in 1910) when Houser discovered that "the Gary Land Co. would not permit us to erect any temporary chapel for our work." Since the Gary Land Company permitted Christ Church to erect a temporary chapel only a year later (in December 1907), Houser's account is mystifying. Perhaps U.S. Steel changed its policy in order to encourage the establishment of churches within the First Subdivision.[10] Presbyterian work at Gary centered on Tolleston for a year after October 1906, and "the work at Gary was suspended so far as any attempt at public services" was concerned.[11]

Houser continued to visit Gary during that year, however, eventually securing thirty signatures to a petition requesting the Presbytery of Logansport to begin a church in Gary. As local Presbyterian historian, William Joder, wryly noted, "Many of these signatures later turned out to be nothing more than the registering of no particular objection to the proposal." On October 25, 1907, two representatives from presbytery held a meeting in the Delaware Hotel in order to organize a Presbyterian church, but Gary's primitive conditions frustrated their efforts. Houser described the scene as follows: "A fierce storm was raging that night and the darkness of the unlighted streets was intense, so that going out was difficult and dangerous. On this account only a very few were present." Although one deacon was elected, he was, in fact, absent and could not be ordained at that time, and the organization of the church could not be completed. This first attempt to form a Presbyterian church was a failure. As winter approached, no suitable meeting place could be found, and no regular services were held until the spring of 1908.[12]

Presbytery had not forgotten Gary, however, and a February 18, 1908, letter from Houser referred to a meeting called to "thrash out the Gary matter." That meeting, on February 24, 1908, heard enthusiastic reports on the Gary mission field from Houser, Dr. George Knox (who had preached in Gary on occasion), and Dr. Henry Webb Johnson of South Bend. Those in attendance decided to ask the denomination's Board of Church Erection for $5,000 for the Gary work. Their request was approved, apparently on the condition that the Synod of Indiana raise an equal amount.[13]

Their fund-raising efforts continued at least into the fall of 1908, and their letters referred frequently to them, including their own pledge payments of $100 and $200. Henry Webb Johnson of South Bend wrote: "While I have subscribed $100, I deem the work so important at Gary that I will give more if it is needed. It is a great opportunity for our Presbytery to plant a church in that growing city." Some thirty-two churches in the presbytery were solicited for amounts ranging from $10 to $500 for this "greatest missionary field known." Fund-raising efforts even went beyond the local presbytery. The New Albany Presbytery, for example, attempted to meet its goal of $100, and its fund-raising letter indicated vividly the missionary enthusiasm for the work at Gary:

> Gary is a new city. The manufacturing plants now in operation, and those under construction, when finished, will give employment to 100,000 men. Eighty saloons have recently been put out of business, so Gary is a Dry City. We now have a great opportunity to give them the Gospel. The General Assembly last May at Kansas City, because of the unprecedent [*sic*] opportunity, directed the Board of Church Erection to give $5,000 for a building at Gary, on condition that the Synod of Indiana raise $10,000.00. . . . Will you invest $5.00 in this great Home Mission work, the greatest that has ever come to the Synod of Indiana?[14]

In spring 1908, the Presbyterians rented the Broadway Theater for their morning service, one of several Gary religious groups to use it. Although the theater was more suitable than several other options, it was not without its drawbacks. In order, for example, to clear the hall for the regular show, the management extinguished the lights, even when the service was still in progress. Some mothers complained that their children hid under the seats after church so as to stay and see the movie, and, on one occasion, an electric piano, which had ceased playing during a power failure the night before, resumed in the middle of the Sunday service with "Hail, Hail, the Gang's All Here."[15] Moreover the congregation considered the five-dollar rent for the theater for only two hours on Sunday morning to be exorbitant. Finally it was impossible to hold Sunday evening services there, services which, some were convinced, would better meet the needs of steel men who had to work in the mills during the day on Sunday.[16]

So with the promise of over thirteen thousand dollars in denominational funds to back them, Gary's Presbyterians arranged to purchase three lots at Sixth Avenue and Monroe Street from the Gary Land Company and started planning for a building.[17] By September 1908 their plans were complete, and bids were in. But although the congregation hoped to be in the chapel by Thanksgiving, construction had not yet begun. Strained relationships with presbytery officials were partly to blame. Since the Gary work was a missionary enterprise, denominational officials had been involved from the beginning. Houser, for example, represented the synodical office in Indianapolis. But despite the commitment of these officials to the mission field at Gary, their willingness to work with the Gary Presbyterian leaders was often suspect. For example, suspicion of the local leadership was reflected in the synod's decision that the actual title to the property should be vested in the trustees of the synod, not in the local church, at least for the time being. George Knox advocated this position, for example, in a letter to John Vanatta on July 23, 1908:

> If the property is in the hands of their trustees they can do as they will. I have always thought since the church was organized so loosely and the Board and the Synod furnishing nearly all the money that for a time the Presbytery or the Synod should hold the title to the lots and the property and safeguard the money put in by the Synod and the Board. This is specially true since the men who now run the Gary church are not the men who will be or should be in charge after the operating force comes on the ground and the steel plant is in full operation. The character of the church may be wholly changed within a year or in their rule or ruin policy when they ignore the councils of the committee and the Presbytery they may keep out of the church those who should come into it. Findley says even now many Presbyterians on the ground are going over to the Congregational Church.[18]

Ah, Findley, the bone of contention! It was not, after all, the building program alone that soured the relationship between local leaders and the presbytery. But the building coincided with a complicated and fascinating tale over the selection of a pastor, a tale that reveals much about the interplay of denomination, local lay leadership, and clergy. In the end, the Gary leaders selected their own pastor and built their building too.

As noted above only a few services were held during the winter of 1907–1908, with Houser or Knox in the pulpit. But the church rented the Broadway Theater for services in the spring of 1908, and, during April, May, and June, the Reverend F. A. Hamilton filled the pulpit. Apparently Hamilton had been selected by presbytery as the Gary pastor and forced on the congregation against its will. If so, it was an unfortunate decision.[19]

Hamilton and his family came to Gary from Grand Rapids, Michigan. According to the *Northern Indiana,* he enjoyed considerable early success in fund-raising and was popular with his parishioners, but "then the shock came." "Rev. Frederick A. Hamilton, the pastor of the First Presbyterian Church in Gary, was not allowed to preach Sunday. . . . This decision was reached at a meeting of the Gary Presbyterians Friday night, as a result of the unfrocking of the popular man in Grand Rapids, where he was charged with cigarette smoking, taking liquor to excess and slumming tours." In this article the paper appeared to take Hamilton's side; under the main headline, "Rev. Hamilton Falls Down," the paper printed secondary headlines, "Congregation With Him" and "Envious Critics Who Would Like the Post Pulling Wires Vigorously." By August, however, the *Northern Indiana* reported, also on the front page, charges of "intoxication, entering a house of ill fame and contracting bad debts." Hamilton defended himself by claiming "that he drank but one bottle of ale on a dining car" and that he went to a brothel twice "to rescue a white slave and in company with his wife."[20] The church was not impressed.

Hamilton remained in Gary during July and attempted to fight the charges, but his conduct, according to Houser, was "so thoroughly bad that he is respected by nobody."[21] When Hamilton left town suddenly in early August, leaving behind an unpaid hotel bill of four-hundred dollars, along with his clothes, books, and typewriter, the *Northern Indiana* reported that he had a history of bad debts in at least ten cities from Philadelphia to Chicago. Of the debt owed to hotel owner O'Donnell, the paper quipped, "There are still several people in Gary who have faith in their late pastor. Whether Mr. O'Donnell possesses faith of the same variety is not known."[22] The affair created such a sensation in the region that a Presbyterian minister from New York State read about it in the newspaper while visiting his sister in Chicago.[23]

Meanwhile several presbytery leaders, including George Knox, decided that the Gary church should accept the Reverend John Findley as Hamilton's successor and do so by July 19. Said Knox: "If possible let us fix Findley at Gary at once." Two others, Dr. Henry Webb Johnson and the Reverend A. M. Smith, wrote letters to the church strongly endorsing Findley, but "the wording was such that Gary men read into them the command to take Findley" and a threat to withhold funding if they did not. The leaders at Gary resented the advice. As Johnson subsequently admitted, "There are some Scotchmen in the church at Gary that are difficult propositions to handle." These "Scotchmen" gave Findley an extremely cool reception when he came to fill the pulpit on July 19, a reception not lost on the Reverend Mr. Findley. Although he conducted "an excellent service on Sabbath," he was obviously not the man for the Gary Presbyterians.[24]

But by July 19, in any case, they had made up their own minds concerning their next pastor. As it happened, the New York pastor who had read about Hamilton in the Chicago paper was seeking a new call. So it was that Frederick E. Walton took the train to Gary "to see if there might possibly be an opening for him." Other accounts say Walton came out of curiosity "to see what was going on in a place which would grow from zero to fifteen thousand in population in two years." He met with Dr. E. E. Geisel, a trustee of the church, and Geisel introduced him to Houser who was visiting Gary at the time. Two facts about Walton, a thirty-nine-year-old Union seminary graduate, impressed Houser. First, he had spent the previous twelve years at Hornell, New York, serving a mission church that grew from some forty members to over five hundred. Second, he came from a family of some means and was willing to work initially for a very low salary. Both factors apparently impressed the Gary church leaders as well, despite their judgment that "Findley was a better preacher than Walton." Consequently on Monday, July 20, they selected Frederick E. Walton as their pastor.[25]

The decision angered the leaders of presbytery who had sought to place John Findley, a known quantity, in the Gary pulpit. They simply did not trust the local leaders in Gary to make a wise decision. As George Knox wrote to John Vanatta in July 1908, "The men who now run the Gary church are not the men who will be or should be in charge after the operating force comes on the ground and the steel plant is in full operation."[26] Admittedly mobility in Gary was high, but mobility was more characteristic of the laborers than of the middle-class supervisory and professional men represented in the Presbyterian leadership at Gary.

In fact, the argument over Gary appears to have centered as much on the character of the laity as on the qualifications of Walton. To presbytery they appeared to be stubborn Scots who would not accept guidance. Their great defender in all this controversy was Houser who, significantly, appears to have spent more time at Gary than the others. To Knox's objections, Houser retorted bluntly: "You are in error when you say those men are not fit to handle the property of Gary church. I have never found the same number of men having comparable experience in affairs of business in any of our new churches. . . . Mainly they are Supts. of departments in the steel mill and the Gary Land Co.—Dr. Geisel being an exception and he is a prosperous physician. You see they are men of affairs; in their business they think matters over and are in the habit of having their conclusions respected." The Reverend J. B. Donaldson concurred with Houser in a September 4, 1908, letter to Vanatta: "These men are superintendents: all of them; accustomed to taking and managing great enterprises. They do not like to be ignored, though they do not show any bad spirit about it." Sociologically, Houser and Donaldson had correctly identified the Gary Presbyterians. From the very first it was a church of "superintendents"— mid to upper management in the mills—and professional men. That fact both insured the congregation's position of prominence in the community and perhaps contributed to its somewhat limited vision in living out its faith in a city like Gary.[27]

Once they had decided for Walton, then, Walton it would be. But there was one problem—Walton was a bachelor. Advised that life in Gary would be far more comfortable for a married man, Walton reported that he was already engaged. A more disturbing aspect of Walton's bachelorhood, however, was a report from New York regarding his relationships with older women. A. M. Smith, a steadfast opponent of Walton, wrote to John Vanatta, the treasurer of presbytery, on July 29, 1908, with charges he attributed to "the Synodical missionary of New York" to the effect that Walton "has a mania of courting old women, inducing them to take him with them and going on long journeys to Florida and to Europe." Then Smith went on to blast his own denominational colleague: "Houser let

Walton into Gary before he knew a thing about him. He was at Gary when Hamilton was called and urged the people to make their invitation unanimous. I am about ready to tell Houser to get out of Gary and give someone else a chance." Given the charges, local presbytery officials made inquiries about Walton. The overwhelmingly favorable response convinced even such Walton foes as A. M. Smith and H. W. Johnson. Smith, in fact, acknowledged, perhaps sheepishly, to Vanatta on August 7, 1908, that he had received "letters regarding his relationship with the old ladies which clear up the matter with me. They were relatives of his mother and had taken a great liking to him." A few days later Smith wrote Vanatta again reporting that he had received some twenty letters from New York concerning Walton, only one of which was unfavorable. He conceded: "I cannot get a trace of any scandal and inasmuch as the Gary Church wants him I have decided to withdraw any objection and I believe the only thing we can do is to recommend him if he brings the proper credentials to our presbytery, not before." The matter, once settled, faded into official obscurity. Walton arrived in Gary in August 1908, accompanied by his bride, Mary, who remained an influential force in the Gary church until her death in 1946.[28]

Despite occasional grumbling from some members of presbytery, Walton became immensely popular in Gary and was remembered in succeeding historical accounts as the revered and successful founding pastor. Indeed, the communion service he held on October 18, 1908, in the Broadway Theater came to be the official founding date for the church since it was at that time that members were received, trustees were elected, and two elders and a deacon were ordained. Of any earlier organization, "there was not a record anywhere."[29]

Twenty-nine (thirty in some accounts) members were received that day. Gary, still virtually a construction camp, had a population of some seven to eight thousand, most of whom were young men. Elder James McCorkle was said to be one of only "three gray-haired men in Gary." Despite the promise of wealth that drew people to Gary, Walton reported that "the people are poor and our houses are being built by outside capital and exorbitant rents are being charged." But notwithstanding the poverty and frontier conditions Gary's citizens were taking some steps toward respectability. In January 1909 Walton reported that "a room has recently been opened as a public library and reading room" and "our saloons are now reduced to about 40." He went on to report the efforts of at least five other

Reverend Frederick E.
Walton, pastor of First
Presbyterian Church,
1908–1925. Courtesy of
First United Presbyterian
Church, Gary, Indiana.

Protestant congregations and a Polish Catholic one to begin work in Gary.[30]

A list of the church's charter members confirms that they were not a random sample of Gary's polyglot population. Virtually all had either British or German surnames, and had come to Gary from other churches in the Midwest—Joliet and Chicago, Illinois, and Donora and Clairton, Pennsylvania, for example. The only immigrants as such were from Scotland. There were Scots in the church after all! An example of the church leaders was A. R. McArthur, the son of a Scottish immigrant. He grew up on a farm, graduated from the University of Wisconsin in 1900, and began work with U.S. Steel in Gary in 1910, eventually becoming chief mechanical engineer of the Gary Tin Mills. An enthusiastic participant in civic affairs, he served as president of the Board of Education for twelve years. He was a leader in the Gary church as well, serving as elder and Sunday school teacher for many years until his death in 1929.[31]

Subsequent congregational growth continued, principally among Gary's native, white, middle-class population. Synod minutes in 1908, for example, described the church as "for the English speaking people." Years later, Lillian Call reported that the church membership included business persons, superintendents from the mills, and even a few mayors of Gary. Although basically "middle class," they were generally younger family people with no inherited wealth.[32] Except for Persians, about whom more later, names of immigrants appear only occasionally in the records. But the Session Minutes for March 27, 1910, recorded that "Joseph, the infant son of Mr. and Mrs. Cormos was baptized at the home of the parents, they showing themselves through the aid of [an] interpreter to be very devout Christians and making a very good confession of their faith in Christ." In 1917 a foreign-born member named Hosama was even elected to fill an unexpired term on the Session, but the church records indicate he was suspended in March 1919.[33]

If ethnically homogeneous, the early members of First Presbyterian Church were denominationally diverse, the Session Minutes for 1908–1909 recording new members from Congregational, Methodist, Baptist, Disciple, English Lutheran, Reformed, and Brethren churches. Although less mobile than the laboring classes in Gary, the Presbyterians moved too, and the Session Minutes recorded the movements of members far and wide, many to Chicago.[34]

But despite mobility, growth was rapid. In January 1909, Walton reported a church membership of sixty in the first three months. By April 1909, the membership totaled eighty-four, which grew in successive years to 220 (1910), 322 (1911), 404 (1912), and 527 (1913). By November 1917, Walton had added 1,100 members (581 on confession of faith and 518 from other churches) and lost 400 by removal or death, leaving a total of over 700. By 1920, membership had topped one thousand. As the *Gary Daily Tribune* editorialized on the occasion of Walton's tenth anniversary in Gary, "He has met with marvelous success in his ministry. His church is one of the most flourishing in the city."[35]

Organizational growth was as rapid as membership growth. As the various congregations in Gary functioned as subcommunities in the midst of the city, so a variety of organizations within the congregations constituted another layer of subcommunities. First Presbyterian Church was no exception, and a 1917 historical summary exulted in the fact that the church had a "closely graded Sunday School . . . three Christian Endeavor Societies, the Junior, Intermediate and Senior. There is a Women's Society of more than 200 members divided into four circles, besides a flourishing

Woman's Missionary Society. The men are organized into a Brotherhood and have met weekly during the past winter."[36]

In addition to these official organizations, other organizations were important to many within the church for many years. Classes and groups such as Alpha Class for women and Tri Mu for men started out as children's Sunday school classes and continued for years, changing function as their members aged. Alpha Class, for example, began in 1917 as a group in their middle teens with the goal of developing "a spirit of Love and Loyalty among its members and to be of service to the Church, the Sunday School and the girls throughout the City of Gary." Later on they raised funds for the church, developed a glee club, and held an annual Brides and Babies Party, since "so many of our members were now of marriageable age." As they acknowledged, "since one of our considerations was to promote a closer union between the young women of our church, our social meetings have been very important." But they undertook a number of service projects as well, providing funds for an Armenian orphanage and contributing to a milk fund for the Neighborhood House nursery, among other activities.[37]

Of special importance to First Presbyterian Church was Tri Mu, which began in 1909 as a Sunday school class for ten-to-twelve-year-old boys taught by the pastor's wife, Mary Walton. Members later recalled fondly their early meetings in a tent on the church grounds, the doughnuts and coffee prepared by Mrs. Walton, and the hymn singing in the Walton home, with Mr. Walton at the piano. The boys were old enough to serve in the military by World War I; ninety-six class members served in that war, and at least one died there. By 1934 Tri Mu had become a men's Bible class which, among other activities, sponsored a Boy Scout troop. At Tri Mu's thirty-second anniversary in 1941, sixty-five current and former members attended. "The boys of 1909 and succeeding years, now numbering some of the city's leading business, professional, and industrial men, sang the old hymns and heard a Bible lesson by the class's original teacher, Mrs. F. E. Walton, who still instructs the group each week." Gary's pervasive racism was, unfortunately, reflected in Tri Mu's annual minstrel shows which began in 1921 or 1922 and continued at least until 1934 as a high spot in the church's social year. Yet on the other hand, they also heard from Mrs. Walton lessons on Christian brotherhood and race relations in which they discussed "what should a Christian do when a Negro is refused food in a restaurant where it is perfectly legal for him to enter and buy food?" "How far," she asked her charges, "is our church willing to go in the actual practice of racial brotherhood?" As members recollected in a 1958 historical pageant, "Young men coming to Gary found themselves welcomed into this friendly group where Christian living was learned and practiced. Once a Tri Mu, always a Tri Mu because of the influence of Mary Walton."[38]

By 1931 the church numbered some twenty-six such organizations "which function as 'units,' raise certain funds, and expend them in social and spiritual channels." In twenty years, for example, the Missionary Society raised almost ten thousand dollars for missions. Members' long-term loyalty to these organizations bespeaks the importance of such groups, both to individuals and to the church.[39]

Church discipline was also part of the Presbyterian experience in Gary, especially when members requested letters of dismissal to another church. In May 1916, for example, the Session refused to grant letters of dismissal to Dr. E. E. Geisel and Mr. J. A. Umpleby. Geisel, a charter member and trustee, grew up in Minnesota, came to Gary in 1907 as Gary's fifth physician, and was active in the founding of the congregation. He "had subscribed to the building fund of the church and had refused to pay the same and would not give the trustees any reasons for not doing so." The matter was later resolved, and Geisel was readmitted to church membership. Umpleby's case was more serious, however, inasmuch as "he ran a pool room and gambling place while living in Gary." That would hardly do for a group that a year earlier had discussed the issues of dancing, card playing, and prohibition.[40]

Ministerial Leadership

The "new urban history," like the new social history generally, has attempted to do history "from the bottom up," preferring to study the common people instead of leadership elites. There is, of course, much to be said for this approach. As the new social historians have noted, traditional historical writing often ignored the experience of marginalized groups, including racial minorities and women, and attempts to remedy the situation have enriched immeasurably our historical understanding. But as with many such methodological shifts, there is a danger of going too far. Leaders are important, not just to themselves, but to the communities they lead, and to know something about their story is to know something about the community's story as well. Amateur congregational history, too, often has been criticized for excessive attention to the minister at the expense of men and women in the pews. But these amateur historians often have focused attention on ministerial leadership for some very good reasons. As a rule leadership is tremendously important in religious organizations, and to overlook the leader in American congregations is in a sense to overlook the congregation.[41]

As the pastor of a large, growing church, Walton assumed a prominent role in Gary's public life. Despite the fragmentary character of the church records during the Walton years, three aspects of Walton's public role (and that of the church) stand out—Walton as a pastor, Walton as a Protestant leader, and Walton as a public figure.

Like any other local pastor, Walton was expected to minister to the needs of his parishioners, to strive to increase their number, and, if necessary, to build an adequate physical facility. Walton succeeded on all three accounts. Throughout his years in Gary, Walton established a reputation as a friendly, hospitable man who "took in anybody." That spirit of generous hospitality, in the midst of a raw, rough city of strangers, impressed the people of Gary. According to Lillian Call: "The Waltons had open house all the time. They brought newcomers to Gary to their home and to the church. Many small groups met in their home before they were able to get their own meeting places." She remembered with particular fondness the Waltons inviting the church's young people to their home after the Sunday evening service to sing around the piano and enjoy the fire in the fireplace. As Joder noted, in addition to using his own home, Walton, ". . . seeing the lack of wholesome social life in the new town, inaugurated a successful series of receptions in various homes. These entertainments, given by local talent, were so popular with the general public that standing room was at a premium. In the meantime, the congregation grew in number along with Gary's phenomenal growth."[42]

But the job called for more than hospitality. In a tribute after Walton's death, his successor, Frederick Backemeyer, spoke of the many responsibilities the Waltons assumed upon arriving in Gary: ". . . making friends, helping newcomers, organizing the church, receiving members, building up the Sunday School, planning a permanent building, and doing the thousand and one things that an energetic pair would do in a pioneer movement, believing that the future would demand spiritual as well as economic forces."[43]

Walton's 1922 report to the congregation reflects his basic humility as he oversaw this increasingly large and complex church organization. He expressed gratitude for the work during the year by the various organizations, noting that they had worked together "in excellent Christian harmony." He praised the revival of the men's club, which had come to the attention even of "the business men of the city." The only weak link he noted, to be repeated again and again by Gary ministers, was the Wednesday evening prayer meeting, which was poorly attended. He concluded: "With so many people as God has given us, what is there too hard for us to undertake? The Elders desire to express their gratitude to all who are giving and working so much to help in this great work. Let us strive to have the Spirit of Christ prevail more and more until the world outside, seeing our good works, shall learn to glorify our Father which is in Heaven." All the praise he reserved for others, calling no attention to his own accomplishments.[44]

These accomplishments were considerable. As table 3 indicates, donations to meet congregational expenses had increased from $1,100 in 1909 to $17,386 in 1922, and missions giving had increased from $87 in 1909 to $2,309 in 1922. First Presbyterian Church had grown from 84 members to 1,318 during those years; some 245 of that number represented adult baptisms. The increase in membership reflects Walton's success as an evangelist. Indeed his successor proclaimed that "the finest tribute we can pay him today is to say that he desired to win people to Christ and to the church he loved." He did not, however, love revivals. Although the Session Minutes occasionally mentioned evangelistic services, more often than not these services were in cooperation with other groups, such as the Federation of Churches in Gary. Walton himself was less than enthusiastic about traditional revivals. William Clark, later pastor at City Methodist Church, recounted a time when ". . . a tent evangelist came to Gary, and many of Walton's own congregation went there and kept urging Walton to go there. Walton had little time for that method but decided to be fair minded he should go. Being a canny Scot he took an aisle seat. When a young woman seeking converts asked him, 'Sir, are you a Christian?' he replied, 'I was, lassie, when I came in here.' "[45] But revivals or no, the church grew, repeatedly outgrowing its physical quarters. As a pastor, then, Walton also had to be a builder.

In Gary's early days, a church building was almost a condition of survival. Without one, Gary's Presbyterians had to suspend services during two consecutive winters (1906–1907 and 1907–1908). But before the

Table 3. First Presbyterian Membership and Finances, 1908–1975

Year	Members	Receipts	Year	Members	Receipts
1908	35	——	1942	1,460	19,505
1909	84	1,100	1943	1,474	22,651
1910	220	3,462	1944	1,570	23,806
1911	322	3,572	1945	1,612	26,477
1912	404	5,116	1946	1,615	27,482
1913	527	9,180	1947	1,595	31,264
1914	550	32,769	1948	1,570	26,206
1915	460	9,340	1949	1,628	39,000
1916	575	8,600	1950	1,615	42,487
1917	678	8,557	1951	1,655	46,937
1918	837	11,708	1952	1,731	46,700
1919	842	14,180	1953	1,805	59,425
1920	1,056	17,520	1954	1,766	61,960
1921	1,204	19,110	1955	1,793	75,105
1922	1,318	17,386	1956	1,781	75,779
1923	1,412	16,014	1957	1,701	75,139
1924	1,420	18,320	1958	1,631	92,770
1925	1,425	16,400	1959	1,650	92,886
1926	1,286	15,981	1960	1,643	95,533
1927	1,325	21,000	1961	1,532	126,683
1928	1,377	29,931	1962	1,456	111,303
1929	1,430	24,651	1963	1,403	85,009
1930	1,385	23,507	1964	1,337	82,593
1931	1,441	22,000	1965	1,253	78,358
1932	1,382	15,700	1966	1,148	85,697
1933	1,302	13,000	1967	1,066	96,716
1934	1,370	13,221	1968	1,077	79,776
1935	1,408	13,419	1969	960	——
1936	1,439	14,997	1970	722	80,848
1937	1,451	15,097	1971	595	65,057
1938	1,450	18,017	1972	480	53,766
1939	1,444	22,961	1973	334	56,397
1940	1,458	19,225	1974	348	188,244
1941	1,455	18,510	1975	314	130,419

Source: *Minutes of the General Assembly of the Presbyterian Church in the United States of America* (Philadelphia: Office of General Assembly)—from 1908–1957; *Minutes of the General Assembly of the United Presbyterian Church in the United States of America* (Philadelphia: Office of the General Assembly)—from 1957 to 1975.

third winter came, they worshipped in a roofed-over basement which, if not elegant, at least kept out the cold. Walton knew the importance of building and building quickly. In a revealing letter to George Knox on January 22, 1909, Walton pleaded for the denomination to pay its share of the construction costs promptly: "We must have money right away or stop the work." One source of controversy, however, was the church's decision in 1909 to buy an expensive red Wilton carpet for its first building. Vanatta, who was assisting with fund-raising efforts, pointed out that few of the churches he was soliciting had such expensive carpets and advised that the church would "have to learn economy sooner or later." At least two of the congregation's six trustees, including E. E. Geisel, agreed it was an unwise decision but reminded Vanatta that the Waltons had agreed to raise the money for the carpet themselves. It must have been a sturdy carpet, for it remained in the chapel twenty-five years later, and it was still remembered over fifty years later. A building was also, however, an assertion of denominational pride, as Walton's letter made clear:

> The Congregationalists are hurrying to complete their chapel and if possible to dedicate before we can so as to get-the-start-of us by way of local help among the business men. They hold their services in a hall however. The Episcopals worship in a portable wooden building the only one permitted by the Steel company. The M. E. [Methodist Episcopal] Church has made no move toward building. Neither have the Christians who worship in a portable school building which is liable to be moved any week and which holds only forty, and the Baptists are in a five-cent theatre. We meet for our services in the basement of our church, which is so difficult to gain an entrance to, that it precludes all possibility of growth.

Both survival and denominational pride required a building. Consequently Presbyterian hearts were glad when the building, subsequently known as the chapel, was dedicated on March 28, 1909. They were also generous, raising $2,300 that day. The chapel, replete with the controversial red carpet, seated 266; it served the congregation for five years.[46]

The anticipated growth came quickly. Between 1910 and 1914 the membership increased from 220 to 550, and the need for more room became obvious. One member, for example, recalled a men's quartet practice held in the coal room for lack of any other available space, and worshipers regularly crowded onto the edge of the rostrum or into the choir loft. So in February 1912, the Session voted unanimously to build an extension "that

Presbyterian Church (the chapel) under construction, 1910. Courtesy of First United Presbyterian Church, Gary, Indiana.

would harmonize with the present building." Once again the Gary Presbyterians turned to their denomination for assistance, and once again received a ten-thousand-dollar loan from the Board of Church Erection in New York. Significantly for a church in Gary, there is no record of an appeal to or help from U.S. Steel. Ground was broken that fall and the building was ready for Easter services, April 12, 1914. It increased the seating capacity to nearly a thousand and served the congregation's needs until it was gutted by fire in 1947. Later a small addition was made to the chapel, and in 1920 a Parish House was purchased.[47]

In addition to his responsibilities as a pastor, Walton was also active as a leader among Gary Protestants. He made his pulpit available, with Session approval, to such groups as the Salvation Army, the YMCA, and the Anti-Saloon League, provided that no collection was taken. He even cooperated with city-wide evangelistic services despite his personal coolness to revivalism. With other Gary ministers he supported the weekday church school experiment, but in 1915 the Session balked at the idea of providing support for the schools, due to "the financial depression during the past 18

This photograph of the City Water Tower in Jefferson Park was taken on July 14, 1910. First Presbyterian Church is visible in the background. Courtesy of Calumet Regional Archives, Indiana University Northwest.

months." They did agree, however, to furnish the room at no charge, and in April 1919 the congregation approved a payment of thirty cents per member ($240) to the Board of Religious Education for support of the weekday church schools.[48]

Moreover First Presbyterian Church supported the work of the ecumenical Gary Church Federation. In April 1918, the congregation approved a contribution to the federation of fifty cents per member provided that other churches did likewise. Later that year, Walton reported to the Session on a church federation for the entire Calumet Valley, organized "for the purpose of doing work among the foreign people of the Valley." Walton's ecumenism extended beyond the Calumet Region, and he supported both the ecumenical Interchurch World Movement and the denomination's New Era Movement. Church records portray Walton as a man actively engaged in cooperative efforts with other churches both locally and nationally in addition to his work at First Presbyterian Church.[49]

Finally, in addition to his roles as pastor and Protestant leader, Walton was a public figure and a minister to the wider community in Gary. Although his own congregation was principally a middle-class, English-speaking organization, Walton's vision of the church's role in the community extended to other elements of Gary's diverse population as well. Particularly important to First Presbyterian Church was the Assyrian Presbyterian Church, in which Walton had an abiding interest. Many of Gary's Persian immigrants had been Christians in the old country. In May 1910, seventeen of them organized a mission which grew into the Assyrian Presbyterian Church. In 1927, after sixteen years worshipping in the First Presbyterian building, the Persians built their own building a block or so north, with some help from U.S. Steel. The Waltons were vitally interested in the Persian congregation, which in turn regarded them with great affection, even after Walton's death. In a 1926 letter to First Presbyterian Church, the Assyrian congregation acknowledged that ". . . we cannot forget the blessed memory of Dr. F. E. Walton who, with his dear wife, have been as a father and mother to us in our infancy as a mission and under whose care we have grown to be organized into a separate Presbyterian Church."[50]

Walton's concern extended to other groups as well, and in 1909 he was instrumental in the establishment of Neighborhood House, Gary's first social settlement. The original idea, however, came from Kate and Jane Williams of Lima, Indiana, who by January 1909 had expressed to their pastor an interest in beginning kindergarten classes in the new city. Knox reported this interest to Vanatta as follows: "I had a letter from Bro. Ferguson of Lima saying a lady in his church wished to put in a kindergarten work and teacher at Gary. She would also be a Primary Teacher on Sabbath. This would be a splendid thing for our Gary work."[51] The next month they toured Gary's infamous Southside with Walton and George Knox and met with William Wirt concerning their proposal to set up kindergarten classes for immigrant children. Wirt agreed to provide a portable building, and classes opened in May 1909. Although it was supported principally by the Synod of Indiana, Neighborhood House also relied on First Presbyterian Church. Several church members served on the Neighborhood House Board over the years, and both members and organizations provided financial support as well, especially in its early years. For example, in 1925–26, the Ladies Aid gave $10 to Neighborhood House for a dentist's chair.[52]

Although Neighborhood House presupposed Americanization of immigrants as the ideal, it rendered impressive service to many Gary newcomers from its inception in 1909 to its demise in 1973. As African Americans moved in greater numbers into Gary's Southside, Neighborhood House extended its services to them as well. In 1919, however, six blacks who had been attending church services at Neighborhood House were rebuffed in their attempt to join First Presbyterian Church. Unfortunately, Walton's position on this issue is unknown, but in general he appears to have been supportive of the work of Neighborhood House. According to Ruth Crocker, Walton also attempted unsuccessfully to establish a settlement house for blacks as early as 1916. She quotes Walton from the *Gary Daily Tribune* of July 20, 1916, as follows: "If Gary is to become a clean, well-governed city we must look after our colored people. . . . It is unfair to criticize them and to exploit their weakness and faults if we do nothing for their moral and social uplift." His rather patronizing appeal, however, raised only $250. But as Rod Frohman, a later minister of First Presbyterian Church, observed, "Although Walton's ministry with the poor was conducted in nineteenth-century aristocratic style it is significant that it was done at all. That this ministry was started and conducted while a massive building program was underway is further tribute to Walton's sense of justice."[53]

But Walton's ministry to the wider Gary community was not limited to Gary's immigrant and poor population. Indeed his position and personality made him perhaps Gary's principal Protestant voice. In this capacity he contributed to Gary's nascent cultural life, commented publicly on issues of morality, and interpreted religion to the wider community.

In actuality Walton was only the first of several Gary clergymen, including Rabbi Garry August of Temple Israel and William Grant Seaman and William Clark of City Methodist Church, who became important cultural figures in the new city. Their cultural influence may say more about Gary's primitive state than it does about the sophistication of its clergy, but nevertheless they were important cultural figures in their time. Whereas others made specific contributions—to the symphony or literature or the theater—Walton's contribution appears to have been more diffuse. His successor, Frederick Backemeyer, suggested as much in a tribute to Walton: "He was an intellectual leader. With a fine training in the arts, with degrees that speak of his wide knowledge and scholarship, with a musical talent that was unique, he made his contribution to the cultural life of the city." Indeed Backemeyer went so far as to put Walton's aesthetic contributions on a par with his evangelistic ones, noting that through his efforts "men, women, and children were won to a love of things beautiful, to the Christian life, and to the church."[54]

Along with other Gary ministers Walton participated prominently in discussions of certain public issues, particularly concerning questions of morality and civic life. To all appearances neither Walton nor his contemporaries thought it should be any other way. In fact, the prominent minister was expected to be a public voice, to speak to the city as well as to the congregation. Walton, in particular, was regarded as both influential and thoughtful in his civic responsibilities. On his death on January 1, 1925, the *Post Tribune,* in a front-page story, said of Walton that ". . . his foresight and depth of thought established him, soon after his arrival in Gary, as leader of the city's ministers. . . . throughout the entire period of 16 years he was a consistent worker for the civic and religious advancement of Gary and its citizens." To William Joder, Walton was a tireless advocate of his church as well as a champion of "every cause of civic righteousness." To Backemeyer, Walton was "a true citizen. Everything that had to do with the welfare of the community engaged his interest and his zealous attention. If it was good for Gary, he was for it." Some of the causes on which he spoke out—he was, for example, against Sunday baseball—hardly seem worth the effort today. But his consistent advocacy of righteousness in the public arena made him an important and revered figure in Gary's public life.[55]

Finally, Walton was an interpreter of religion to this wider community as well as an advocate of civic righteousness. Or, perhaps better, he insisted that religion, interpreted in a broad, ecumenical fashion, was essential to civic righteousness. For example, in his rather eloquent baccalaureate address to Emerson High School's 1918 graduating class, Walton reflected on the Great War still raging in Europe and asked why it had happened. Walton claimed that Western civilization had misplaced its hope in business, science, education, and law, only to find that none of them could ensure peace. Said Walton, "it is a good thing for us Americans especially to recognize the fact that business and money-making is not everything." Referring to the communications revolution of his era, he reminded his young hearers that "it is true that we can speak and men can hear us from the other side of the world, but the matter of importance is not how far we can be heard, but what is our message." Consequently, Walton claimed that "we shall never have a lasting peace until religion is a matter of the life of the whole nation and of every nation." Defining religion as love of God and neighbor, Walton insisted that religion must permeate all of life, even the political realm, if peace is to prevail. Significantly Walton defended religion in broad, ecumenical terms. Not only did he avoid any specifically Christian references, referring to Jesus, for example, as "the Great Teacher," he explicitly praised the Jews as a people who knew what it meant for religion to inform their national life.[56]

Walton's ministry thus extended far beyond the pulpit of First Presbyterian Church and extended to all of Gary. When he died on New Year's Day, 1925, at the age of fifty-five, much of Gary mourned. Said the *Post-Tribune*: "For thousands of Garyites the joy that usually accompanies the welcoming of a new year was laden with sorrow for a friend and advisor, called to his eternal reward."[57] Somewhat like Tom Knotts in the political realm, Fred Walton was something of an opportunist who got in on Gary's ground floor and played an important role in shaping the city's future. In those early days he both reflected and contributed to Gary's aspirations to urban greatness, sponsoring socials, supporting music and the arts, even raising money for a luxurious red carpet for the church. As the much-revered founding pastor, Walton left behind not only a flourishing First Presbyterian Church, but a legacy of active ministerial involvement in the broader communal life of a city in which major Protestant churches still had a significant place in the community's public life.

THE BACKEMEYER YEARS

By all accounts, the Walton years were a challenging precedent for his successor, Frederick W. Backemeyer. Under Walton's leadership the congregation had increased from the thirty charter members of 1908 to over fourteen hundred in 1925. As even the printed program for Backemeyer's installation service noted, "this Church is largely what Dr. Fred E. Walton made it."[58] This fact, apparently, was never forgotten, at least by the older members who looked back fondly on the Walton years. Even Backemeyer himself in a 1930 sermon suggested an almost apostolic succession from the founder by referring to his frequent conversations with Walton about the church when Backemeyer was a denominational official in Indianapolis. Walton cast a very long shadow indeed.[59]

But Backemeyer was not intimidated. As William Clark, one of his Gary ministerial colleagues, observed much later, "Backemeyer followed a success," but "by his own diligence and ability he established himself and built well on the foundations Walton had laid." His style and personality were

Dr. Frederick Backemeyer, pastor of First Presbyterian Church, 1925–1954. Courtesy of First United Presbyterian Church, Gary, Indiana.

certainly different. Even photographs of the men suggest the difference: Walton, with his nineteenth-century mustache and almost dapper, angular good looks, contrasted with Backemeyer's round, stolid appearance.[60] Whereas Walton was the founder, Backemeyer consolidated the growing church and saw it through its continued growth and maturity, despite the Depression and war.

The choice of Backemeyer for the congregation's middle years was, in the long run, a good if unexciting one. He presided over a period of continued growth and development in both membership and church organization. Whereas Walton had been cool toward revivals, Backemeyer regularly conducted evangelistic services on college campuses and Indian reservations.[61] Despite the Depression and the pervasive racism in Gary, there is little evidence of Backemeyer speaking out on either the economic situation or race relations. Nor did he have much to say about the distinctive role of the downtown church in the modern city. But on some issues, namely peace, prohibition, and political corruption, he could rise to prophetic fervor.

The Backemeyer years (1925–54) were years of maturity for First Presbyterian Church, stable years that many members would later recall as "the good old days."[62] Despite continued growth and institutional health, however, the church did not hold as prominent a place in the life of the community at the end of this period as it had at the beginning, and it was obviously unprepared for the rapid social change in Gary in the 1950s and 1960s. But the Backemeyer years do illustrate a rather traditional Protestant evangelical style of relating to the city, a style that proved to be inadequate for the postwar American city. They were years of institutional maintenance and of a lively, if somewhat selective, public ministry dealing with peace, prohibition, and political corruption.

Institutional Maintenance

Midway between Walton's death and Backemeyer's arrival, the Board of Trustees of First Presbyterian Church wrote to all church members urging support for a budget of $25,000. Said the board: "As a congregation, we must realize we have graduated into the class of a city church in a rapidly growing community and must look forward to doing big things." The "worship of bigness" in Gary in the 1920s characterized the Presbyterians as much as any other religious group. It also characterized Frederick Backemeyer, the man they chose to be their pastor in September 1925.[63]

A minister's son, Backemeyer was born in 1884 in Nebraska and educated at Morningside College in Iowa and at the Presbyterian (later McCormick) Theological Seminary in Chicago. After receiving an honorary doctorate from Hanover College in 1925, he was referred to as "Dr. Backemeyer." Prior to coming to Gary he served churches in Monticello and Indianapolis, Indiana, and, from 1919 to 1925, served the denomination as executive secretary of the Synod of Indiana. In January 1926 Backemeyer married Alma Korengel, who became an active participant in Gary religious and civic life. On November 1, 1925, he began his ministry in Gary and preached to a full sanctuary on "The Church's Ministry of Joy."[64]

Backemeyer's intense interest in membership growth was reflected in the meticulous records he kept of additions to the congregation. In his Pastor's Register he tallied by hand additions to the church by transfer of letter and by confession of faith for each year of his pastorate, 1925–54. His running tally showed a total of 3,462 additions during twenty-nine years in Gary.[65] Clearly Backemeyer regarded church growth and evangelism as an important aspect of his ministry. Moreover, as the total of 3,462 additions would indicate, he was good at it. But during these years there were significant losses as well, and the net growth was much less than these figures would suggest. The U.S. Religious Census, for example, records a total Presbyterian growth in Gary of only 138 between 1926 and 1936, from 2,235 to 2,373! Obviously Backemeyer had to fight hard to hold his own, but he did so, in good times and bad. Whereas he took over a church of some 1,400 members, he left it with some 1,800, despite a dip to 1,300 in 1933. Backemeyer finished his ministry on a high note with additions to church membership of 144 in 1952 and 156 in 1953, making them two of his six best years in this respect.[66] But First Presbyterian Church's participation in the nationwide church growth of the 1950s ended abruptly not long after Backemeyer's retirement.

Financial growth was even more mercurial than membership growth, as indicated by table 3. Backemeyer assumed the pastorate during the affluent 1920s, carried it through the Depression and World War II, and left it during another period of prosperity in the 1950s. Financial affairs at First Presbyterian Church were particularly difficult during the Depression, especially between 1931 and 1934, years in which receipts dropped from $22,000 to $13,221. In March 1933, Backemeyer offered to take a hundred-dollar-per-month salary cut to a total of three-thousand dollars for the year, and his offer was accepted by the board.[67] The board must have appreciated his sacrifice for it restored his salary to the earlier level long before the budget returned to that level. Prosperity returned slowly until World War II, from which point receipts increased regularly through the end of Backemeyer's pastorate. But during the 1930s one of Backemeyer's major concerns, in addition to church growth, was financial survival.

Organizationally, during Backemeyer's pastorate, the church remained vital. In addition to the plethora of existing groups a World Service Club, a missionary society of sixty business and professional women, was in place by 1931. Descriptions of the church indicate it was a very busy place each week: ". . . five large social groups among the women, one new 'circle' just organized, a thriving Men's Club, a strong Young People's Department, a group of seventy-five High School age boys and girls known as 'Tuxis' and the Pioneer Club make up the social activities of the weekly program of events."[68] The congregation continued to support Gary's weekday church schools, even approving its $150 apportionment in 1933, in the depths of the Depression.[69]

During his long tenure Backemeyer made or participated in a number of adjustments in the church's program. One of the first was to change the Sunday school hour from 12:15 to 9:45. As Joder recalled the discussion concerning the change, "much goodnatured banter passed between the respective camps of the 'sleepers' and the 'eaters,' but before long everyone became reconciled to the change," which resulted in an increased Sunday school enrollment.[70]

Backemeyer made changes as well in both the Wednesday and Sunday evening services—several changes in fact. In many Protestant churches, including City Methodist Church, these two traditional services became problematic in the 1920s and 1930s. At First Presbyterian Church, the Sunday evening services were usually cancelled during July and August, and in 1938 the church participated in a popular series of cooperative Sunday evening services known as "Garytown Church Nights." In 1943 Backemeyer proposed a series of lay-led Sunday evening services from February through April in addition to a series of four large "fellowship" meetings on four Sundays in November and December. Sunday night remained a problem.[71] Wednesday night was another one. Even Walton had complained in 1922 about poor attendance at Wednesday night prayer services, and the situation remained problematic for Backemeyer. Consequently in 1928, at Backemeyer's suggestion, the Session voted to change the Wednesday night program from a prayer service to a "Church Night" service including devotionals, committee meetings, and occasional dinners. Again in 1938, 1943, and 1944, he made further suggestions for changes in the Wednesday night program, tending toward educational meetings at that time, and in 1953 the church held a series of Family Suppers to study Africa. The repeated discussions of Wednesday night services in the Session Minutes suggest that this was a persistent and recalcitrant problem for Backemeyer.[72]

As did Walton before him, Backemeyer relied heavily on the support of lay leadership, including a number of women and men who were also prominent industrial and civic leaders. Like the neighboring City Methodist Church, First Presbyterian Church remained predominantly a church of the American-born middle and upper middle class. For example, Mrs. W. W. Gasser, wife of the president of the Gary State Bank (the only Gary bank to survive the Depression) was the first president of the Women's Association in 1946. Peter W. Seyl, manager of American Bridge Company, was a prominent lay leader in the church as well. Members of the Session and Board of Trustees included lawyer Fred Seabright, builder Jay

Grantham, Clarence Goris (vice president of Gary Heat, Light, and Water Company), C. J. Kennedy (chief engineer at American Bridge Company), S. M. Jenks (general superintendent at Gary Works), and W. W. Gasser, the banker.[73] The influence of some of these men was apparently responsible for a gift to the congregation from U.S. Steel of thirty-five thousand dollars toward the rebuilding of the church in the late 1940s, a time when contributions from that source were extremely rare in Gary. In a letter to company officials the church acknowledged that ". . . it is, of course a matter of common knowledge that we have great friends in the leaders of your Corporation. Your past interest has shown that, and we, as a Board of Trustees, desire to speak this word of gratitude to every one of your officials who in any way wielded his influence on our behalf in securing for us this splendid gift."[74] First Presbyterian Church remained, that is, an upper-middle-class, white church throughout Backemeyer's pastorate.

As such it also continued to be an influential participant in various ecumenical activities in Gary, such as the weekday church schools, ecumenical evangelism campaigns in 1926 and 1932, and in the founding of the Gary Council of Churches in 1938. Although, in comparison with City Methodist Church there is less evidence of participation in Race Relations Sundays and exchanges with immigrant churches, First Presbyterian Church did pass unanimously a resolution on race relations in 1939 as part of the Gary Council of Churches' first Race Relations Sunday.[75]

As noted above, one of Walton's early accomplishments in Gary was the construction of a building, a significant event to both church and community. But the church's growth and its crowded schedule of activities required several additions to the church property. The congregation purchased two adjoining houses in 1920 and 1944 and in 1945 appointed a building committee to plan for the construction of an educational wing to the church.[76]

But, ironically, "as Gary began its observance of national fire prevention week," a fire gutted the main church building on October 6, 1947.[77] A large crowd, including men leaving the mills after the midnight shift change, gathered in Jefferson Park to watch the spectacular blaze. A church pageant eleven years later recounted, perhaps apocryphally, that "many who remember that fateful night will recall Dr. Backemeyer quietly saying, 'from the ashes we will build.' "[78]

And build they did. Within eighteen hours, the Board of Trustees met to discuss the rebuilding and decided to combine the plans for the educational

Photograph of interior of First Presbyterian Church, with Dr. Backemeyer in the pulpit, taken prior to the October 1947 fire. Courtesy of First United Presbyterian Church, Gary, Indiana.

building with the reconstruction of the sanctuary. It proved to be a major financial undertaking. Although the church realized almost $100,000 from insurance on the burned building, it spent approximately $275,000 in the reconstruction. For two years the church held services in the neighboring Masonic Temple. But on November 20, 1949, the congregation processed down the block to its rebuilt sanctuary, and on December 10, 1950, the new building was dedicated. Three years later the church held a mortgage-burning ceremony, completing the project.[79]

The result was, and is, a beautiful building, "one of the most beautiful of the remaining old buildings in downtown Gary."[80] Quite consciously Backemeyer attempted to adorn the building with a rich panoply of traditional Christian symbols. In fact in 1941, six years before the fire, he had introduced for the first time a cross and candles at the altar. The reconstructed sanctuary featured a divided chancel as well as a "Perpetual Lamp" representing "the ever-present Spirit of God."[81] Backemeyer was thus able to rebuild a building in addition to his efforts to increase church membership and to achieve financial stability. But though much of his energy necessarily went into these efforts of institutional maintenance, he carried out as well a substantial, albeit selective, public ministry, the content of which reveals much about the ministry of First Presbyterian Church under his leadership.

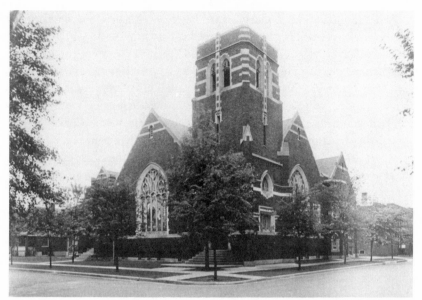

First Presbyterian Church, circa 1940. Courtesy of Calumet Regional Archives, Indiana University Northwest.

Public Ministry

I have claimed that First Presbyterian Church represented especially the Protestant evangelical tradition which dominated the American landscape in the nineteenth century. At the very least this tradition emphasized the importance of evangelism, conversion, and individual morality. It also, however, supported various Progressive campaigns for social reform, such as prohibition, although with a frequently pronounced individualistic bias. As illustrated in the career of Frederick Backemeyer, this tradition remained strong well into the twentieth century, although its position of dominance was clearly eroding. Backemeyer was certainly a far more traditional Protestant minister than William Grant Seaman, his contemporary at City Methodist Church, but he was not reluctant to challenge the status quo when action was required. In keeping with his rather traditional conception of the role of the urban church and the urban pastor, he tended to speak out on public issues that had strong implications for individual morality as well. The three areas that most engaged him were peace, prohibition, and political reform.

As noted in chapter 3, Gary prided itself on its patriotism. Protestant church leaders vigorously supported the U.S. cause in World War I, and the Session of First Presbyterian Church voted "to hang the American flag in a conspicuous place behind the pulpit and to sing America at one service at least each Sunday."[82] Backemeyer, of course, came to Gary seven years after that war ended, concurrently with a widespread reaction in liberal American Protestantism against war and unexamined patriotism.[83] Backemeyer shared that reaction and continued to express an abhorrence of war long after that trend in Protestantism had abated. But the Session Minutes suggest that his views may not have been shared by all members of the congregation. In October 1940, for example, as the conflict was intensifying in Europe, Backemeyer went before the Session to request ". . . authority to secure from the Philadelphia office of the General Assembly blank forms for the registration, in that office, of young men of draft age who desire to identify themselves as conscientious objectors to war. These forms have been made available by the General Assembly, and are acceptable to the Government of the United States, under the Selective Training and Service Act of 1940. *After considerable discussion* . . . such authority was granted" [emphasis added].[84]

A year later Backemeyer took his peace sentiments to the pulpit, reading an open letter to President Roosevelt on Sunday morning which urged the United States to stay out of war and then preaching a sermon on "The Peace of Christ." A month later, only a week before the Japanese attack on Pearl Harbor, the Session authorized Backemeyer to invite the Lake County Ministers' No War Committee to hold a meeting in the church "in opposition to our country's entry into war." But the Session stated explicitly that the speaker for the meeting should be "an outstanding Christian leader who will present *a talk based on sound Christian reasoning, rather than on emotionalism*" [emphasis added].[85] I have found, however, no record of that meeting being held.

During the conflict, First Presbyterian Church followed the example of other churches throughout the country. In 1942 it established an honor roll of church members in the service, and in 1943 it raised nine hundred dollars for the National Wartime Service Fund. Throughout the war the congregation sent the church newsletter to its members in the services "to keep in touch with these loved ones as best it could."[86] Backemeyer's peace sentiments were not, however, quenched by World War II. In the midst of the days of the Korean War and McCarthyism, Backemeyer addressed

Gary's Rotarians on the relationship between Christianity and peace, bluntly restating his own position: "Again we stand in the terror of another war. . . . Will we never learn that war always breeds more war and that lasting peace can be built on good will, understanding, and justice? . . . I am getting woefully tired of those propagandists who are forever trying to imply that if a man is for peace, he must be a communist."[87] Backemeyer's peace stand was a lasting legacy to First Presbyterian Church and was echoed in the Vietnam era as questions of conscientious objection, war, and peace arose once again.[88]

Backemeyer, the peace advocate, was also a lifelong champion of prohibition, another legacy of his evangelical tradition. Vice president of the Indiana Anti-Saloon League, he exemplified the way in which the prohibition forces often made the anti-liquor crusade the centerpiece of a broader social agenda. It was not just booze that Backemeyer opposed but the connections between alcohol and all manner of social evil. Backemeyer saw the crusade as a way to protect women and children from the nefarious effects of the distillers and to protect the republic at large from the unavoidable links between alcohol and individual and political immorality. The brewers, said Backemeyer, "want to establish once more the beaten path between the saloon and the house of prostitution; they want to appoint mayors, control cities, rule and ruin as they did before."[89] As a pastor Backemeyer spoke regularly on these matters to his congregation and other church audiences.

But he encountered probably his largest and most hostile audience at the "memorable debate" on the evening of April 7, 1932. The sponsoring American Legion expected this public debate on prohibition to fill Gary's four-thousand-seat Memorial Auditorium, with proceeds going to the local Red Cross for local Depression relief efforts. In fact it drew only about half that. But what it lacked in numbers, the debate made up in enthusiasm and ballyhoo, proving to be one of the most celebrated events of the decade in Gary. It was not, however, a short evening. Both Backemeyer and his opponent were allotted a full hour—thirty-five minutes for opening arguments and twenty-five minutes for rebuttal. No winner of the debate was to be chosen. But in an informal poll before the debate, the moderator, Reverend James Foster of Christ Episcopal Church, discovered "a wet majority of unmeasured proportions, with only three persons acknowledging a neutral stand on the issue."[90]

As if these odds were not bad enough, Backemeyer's opponent was the moderator's best friend, Rabbi Garry August of Gary's Temple Israel. Although the *Post-Tribune* referred to the combatants as "the two silver-tongued orators of Gary's ecclesiastical world," Backemeyer was clearly no match for August. Whereas Backemeyer "read his opening speech . . . with an intense earnestness," August threw his prepared remarks away and spoke impromptu for his half-hour. As the reporter observed, even Backemeyer's "graying hair and gray attire" contrasted sharply with "the dark looks and habiliments of his adversary." In the account of the debate Backemeyer appears to have been stodgy, formal, and a bit thin-skinned, whereas August was witty, charismatic, and lively. Backemeyer never had a chance.[91]

August was already known as an orator when he came to Gary from Joplin, Missouri, in 1926, and a contemporary account of August portrays him, in stereotypical terms, as a very good speaker indeed:

> Being a Jew, he must talk with his hands. They flutter all about him, the long white fingers interweaving and unlacing the accusing forefinger writing ceaselessly in the air. He is an actor, a magnificent actor. His voice is deep, resonant, and he plays upon it with the skilled artistry of the finished actor. . . . He cannot stand still, caged by a pulpit. Now he is on this side, now the other, but he moves majestically, determinedly, not in aimless hysteria. . . . It needs no label to proclaim his intellectual kinship to the berated Mencken.

In fact, it was after an address to a B'nai B'rith meeting in Kansas City that a representative from the Gary congregation invited August to come to Gary. Of that address, August later remarked, "If you have an audience in front of you, and you're a good speaker, you can give them all sorts of hooey. I don't care if they're professors, they'll eat it up."[92]

While Backemeyer remained chained to his text, August "did not remain behind the pulpit for long, ranging out to the edge of the rostrum, walking back and forth, stirring rippling laughter with his jibes and jests." Underlying the debate, it appears, was a personal animosity between the two men. When he came to Gary, August felt snubbed by both William Grant Seaman and Frederick Backemeyer, whom he characterized as the clerical "king-pins." During the debate, August acknowledged that he had "no use for two-thirds of the ministers in the pulpits today," and, although he weakly praised Backemeyer as "a man of fine courage and friendly personality," it is clear he numbered his Presbyterian colleague among the two-thirds.[93]

The course of the debate, given the audience and the debaters, was predictable. Backemeyer made his case against the social evils of alcohol and the criminal intentions of the brewing industry and linked Prohibition with other laws which curtailed personal liberty for the good of society. August, on the other hand, derided Prohibition as a silly, unenforceable law that abridged individual freedom and failed to eradicate alcohol consumption. August concluded by offering to send Backemeyer instructions on how to introduce his two sons to some of life's pleasures, "among which will be a nice, foaming glass of beer," an offer Backemeyer bitterly resented.[94] The debate solved nothing, of course, but it did illustrate graphically the depth of Backemeyer's convictions on this issue, his courage in advocating it, and the absolute hopelessness of the cause which by 1932 was on the verge of defeat.

But his campaign against political corruption, the third major area of his public ministry, remained timely throughout his ministry in Gary. By the time Backemeyer came to First Presbyterian Church in 1925, the nineteen-year-old city already enjoyed a nineteen-year-old reputation as a wide-open town. Part of this reputation was based on the abundance of saloons, brothels, and gambling dens in Gary, and Backemeyer, prohibition crusader that he was, was quick to take aim at them. But, throughout his career in Gary, he also took aim at what he regarded as political connivance in and protection of the vice trade. In 1932, for example, he attacked Mayor R. O. Johnson on this account in a sermon entitled, "What's the Matter with Gary?" Johnson publicly rejected Backemeyer's charges at the next meeting of the city council.[95]

Backemeyer mounted the pulpit in a similar cause in 1938 during the administration of Mayor Barney Clayton in a sermon entitled, "Washing Up the World." In a front-page story, the *Post-Tribune* recounted Backemeyer's charge that "Gary needs a great cleansing" and his insistence that the church had the right to speak out on civic matters. Cooperating with the Ministerial Association in its campaign against gambling, Backemeyer preached on current events three weeks later. Once again his sermon, "Who Is Responsible for Gambling," was reported on the first page. Denying he was politically motivated, Backemeyer reminded his hearers that "in every administration during which gambling and vice have controlled the city . . . this pulpit has spoken freely and emphatically." In a 1941 sermon celebrating the thirty-second anniversary of Tri Mu, Backemeyer's calls for reform became very specific indeed, as he urged the members to clean up the 2800 Club, a gambling establishment on Ridge Road. As Frohman noted, Backemeyer's stand was a courageous one since he was attacking some of the major activities of organized crime in Gary.[96]

But it was perhaps Backemeyer's response to the senseless murder of popular high school teacher Mary Cheever that best illustrates his attacks on political corruption. On March 2, 1949, Cheever, a long-time member of First Presbyterian Church and a friend of the Backemeyers, was robbed and murdered. At her funeral, Backemeyer delivered "a dramatic appeal for civic righteousness" to the overflow crowd. Acknowledging Gary's unsavory reputation, Backemeyer placed the blame squarely at the feet of local politicians and called for "some first-class, immediate resignations in our city hall and in our police department." Assuming those resignations would not be forthcoming, Backemeyer called for a crusade uniting all elements in Gary's population, a crusade that presumably would throw out corrupt public officials and elect righteous ones. Gary's lawlessness, Backemeyer claimed, was not beyond correction. "All it takes is a set of public officials who have at heart the interests of the people of Gary, and not of the combines of lawlessness. . . . It could be stopped instantly if those responsible had the courage of moral righteousness and of the fear of God." Only then, said Backemeyer, could Gary become "the kind of city God intended it should be—a city of great and honorable industry, a city of great educational ideals and standards, a city of churches and of spiritual integrity, a city of personal and collective achievements—and above all, a city in which righteousness dwells, and in which peace and purity will make their home."[97]

Later that afternoon, nearly two thousand women marched on city hall demanding a clean-up in Gary. The efforts of this Women's Citizens Committee over the next several months led to some action against vice spots, the creation of a special vice squad in the police department, and the establishment of a Gary Crime Commission, modeled after a similar organization in Chicago. Backemeyer served on the Crime Commission and his wife, Alma, was one of the founders of the Women's Citizens Committee. Unhappy with the pace of change, the women took to the streets in July 1949, picketing for two days some eighteen of Gary's vice spots in Operation Shoe Leather. Thereafter they turned to direct political action, seeking to oust the incumbent county prosecutor in favor of Republican candidate, David Stanton. Wiretaps of conversations between the county prosecutor's Gary deputy and the leading syndicate figure in Gary destroyed the prosecutor's chance of reelection, and massive ticket-splitting led to Stanton's election, despite a Democratic landslide elsewhere in the county.[98]

Appropriately enough, Backemeyer's twenty-fifth anniversary at First Presbyterian Church occurred the Sunday before the election, and Backemeyer took the occasion to press for political reform. Although he did not mention Stanton by name, he wrote an article in the Sunday bulletin for November 5, 1950 entitled, "Our Civic Duty!" which included the following:

> It seems out of place to inject into the happiness of our observing our Twenty-Fifth Anniversary as Pastor and People, the idea of cleansing our city and county of the corruption that has run rampant. . . . This program of "cleaning up" can be done most easily and efficiently if the good people of the County will only vote good men into office! We have that opportunity on this coming Tuesday. . . . When men who have held office, and have violated their sacred trust, are found out, and then proceed to intimidate and browbeat those who would place decent men in office . . . is any further evidence needed to establish guilt? . . . Let us go to the polls this week determined that these things shall come to an end![99]

Notwithstanding Stanton's election and the efforts of the W.C.C., Gary's reputation for vice and political corruption continued into the 1950s. On his retirement in 1954, Backemeyer repeated his conviction that political reform was overdue in Gary: "It seems to be inherent in Gary that low ideals prevail and that selfish interests are bold in their grasp of possessions and power. First class men, clean and high-minded citizens who have Christian convictions are not encouraged to hold office. This is an intolerable situation and constitutes the greatest reflection upon this otherwise great community." Despite his lifelong "war against crime in his city," Backemeyer left First Presbyterian Church convinced that the job was not yet complete.[100]

But his long struggle against political corruption, as well as his efforts on behalf of peace and prohibition, do illustrate Backemeyer's views on the role of the church in the city. As noted earlier, Backemeyer left little in the way of systematic reflection on these matters. But, as an evangelical Protestant, he considered the church to be an important agency for civic righteousness, principally by means of its influence on individuals. Churches did, of course, serve society by maintaining social institutions, such as settlement houses. But they served best by nurturing Christian men and women of character and conviction. During the chamber of commerce's Civic Week membership drive in 1927, for example, Backemeyer satirized some of the week's booster rhetoric and articulated his own vision of civic righteousness: "Talk about 'community service!' Talk about 'municipal evangelism!' Talk about the 'gospel of civic welfare!' There is but one evangelism, the evangelism of the Cross; and there is but one gospel, the gospel of the Son of God. And Gary will attain civic righteousness only as this evangelism and this gospel grips and controls the individual lives that make up our city's population." Thus, in assessing the career of his predecessor, Fred Walton, Backemeyer acknowledged his many contributions to the city of Gary but concluded that "the finest tribute we can pay him today is to say that he desired to win people for Christ and to the church he loved."[101] Backemeyer's carefully kept records of additions to the church suggest that he wanted to be judged by the same criterion. Good Christians, thought Backemeyer, make good cities.

But, on the other hand, Backemeyer knew that political action was sometimes required in the modern city, and he was not reluctant to involve the congregation in it, as his efforts against political corruption attest. The urban church was in a strategic position, and, although it could not coerce the body politic to do its bidding, it did have a right to speak out on issues of human welfare. In a 1935 address to the Lions Club on "The Church and Politics," Backemeyer claimed that there was "an overlapping belt in which the church and politics must meet."[102] Predictably, Backemeyer's basic conservatism recurred even here. As in his campaigns against political corruption, the goal of political action was to influence individuals. Corrupt politicians should resign; honest persons should run for public office. Even political reform was basically a matter of individual morality. But, as the pastor of a leading downtown church, Backemeyer was politically astute enough to know that concerted public action was necessary if the church were to have its proper influence on the city.

Backemeyer was thus well aware of his public role in Gary and the role of the congregation he led. Although his response to the city and the church's role in it was consistent with his evangelical heritage, his long and energetic career at First Presbyterian Church illustrates the significant contribution that even traditional Protestantism made to public life in Gary in its first four decades. Even as Protestantism's role in America was changing during the twentieth century, the First Presbyterian Church in Gary remained an influential and active voice in the community.

CHANGING TIMES

By the late 1950s, however, that voice began to fade, even as Gary began to change rapidly. The story of First Presbyterian Church, as indeed that of many urban congregations during these years, is quickly told. As the city changed racially and socioeconomically, the congregation, reluctant to adapt to the new conditions, began a steady decline. Within a decade and a half it had shrunk to a fraction of its former size and influence. Interestingly it was during those years that the congregation became more attentive to the nature of the city and intentional about the church's responsibility to the modern urban social order. Unlike many similar churches, First Presbyterian Church did survive, by merging with three other struggling Presbyterian congregations in Gary. But its new role in a new Gary was not one that Walton and Backemeyer would have recognized; the First Presbyterian Church was no longer at home in the city.

In retrospect, Backemeyer left First Presbyterian Church at the crest of the wave, but the wave receded slowly for a few years. At his departure, the membership exceeded 1,800, and it continued to hover just under that figure for three more years: 1,766 in 1954, 1,793 in 1955, and 1,781 in 1956. But membership plunged to 1,631 in 1958, the church's fiftieth-anniversary year, and the slide continued relentlessly for over twenty years.[103] The brutal fact was that the First Presbyterian Church, which had been one of Gary's most influential churches for a half-century, consistently declined in membership, Sunday school attendance, and in giving after the mid-1950s. For everyone involved, these were difficult, as well as changing, times.

But there was little premonition of the decline when the Reverend Victor Brown became pastor in January 1955. A 1939 graduate of McCormick Theological Seminary, Brown had served churches in New York City; Burlington, Iowa; and Evanston and Arlington Heights, Illinois, before coming to Gary. Church records portray Brown as a thoughtful, well-educated, and well-liked pastor who attempted to lead the church responsibly as the nature of the challenges facing it gradually became clear.[104] Brown's report to the church in January 1956 stated that 1955 had been "a good year." A Planning Committee appointed in 1956 to study the problems and needs of the church concluded that the major problems were parking and overcrowding and recommended the purchase of additional property for expansion. Although the committee members discussed the possibilities for growth in a downtown church such as First Presbyterian Church, they concluded that "there is no evidence that the church membership is on the decline." According to the Planning Committee, "present indications warrant an optimistic outlook on the possibilities of growth, with the First Presbyterian Church playing an increasing part in the spiritual life of the community."[105]

When the congregation celebrated its fifty years in Gary with a week-long celebration in October 1958, the church was described enthusiastically as "a zealous, faithful clergy and congregation which realizes the importance of Gary today." But Brown's report to the congregation three months later revealed a membership of 1,631, a decline of 70 during the anniversary year. By the end of Brown's fifth year, he reported on a number of new organizations that had been added to the church and the addition of a second Sunday school session and an early worship service on Sunday, but he also acknowledged that "much remains to be done."[106]

Later in 1960, the appointment of a Long Range Planning Committee signaled clearly the church's realization that its situation had changed and that it needed to reassess its ministry to the community. The committee's task, in Brown's words, was "to study and recommend a program to accomplish our mission in a changing neighborhood and community."[107] The committee met for almost four years. The record of its deliberations suggests not only the nature of the socioeconomic changes in Gary and their effects on the church but also the efforts of the congregation to take a new look at itself and its mission to a quite different city than it had known.

During 1962 Brown and the members of the Long Range Planning Committee began to meet twice monthly, studying the problems facing Gary and the church with the aid of invited guests, directed reading, and special seminars. In January 1963, they reported to the church on their deliberations, but, as Brown acknowledged, "About all we have discovered thus far is that we have problems; the answers are still to be found." The problems included declining church membership and Sunday school attendance, reduced financial support, aging church membership, and a changing community. Membership had declined from 1,631 in 1958 to 1,403 in 1963. Giving had declined from $126,683 in 1961 to $111,303 only a year later. Many younger members were moving to the suburbs, and those left behind were older and less able to provide needed leadership.[108]

After a long study of the nature of the church, the committee agreed on a statement of purpose for the church which was adopted by the Session: "To introduce Jesus Christ to those who do not know and love him; to deepen the faith and commitment of those who already know him, and to demonstrate Christ's way of love in service to the world." Consistent with this purpose they discussed ways of increasing church membership and revitalizing church programs in education, worship, and so forth, and they discussed several mission projects and the creation of a Social Service Committee.[109] But in general the Long Range Planning Committee was long on discussion and short on action, and there is no record of its meeting after Brown's departure in mid-1964.

The committee did, however, accurately identify some of the problems facing the church, problems which continued to defy solution: membership and financial decline on the one hand (see table 3) and a changing community on the other. This relentless decline was the most obvious sign of the church's problems and was extremely frustrating to its ministerial leadership. As Brown noted in January 1964, "Like so much of our world, the Church is also undergoing change. As is true in all cities, one group of people is moving out of our cities while others, greater in both numbers and need, come in to take their places. These changes can be taken as a concern or a challenge." Brown left Gary for a church in Barrington, Illinois, later that year, leaving the challenge of Gary to his successor, David Haines.[110]

During his three-year pastorate, Haines found the continuing membership slide particularly frustrating. In his annual report in 1967, he tried to be optimistic, reminding the congregation that they still had eleven hundred members on the books and a beautiful building. But a year later he bluntly conceded that, whereas First Presbyterian Church had once been "THE church in Gary," it had lost its prestige, wealth, and influential members. He acknowledged that ". . . times have changed, the community has changed and First Church has changed. When I came to this church two and one-half years ago there were still 1,340 members. Now there are 1,066. (You do the subtracting.) In my eighteen years in the pastorate I have never had this kind of situation to face." After he left in October 1969 to accept a denominational position, the Session discussed his "apparent frustration in not building the membership to its prior levels." As Frohman noted, whereas membership had decreased at an average annual rate of fifty-six during Brown's pastorate, the congregation lost ninety-four members per year during Haines's brief tenure.[111]

There were several familiar reasons for this decline from 1958 to 1970, a period Frohman called the "suburban captivity" of First Presbyterian

Table 4. Pastors, First Presbyterian
Church, 1908–1977

[Frederick Hamilton]	1908
Frederick E. Walton	1908–25
Frederick Backemeyer	1925–54
Victor Brown	1955–64
David Haines	1964–69
Herbert Valentine	1970–77

Source: Frohman, "Pastoral Hospitality with
Worship Visitors in a Multi-Racial Setting,"
D.Mn. thesis, Princeton Theological
Seminary, 1983; Lewis, "At Home in the
City: Mainstream Protestantism in Gary,
Indiana, 1906–1983," Ph.D. diss.,
University of Chicago, 1987.

Church. Many members, especially younger ones, moved to the suburbs or out of the region altogether. New churches were built closer to their homes, leading to a decline in Sunday school attendance from approximately 450 in the mid-1950s to 75 in 1970.[112] Particularly annoying to First Presbyterian Church was the establishment of a Presbyterian church in the Miller area of east Gary, which took "about seventy of our very fine members, most of them being the younger couples whom we had been training and on whom we had been counting for leadership in this Church."[113] The defectors even included three members of the recently established Long Range Planning Committee.[114] In addition to a declining church membership, this population movement resulted in a more dispersed and an older church membership. In 1969, for example, only 54.3 percent of the church membership lived near the church, 37.6 percent resided in the suburbs, and 8.1 percent lived out of state. Some 66 percent of the members were over fifty years old, and 60 percent were female. The congregation continued, however, to be overwhelmingly white, with only nine black members and one Asian in 1969.[115]

This latter fact, of course, suggests another major problem confronting First Presbyterian Church—"the failure, or inability, of First Church to reach those people living in the general area of the church."[116] The population surrounding the church had changed dramatically since the mid-1950s. But it was not simply a matter of blacks replacing whites. Race was, of course, an important issue, especially in the later 1960s. But the membership decline, and indeed the community decline in the neighborhood around First Presbyterian Church, preceded by several years the large-scale movement of blacks into the neighborhood around the church. In 1960, for example, the census tract containing First Presbyterian Church had only two black residents out of a total population of 3,816! A 1964 study of inner city Gary, based on the 1960 Census and conducted by the Indiana Council of Churches, showed serious residential deterioration in the area around First Presbyterian Church, but a black population of only .3 percent. Indeed the principal minority population in the neighborhood was Hispanic, but the study predicted that the Hispanic population would decrease and the black population would increase in succeeding years.[117]

As it discussed the church's future and its mission to the community, the leadership of First Presbyterian Church realized that they must reach out to the black and Hispanic groups around the church. Indeed Victor Brown had raised the issue cautiously as early as March 5, 1956: "Rev. Brown presented for deliberation by the Session the thought that desegregation, although not presently a problem at First Church, may have to be faced by the congregation in the not too distant future." According to Lillian Call, blacks first joined First Presbyterian Church under Brown's leadership. Moreover First Presbyterian participated in community-wide ecumenical services that included African-American churches, hosting, for example, the 1958 Community Thanksgiving Service, which included a combined choir from First Presbyterian, City Methodist, Central Christian, and First African Methodist Episcopal churches.[118]

But progress was slow on this issue at First Presbyterian Church, as it was throughout the state. A 1969 report, for example, showed only 1,000 blacks among 114,380 Presbyterians in Indiana, most of them concentrated in six congregations. The Session itself acknowledged its "failure or inability" to reach blacks and Hispanics but emphasized the need to do so. Some steps had been taken during Haines's pastorate as the church observed "Race Relations Sunday" in February 1966. Two years earlier, Associate Pastor Charles Henderson, who had grown up in the Gary church, emphasized that "Christ was color blind" and that the church must reach out to its neighbors regardless of race.[119]

The desire to reach out to black neighbors, however, was accompanied by anxiety and fear. The Long Range Planning Committee in 1964 expressed the opinion that "there probably will be riots in Gary this summer," but said "we need to be sympathetic to the negro community—we need to try to help work out their problems." In 1969, there was concern over the Black Manifesto, lest some similar disruption were to occur at First Presbyterian Church.[120]

But despite the fear, there was some congregational outreach to the community. A Social Service Committee existed from 1964 to 1967, and its functions were apparently taken over by an Evangelism Committee in 1967. Food collections provided short-term help to people in need, and small-scale tutoring programs sprang up from time to time. Beginning in 1968 Assistant Pastor Gerald Stacy, a former Peace Corps volunteer in Colombia, was particularly active in ministering to the needs of the church's Hispanic neighbors, and his program developed by 1983 into an independent social service agency for the Hispanic community. Despite these forays into their own neighborhood, the church realized that its responsibility to minister exceeded its grasp. But its continuing struggle for survival took precedence as the church tried to decide what to do after Haines's resignation in 1969 precipitated still another crisis. As Leigh Sydes, the clerk of the Session, said in his report to the annual meeting of the congregation on January 27, 1970, the problem the church had confronted in 1969 "of declining membership, of apathy, of neighborhood population shifts—and, finally, the loss of our Senior Minister would be more than sufficient to appall and defeat most men."[121]

A Pastoral Nominating Committee sought a new minister, but it also undertook to discuss systematically the plight and future of First Presbyterian Church, apparently at the request of presbytery. It worked alongside a Strategy Committee, empowered by the Session to meet with Presbytery officials and with similar committees from other inner-city Presbyterian congregations in Gary concerning their future. The Pastoral Nominating Committee's analysis of the situation, reported to the Session in November 1969, soberly reviewed the gloomy facts:

> Five years ago, January 1965, when the last Nominating Committee was at work, First Church showed 1,340 communicant members on its roll. During Victor Brown's pastorate there were two worship services on Sunday morning. Today, the membership is 911, a drop of 429 in a little under five years—an average decrease of 86 per year—7 per month. In January 1965, the Sunday School reported to Presbytery an enrollment of 264 excluding the adult class. Today, the enrollment is 70. . . . Many of you know what is happening to the

environment. One needs only to drive around and through the west side of Gary and count the number of homes that have "For Sale" signs erected in the yards. There are a dozen congregations in our area; they, too, are struggling.[122]

Meeting weekly, the committee consulted with denominational officials and experts on inner-city ministry, studied books on the church and the city, discussed at length the kind of leadership the church needed, and reviewed some forty dossiers of candidates. The process was slow and discouraging. The withdrawal of two of their most promising candidates was frustrating but "makes us more cognizant that the future is not a rosy one for First Church, and that 'good old First Church' is no longer the prestige church of the community."[123]

In light of the discouraging figures on membership and finances, the committee proposed that presbytery undertake a study of all five Presbyterian congregations in inner-city Gary, a study which Victor Brown and the Session had suggested as early as 1960. Moreover the members urged the congregation to select a minister who would lead them in new directions rather than a "'Preacher' to carry us on in the old tradition." The efforts of this committee represented an impressive attempt to reassess the mission of First Presbyterian Church to the community during exceedingly difficult times. Their efforts to secure pastoral leadership ended successfully on April 19, 1970, when, by a vote of 217 to 2, the church voted to call the Reverend Herbert Valentine.[124]

Valentine inherited a struggling church engaged both in creative reflection on its future and in internal bickering that reflected, no doubt, the frustrations inherent in its difficult situation. As in many congregations, the music program was one source of contention. During April and May 1970, for example, the Session considered complaints that the organ was played too loudly. They prepared a questionnaire for the congregation on this matter, but the questionnaire precipitated still more controversy. Two choir members wrote to the Session emphasizing that musical tastes varied and claiming that the choir "has been the only group in the church which has continued to grow and contribute in spite of the general decline in membership." The Session Minutes record no solution to this particular dispute, but the organist in question abruptly resigned in December when the Session enacted a series of personnel reductions, including a reduction of the organist/choirmaster position to half-time.[125]

A dispute more integral to the church's precarious situation was precipitated in late 1969 when the Session responded to a $10,000 budget shortfall with a decision to withhold for a month a benevolence disbursement to Presbytery of $1,345 until the actual income for the year had been determined.[126] The decision, unpopular with several members of the Session, precipitated an angry letter from a church member who blasted the Session for its decision to withhold the benevolence payment and voiced many of the frustrations and feelings of anguish experienced by members of this formerly prestigious congregation. In January, despite serious cuts to meet revised budget estimates, the Session voted to disburse the $1,345 benevolence payment to presbytery. This decision, in turn, angered the chairman of the Board of Trustees, and he resigned in protest.[127] Such conflicts and internal squabbling, however, did not detract the church leadership from the main question: would First Presbyterian Church survive and, if so, under what conditions?

Indeed the church did survive but only by virtue of a merger with three other inner-city Presbyterian congregations. In his account of the "merger decade" of the 1970s, Roderic Frohman gave a great deal of credit to Valentine and his "progressive ideas about urban ministry." Admittedly Valentine did see to its completion the complex process that resulted by 1975 in the merger of the four churches. But it is only fair to note that merger talk had been in the air since at least 1969, and what might be considered pre-merger discussions had been held with East Side Presbyterian Church as early as 1959.[128]

In fact both First Presbyterian Church and Presbytery tended to consider the five inner-city Gary congregations as a group: First, East Side, Brunswick, Westminster, and Assyrian. For example, the four-person Strategy Committee of First Presbyterian Church, made up of four elders, met with similar groups from the other congregations in a Joint Strategy Committee to discuss their common problems. One proposal called for a "yoke ministry" which would combine their professional staff members under the general supervision of Valentine to meet the pastoral needs of the four churches and the community. Although the Session approved cooperative action in principle, it failed to approve this particular proposal.[129]

But the discussions of merger continued, and Valentine continued his work on its behalf. In December 1971, he preached a two-part sermon entitled "Which Way First," followed by a congregational discussion in January 1972. In the sermon, he emphasized that Christianity originally flourished "because of its successes among the urban people of the Roman Empire." He maintained that: ". . . as in the first century, so it is in the 70s. . . . the test of the vitality of Christianity and of Christians lies in our ability to bring the redeemed life to the masses who are part of our highly urbanized society. . . . To do this I'm proposing that First Church truly become a multi-church with metropolitan interests and characteristics." Citing H. Paul Douglass, he emphasized that urban congregations had to adapt to changing conditions if they were to survive. At this time Valentine apparently had in mind an interdenominational merger with City Methodist Church. On January 16, 1972, the congregation met to discuss his sermons, and on January 30 representatives of the two churches met as a "Task Force" and decided to pursue discussion of a merger. The Task Force produced a "Covenant for a Multi-Church," proposing a merger of the two churches by 1973 in order to provide "the most effective Christian witness possible in the downtown area of Gary through the formation of a new church congregation." But by May 1972 these discussions failed, at least partly from a disagreement over which building would be used by the new congregation.[130]

But most merger discussions presupposed a Presbyterian merger with East Side, Brunswick, and Westminster churches. This partly was a matter of geography since all four were neighbors in northwest Gary and had cooperated to some extent for several years. Moreover a merger involving these four congregations would address in some ways the racial issue since Brunswick was approximately one-third black, and Westminster was predominantly so. East Side was a white, working-class church. Any such merger, despite predictable losses of some white members, would result in a thoroughly integrated Presbyterian church.[131]

During 1973, details were completed for a merger of First, Brunswick, and Westminster Presbyterian churches, and on January 1, 1974, the United Presbyterian Church of Gary, Indiana, came into being. The merger covenant statement, ratified on December 9, 1973, signaled clearly the new church's intention to minister to its community: "To be a servant of our Lord is to be visible as Presbyterian Christians to the people around us. To open our buildings and resources. To reach out to the young, to the old, to the poor in spirit, in political, cultural and social activities resisting the blindness of self gain and without any strings attached."[132]

As table 3 above indicates, the merger hardly returned First Presbyterian Church to its former glory, but it did ensure survival, at least for the time being. Membership loss continued at an annual rate of eighty-one during Valentine's seven years. But though the merger did not result in membership growth, it slowed the membership decline dramatically, and between 1977 and 1983 the church lost fewer than forty members. Under the leadership of Roderic Frohman and, as of this writing, Wendy Pratt, it has continued to minister to its community as a genuinely integrated Presbyterian church.[133]

But in 1975 the future of the congregation was uncertain. In contrast to City Methodist Church, its very survival in the face of Gary's rapidly changing social reality was a significant accomplishment. Although no longer an affluent, prestigious church, it still sought to minister to its own members and, to some degree, to those around it in responsible ways. In the process, it was charting new territory for Presbyterians in Gary, who had been among Gary's more traditional mainstream Protestants.

But even in its traditional years, especially before the mid-1950s, First Presbyterian Church had, in fact, significantly influenced the life of its city. In comparison with its Methodist neighbor, First Presbyterian Church played a less prominent urban role and attended to it less explicitly. But it played that role nonetheless. Even traditional Protestantism was at home in Gary.

"Social Gospel Cathedral": City Methodist Church And Progressive Protestantism in Gary

INTRODUCTION

If First Presbyterian Church illustrates the contributions of traditional evangelical Protestantism to Gary's public life, City Methodist Church represents the influence of progressive Protestantism. But in fact, the two congregations were remarkably similar in several ways. Both suffered similar difficulties in their pioneer years and thrived institutionally during the 1920s. In those first few decades, both the "Old First Church" and the "Social Gospel Cathedral" played a significant role in Gary's public life, a role that continued even as they struggled with similar discouragements during the Depression decade. After World War II, however, the speed and nature of socioeconomic change in Gary and the changing role of Protestantism in America more generally forced both traditional and more progressive Protestantism to the periphery of civic life. As the urban crisis deepened in Gary in the 1960s and 1970s, both Presbyterians and Methodists faced difficult decisions common to downtown churches. Unlike many other urban churches, neither followed its membership to the suburbs. First Presbyterian Church managed to survive into the 1990s by virtue of a merger with three other Presbyterian congregations, after rejecting a possible merger with City Methodist Church. City Church, on the other hand, closed its doors forever in 1975, overwhelmed by a rapidly changing urban society to which it could not adapt.

But during its first half century, and particularly during the 1920s, City Methodist Church embodied a progressive Protestant presence in downtown Gary. Even the name "City Church," adopted in 1926, bespeaks the intention of these urban Methodists to minister to the entire city, a goal they could not realize fully. But their attempt to do so illustrates the legacy of the social gospel to twentieth-century urban Protestantism—an ambiguous legacy of both success and failure.

That City Methodist Church was so at home in Gary was principally the achievement of one man, William Grant Seaman, pastor of City Church from 1916 to 1929. Seaman, who had been a pastor, a professor, and a college president before coming to Gary, had a broad vision of what the modern urban church should be and do. He was also a man of tremendous energy in seeking to realize that vision. That he ultimately did not succeed should not tarnish the significance of his attempt and the limited success he did achieve.

But Seaman's ministry did not occur in a vacuum. Indeed the congregation had played an active role in Gary prior to 1916, largely due to the efforts of Seaman's predecessor, Joseph M. Avann (1911–16). Laboring under the difficult conditions of Gary's frontier period, Avann managed to place the First Methodist Church on a solid foundation by consolidating its own position and by extending its influence broadly throughout the young city. His brief ministry laid the groundwork for Seaman's more systematic strategy to transform First Methodist Church into what became known as City Church.

THE FOUNDERS: DEUEL AND AVANN

Congregational Origins

Like their Presbyterian counterparts, the pioneers of First Methodist Church considered the establishment of Methodist work in Gary to be a missionary imperative. In fact, both Presbyterians and Methodists shared an embryonic prehistory in the community Sunday school which met under the trees in the summer of 1906.[1] Although they held no regular services until 1907, the Methodists organized the First Methodist Episcopal Church of Gary on October 5, 1906, in a hall above the Binzenhof saloon.[2] Even at this first meeting, the Methodists included some of Gary's leading citizens among their number. For example, the church's first three trustees were John Sears, James Hyman, and C. Oliver Holmes. Sears, a resident of the area before the founding of Gary, was one of the original three members of the town board. Hyman was the cashier of the Gary Land Company. Holmes was perhaps the most prominent layman of First Methodist Church until he moved to Indianapolis in 1940. An opportunist of the first order, he quickly became involved in numerous aspects of Gary life. Twenty-five years later, he described this early involvement as follows:

> . . . as stenographer for the Gary Land Company, to A. F. Knotts, their first manager, and others; as town clerk from 1906 to January 1910; as one of the organizers and for some seven years a member of the Gary school board; as one of those who helped in the promotion of the first Sunday School north of the Wabash and in the fall of 1906 assisted in organizing the First Methodist church; as special writer (a column a day) for months for the Lake County Times at Hammond; quite often assistant to the postmaster; later an organizing and charter member of the Gary Y.M.C.A., the Gary chapter American Red Cross; the Associated Charities; the Gary Commercial club; the Central Trust and Savings bank; the Methodist hospital; the Gary board of religious education, and others, there wasn't much that escaped our being interested participants.

Holmes became a prominent banker in Gary and served as state senator from 1920 to 1932. The early minutes of the church's Official Board show him as a regular and active member of the board, a pattern that continued throughout his career in the church.[3]

Deuel

The infant church held services infrequently during the winter months and was described in one historical account as a group "that came together on call," until the April 1907 arrival, fresh from the Garrett Biblical Institute, of the Reverend George E. Deuel and his wife. Deuel later claimed, perhaps inaccurately, that he was "the first pastor of any denomination to be appointed in the city."[4]

Like the Presbyterians, Methodist regional denominational officials considered Gary to be a strategic mission field and worked hard on its behalf. For example, the 1907 Northwest Indiana Annual Conference of the Methodist Episcopal Church passed a resolution recognizing "the new and rapidly developing city of Gary as truly missionary ground as any location in the U.S." and solicited assistance from the Board of Home Missions and Church Extension in securing a building and supporting a pastor. The minutes for 1907 report that the Gary church had only eight members and twenty-five dollars in total receipts. Indeed until 1911, First Methodist Church was regarded as a missionary charge and received some denominational support for its current expenses.[5]

The Deuels, both husband and wife, vigorously pursued their responsibilities in this frontier community, conducting regular church services at a variety of locations, including the school building, an old factory building and, in the winter of 1908, the Hodges and Ridgely building on Broadway. By 1907 the old factory building at Twenty-Second and Jefferson, which had once been a piano stool factory and later became a street car repair barn, housed the Deuels and at least two other families in "the only brick building in the city." For a time the Methodists held their morning services there and their evening services in the schoolhouse at Third Avenue and Broadway. The Reverend L. W. Applegate, who began Episcopal work in Gary in 1907, later commented on Deuel and the remoteness of his residence: "I often wondered how many would be willing to go so far to attend a service, but I admired the man who would work against such odds—and my admiration grew when I called on him and found that he and his brave wife made their home in that same factory building in a curtained corner."[6] Though few in number, the Methodists under the leadership of Deuel and Holmes spearheaded the successful 1908 campaign to close Gary's saloons. According to congregational historian Beatrice Lewis, this prohibition drive caused controversy in the church as well as in the town, and a few members left the church in protest.[7]

Members leaving, however, was the order of the day in Gary. As Beatrice Lewis noted elsewhere, "Membership fluctuated greatly during these first years; people came and went rapidly making it very difficult to really gain much of a foothold." As late as 1915, the church newsletter apologized for mistakes in the church directory, noting that "our people are constantly moving about." Although some members left Gary discouraged at local conditions, others "were eager for a part in the building of a new city." Growth, however, was slow, and the church reported only thirty-six members in 1908 and eighty in 1909.[8]

By the end of 1909, both the Episcopalians and the Presbyterians had completed buildings. The Methodists had only land—four lots at Seventh and Adams reserved for a Methodist Church by the Gary Land Company.

But since local resources were so meager, a building required denominational assistance. Consequently the years 1908 and 1909 were filled with "urgent requests to the Board of Home Missions at Philadelphia telling of hearts yearning for a church home." As former Assistant Pastor William Switzer put it in 1934, "There was anxious planning, earnest pleading and struggling with meager resources little understood now." District Superintendent A. T. Briggs, who considered the new city an important mission field, supported the church's request for denominational assistance.[9]

Finally in November 1909, Deuel reported that the Board of Home Missions had promised nine thousand dollars for a building at Gary. The gift, however, was subject to some contingencies, and, in 1911, Deuel tried to sell two thousand dollars' worth of bonds in lieu of some of the anticipated money from the board. Denominational assistance, as the Presbyterians well knew, was not without its drawbacks.[10] The building project was a frustrating one. One builder quit, and financial difficulties abounded, leading the Methodist district superintendent to complain: "Why is it that men with their thousands and their millions for commercial enterprises have little or nothing for the building of the kingdom of Jesus Christ? The city of Gary is a sad commentary on the estimate that men of finance and of the church put upon the value of the church to that nerve center of our industrial life."[11] But denominational and local efforts, including several Ladies Aid's fund-raising activities, finally launched the building project in 1910. It was, in fact, quite an ambitious project for a church of just over one hundred members. Planned to cost approximately $25,000 (it actually cost $32,000), the traditional building was designed to seat up to one thousand worshippers for special occasions. In May 1911 partial victory came when the congregation moved into its roofed-over basement while construction continued on the rest of the building.[12]

By this time the congregation boasted one hundred fifteen members and a rudimentary church organization. As in the Presbyterian church, a number of subcommunal church organizations flourished, and by October 1909 the church had a Ladies Aid organization, a Woman's Home Missionary Society, and an Epworth League (a Methodist young people's organization). That year the pastor's salary increased from six hundred to six hundred fifty dollars. The effort of building a church under pioneer conditions took its toll on the pastor's health, however, and Deuel was transferred to Goodland, Indiana, in 1911. He was succeeded by Dr. Joseph and Mrs. Orpha Avann.[13]

Early photograph of Ladies Aid Group from First Methodist Church. The person at the lower right may be the Reverend George Deuel, First Methodist's first minister. Courtesy of Calumet Regional Archives, Indiana University Northwest.

Avann

Joseph Avann's appointment to the new, young city of Gary must have seemed an odd one. He was sixty-five years old and had served churches for over forty years in New England, Ohio, and Indiana, some of them with over a thousand members. But he regarded the appointment to the small church in the five-year-old city as a great honor. As he wrote (in the third person) four years later: "When the appointment was first suggested it was looked upon by some of the preachers as a joke. . . . But however others looked upon it, he thought the appointment an unusually desirable one, for he saw the possibilities it offered. It is not often such an opportunity comes to a man over sixty years old."[14] It was an opportunity he seized with energy and enthusiasm, despite his age and the congregation's transient membership, uncertain finances, and inadequate organization. In meeting these challenges, he led First Methodist Church from its pioneer phase into early maturity, creating in the process a tradition of active congregational and personal involvement in the wider community which characterized the church for decades.

From his relatively brief five-year pastorate, it is clear that Avann thought the church should be an active, integral part of modern urban life. But for the congregation to minister effectively in its urban setting, it required more members, more money, and a more adequate program. Under Deuel's leadership, membership growth had been steady but slow, with 25 members in 1907, 36 in 1908, 80 in 1909, 115 in 1910, and 141 in 1911.[15] Avann and his wife took pastoral calling and membership growth to be a major responsibility, and they enjoyed considerable success. In his monthly pastor's report for December 1911, for example, Avann reported that, in addition to preaching eleven sermons, teaching the children's catechism class, and conducting five prayer meetings, nine business meetings, a communion service, and a watch night service, he had made 120 calls and added sixty-three new members to the church roll during that one month.[16] By February 1912, he reported that one hundred new members had been added since November 1, "so that in this short time the membership has practically doubled." He urged lay visitors from the congregation to call on all new families in their district, and his instructions to them reflected both Gary's frontier ecumenism and its emerging denominationalism, as well as the important role played by women in the congregation: "If they have another church home, do not try to alienate them, but remember all the rest belong to us. Give them a cordial invitation to our services. Introduce them to others and get our ladies to call on them."[17]

The task of cultivating new members occupied both Avann and his wife throughout his pastorate. In December 1913 Avann and the congregation cooperated with the Pastor's Union in a house-to-house religious census of Gary's First Subdivision in an attempt "to increase the interest in church work and also to assist the pastors in getting the names of all persons interested or preferring any particular church." When persons visited the church, care was taken that they "not get away without an invitation to come again." Between May and July 1915, Avann and his wife made 208 calls, and Mrs. Avann alone made up to 300 yearly on behalf of the church.[18] In addition to personal calling, Avann utilized the traditional revival meeting in order to add to the congregation's numbers. In 1915, for example, a month-long revival added fifty members to the congregation, "and the church as a whole was quickened and welded together."[19] All these efforts were wildly successful. In Avann's first year (1912) church membership increased from 141 to 315, and by 1915 it reached 463. According to Avann, "There are twenty-four other Protestant churches in Gary, but not one of them has had the same relative and actual growth." As

Table 5. City Methodist Church
Membership, 1908–1975

Year	Members	Year	Members
1908	36	1943	1,911
1909	80	1944	2,049
1910	115	1945	2,201
1911	141	1946	2,393
1912	315	1947	2,560
1913	391	1948	2,688
1914	393	1949	2,796
1915	463	1950	2,897
1916	474	1951	2,979
1917	524	1952	3,081
1918	585	1953	3,185
1919	605	1954	2,395
1920	1,007	1955	1,851
1921	1,020	1956	1,769
1922	933	1957	1,828
1923	993	1958	1,839
1924	961	1959	1,860
1925	987	1960	1,894
1926	1,037	1961	1,687
1927	1,248	1962	1,684
1928	1,261	1963	1,643
1929	1,316	1964	1,602
1930	1,424	1965	1,594
1931	1,633	1966	1,546
1932	1,587	1967	1,493
1933	1,586	1968	1,393
1934	1,611	1969	1,341
1935	1,629	1970	1,284
1936	1,580	1971	1,241
1937	1,596	1972	1,004
1938	1,620	1973	828
1939	1,636	1974	451
1940	1,674	1975	308
1941	1,674	1976	267
1942	1,819		

Source: Northwest Indiana Conference of
the Methodist Episcopal Church, *Minutes*,
1908–38; Northwest Indiana Conference of
the Methodist Church, *Minutes*, 1939–67;
North Indiana Conference of the United
Methodist Church, *Minutes*, 1968–76. The
figures at the end of each year were reported
in the *Minutes* for the following year.

with the First Presbyterian Church, the Methodist church growth was almost exclusively among Gary's native-born, white, middle-class population on the Northside. For example, a "business directory" printed in the June 1913 *Church Promoter* gave the following occupations for several church members: M. P. Avery, dentist; J. R. Snyder, newspaper publisher; Fishel Brothers, contractors; M. S. Hopper, surgeon; W. H. Bennett, mortician; C. M. Bailey, clothier; C. R. Kuss and C. O. Holmes, bankers; in addition to several lawyers and at least fifteen teachers. The membership directories published regularly in the *Church Promoter* during Avann's pastorate also confirm this membership pattern. Few immigrant names or Southside addresses appear. Indeed the directory in the October 1915 *Church Promoter*, which arranged members by streets, confirms that virtually all the church members lived in U.S. Steel's First Subdivision.[20]

Moreover in Gary's first few years, gaining new members, prominent or not, was only half the battle. As Avann recalled in 1915 in a brief sketch of the church's early history, Gary's extraordinary mobility made membership maintenance as difficult as membership growth:

> It was a shifting population. Many who came went away. There was great uncertainty in the minds of some about the future of Gary. Nearly everyone who was invited to bring his church membership here answered, "we do not know how long we will stay." Scarcely one of the original official board is here now. Fifty persons who have taught in the Sunday school in the last four years have moved away. Of the thirty who were teachers or officers a year ago only eleven are now in town and of the five hundred members that we now have only about fifty were here four years ago.

Consequently the impressive net growth from 141 to almost 500 in four years represents a vigorous and sustained attention to membership growth in the face of considerable difficulties.[21]

But the church required money as well as members, and financial concerns plagued most of Avann's pastorate. In addition to the standard challenge of raising money in a congregation, Avann had to deal with periodic recessions resulting from Gary's absolute dependence on the steel industry. The Church's Official Board in October 1914, for example, noted that the every member canvass for financial support had been fairly successful, "considering the conditions of the times." Likewise the *Church Promoter* in July 1915 observed hopefully that "this has not been a good year to press collections. . . . Now that times are better all who can should meet their obligations."[22] Consequently the church records abound with talk of money, both to meet current expenses and to finish the building, in which they worshiped for the first time on August 4, 1912. In 1911, for example, the church suspended all benevolence expenditures "on account of the erection of the church building," and in February 1912 a special collection was taken to pay for roofing the new building. In 1912 a permanent Finance Committee was appointed, and in September 1914 the Official Board adopted the "every member canvass" plan of church finance, seeking an annual pledge from each church member.[23]

But the pastor and board continued to face the undeniable fact that members often fell behind on their pledges.[24] Consequently the congregation sometimes had to borrow money from local banks, both for building expenses and to meet current expenses and to make up overdrafts, especially during the difficult 1914–15 period.[25] When local sources failed, the church sometimes looked outside the city for help—help that was not always forthcoming. In 1913, for example, Avann reported that an appeal to the Carnegie Fund for money for a pipe organ had been rejected. Not even Judge Gary could be counted on; in 1911 he rejected a request from Bishop McDowell for five thousand dollars for the Gary church.[26]

Although it no doubt complicated his task, Avann did not let the congregation's financial situation deter him from strengthening the church's organizational structure. Deuel had begun the task, and Avann inherited a Sunday school, Epworth League, and two women's organizations. But he continued to add to these organizations, and by March 1914, the *Church Promoter* claimed that "our Church is now thoroughly organized." In addition to the trustees, stewards, and Sunday school, the church boasted an Epworth League, Junior League, Methodist Brotherhood, Boys' Brotherhood, Woman's Association, and two women's missionary organizations—the Women's Home Missionary Society and the Women's Foreign Missionary Society. In the July 1915 issue of the *Church Promoter*, Avann summarized the church's organizational goals as follows:

ALL the Church in the Sunday School.
ALL the Sunday School in the Church.
ALL the men in the Methodist Brotherhood.
ALL the women in the Woman's Association.
ALL the young people in the Epworth League.
ALL Methodists in Gary in the Gary Methodist Church.
ALL Methodist people in Gary right with God.
ALL non-church going people in Gary evangelized.

Like his Presbyterian colleague, Fred Walton, as well as his successor, William Grant Seaman, Joseph Avann placed considerable emphasis on the music program. Despite the Carnegie Fund's refusal to purchase a pipe organ, for example, Avann continued to press the matter and offered to contribute substantially toward its purchase, averring that in his thirty-five years of parish ministry he "had not been without a pipe organ." He lost on this issue, however, when a committee of the Official Board decided not to pursue the matter. Avann's goals for the music program reflected his desire for greater liturgical sophistication in the church. For example, in addition to the pipe organ, he requested the establishment of a children's choir and the chanting of the Lord's Prayer. The latter request was hotly debated, but the board approved it by a vote of six to three.[27]

In addition to his efforts on behalf of membership growth, financial stability, and organizational development, Joseph Avann also urged the church to fulfil its missionary responsibilities and take an active role in Gary. Several of the church's areas of concern were fairly traditional. For example, the Official Board appointed a committee to deal with the "church poor" and agreed to take a congregational vote for the Women's Christian Temperance Union on the subject of national prohibition, and Avann urged the closing of theaters on Sunday.[28] In 1916, the *Gary Tribune* reported approvingly that Avann was not a radical reformer in the pulpit, noting that "once he prefaced a sermon on local vice with a state- ✓ ment that once a year was perhaps once too often to take such topics into the pulpit."[29] Maybe so, but the fact that he preached a sermon on vice in Gary even once in a year places him among the early practitioners of what became a persistent tradition in the Gary Protestant pulpit.

Moreover, he also used his pulpit to address current topics in religious scholarship and politics. During December 1911, for example, shortly after his arrival in Gary, he delivered a series of lectures on "The Making of the New Testament." The previous month he had preached a series of sermons on "Present-Day Religious Thought." What was perhaps more controversial in a steel town, he delivered in January 1912 a series of Sunday night sermons on industrial issues— "Capital and Labor," "Modern Competative [*sic*] Industrialism," and "Brotherhood in the Kingdom."[30] This barrage of sermons and lectures within his first few months in Gary strongly suggests that Avann, while hardly a radical, did consider himself a pulpit activist, consistent with his activist view of the urban church. During his ministry, moreover, the congregation took a major role in two major social initiatives, the Campbell Friendship House and the Gary weekday church schools.

Cooperating with the Women's Home Missionary Society of the Northwest Indiana Conference, the Gary's Women's Home Missionary Society began settlement house work in February 1913 with the opening of a mission Sunday school and a day nursery. In March 1913, the congregation voted to give the W.H.M.S. a site at Twenty-Third Avenue and Washington Street as a permanent home for the Campbell Friendship House.[31] The Gary settlement was named after Abbie J. Campbell, a prominent member of the conference's W.H.M.S. from South Bend. According to William Switzer, the site on which it was built had been donated to the church by Frank Gavit, M. M. Castleman, and Herbert D. Jones "because of their appreciation of the work of Rev. G. E. Deuel and his Church in those pioneer conditions." Gavit was an attorney and winner of the trolley franchise from the city council in 1907; Castleman was a prominent politician and saloonkeeper, known popularly as "Battle-ax." Philanthropy sometimes made strange bedfellows in Gary.[32] Despite initial financial problems, building proceeded, with architect C. E. Kendrick, whose wife was president of the W.H.M.S., donating his services. Friendship House was fully operational by September 1914, ministering to the needs of the "most polyglot, racially mixed 15,000 people anywhere in the Calumet Region." Although several scholars of the settlement movement have emphasized its secular character, Ruth Crocker emphasizes the authentically religious motivations of those women who founded and worked in settlements like Campbell Friendship House. Says Crocker:

> Only by restoring to a central position the not only religious, but missionary, motives of many settlement workers can we understand the depth of commitment of these activists who struggled in the nations' worst slums. Settlements like Campbell House were not only the back-bone of the social gospel movement, and an important element in the movement to Americanize the immigrants, they were also typical settlement houses. Indeed, the strength of the settlement workers' commitment resulted from the fact that they were engaged in a battle not only against poverty, ignorance, and sickness, but also against sin.

This battle was to continue for many years as Campbell Friendship House played an integral role in the congregation's ministry to the immigrant, and later the black, population of Gary.[33]

Perhaps more important to Avann, however, was the program of week-day religious education, an ecclesiastical adjunct of the Gary schools, of which Gary's Protestants were extremely proud. Although, as noted in chapter 4, the weekday church schools were a genuinely cooperative effort, Methodists were among the leaders of the movement from the beginning. Although the official origins of the idea date from William Wirt's 1913 address to the Gary Ministers Association, the idea itself may well have been Avann's, and he was clearly one of its strongest supporters.[34] In fact a cryptic remark in the Quarterly Conference Minutes for November 15, 1911, suggests that Avann may have been among the schools' earliest advocates. In his report at that meeting, he noted that "special classes of children for religious instruction will soon be organized." In fact, it was almost three years before this came to pass. William Grant Seaman later described Avann's role as follows: "Within Dr. Avann's pastorate attention had been called to the fact that the Gary school day made it possible to provide religious education during the week for public school children. While several of the ministers of the city were very active in starting and promoting this work, Dr. Avann was President of the Ministers Association, and in part because of his position and probably more because of his aggressive spirit for the promotion of the Kingdom, he was a leader in the founding of the week-day schools for religious education."[35]

The congregation readily followed its pastor's lead, and the Official Board approved in November 1913 the "action of Pastor and School Board of Gary in regard to religious instruction of school children." The Methodists continued to play an important role, under both the initial decentralized plan and the more cooperative approach adopted in 1917. According to the *Church Promoter* in October 1915, the first year of the schools was a "great success."[36]

Avann did not live to see the conclusion of the schools' second year. But when he died in June 1916, his important role in their founding was duly noted by the newspaper as was his "active interest in all things pertaining to the welfare of the city." In an editorial the newspaper eulogized Avann, who was the first minister to die in the city's young history, as a "staunch" citizen and one whose work had "placed the First Methodist among the leaders of religious thought of this growing population." As Seaman described him, "He was a man of unusual strength of personality, he possessed a scholarly mind, had occupied very important pulpits and always had worked with marked efficiency." He left behind a church that, despite its tender years, was a mature organization in a growing city. He left as well a vision of the church as an integral, active part of the urban community, a vision endorsed and expanded by his successor, William Grant Seaman.[37]

THE VISIONARY: WILLIAM GRANT SEAMAN

Seaman and His Vision

A minister's son, William Grant Seaman was born in Wakarusa, Indiana, in 1866. Described by one of his sons many years later as a resourceful young man, Seaman once worked his way to Europe feeding cattle on a cattle boat, and his musical abilities enabled him to pay his way through both college and graduate school by singing. He received his B.A. from DePauw University in 1891 and the Ph.D. degree from Boston University in 1897. A protégé of Boston professor, Borden Parker Bowne, Seaman wrote his dissertation "On the Supposed Necessity of an Infallible Guide in Religion." From 1893 to 1904 he pastored several churches in Massachusetts. But in 1904 he returned to the academy and to DePauw as a professor of philosophy. A short, gregarious, enthusiastic man, Seaman was nicknamed "Sunny Jim" while at DePauw, where he taught until 1912. During those years he enjoyed close friendships with DePauw's presidents E. H. Hughes (1903–8) and Francis J. McConnell (1909–12), both of whom had also studied at Boston University and later became prominent activist Methodist bishops. Seaman left Indiana in 1912 to become president of Dakota Wesleyan University. But four years later Bishop Thomas Nicholson of Chicago, who had "a warm personal interest in Chicago's new industrial neighbor Gary," asked him to consider the post at Gary. The choice was a brilliant one.[38]

Although Avann had left a far stronger church than he had inherited, the move to Gary must have seemed as improbable for Seaman as it had for Avann five years before. The church had approximately five hundred members but a budget of only $3,500 per year. The building, on which money was still owed, had no educational unit. The city of Gary was only ten years old. But, according to Switzer, "the challenge of the task captured the imagination of that Christian dreamer and promoter," and he decided to make the venture. When he came to Gary in October 1916, he was just short of fifty years old.[39]

"That Christian dreamer and promoter"—repeatedly Seaman was described as a dreamer and visionary. Such terms, of course, are fundamentally ambiguous. On the one hand they connote foolish, unfounded optimism—a charge Seaman apparently faced during his life time and certainly since.[40] But a visionary is also one who sees more clearly than other people what may be and works to bring it about. Seaman was a visionary in this sense as well. He was, according to one of his successors, William Clark, "a leader with a great dream, and he led City Church into a broader sense of mission." But he was also, in Clark's words, "a pragmatic thinker who never lost site of the reality of the goal amid the realities of life." His vision for First Methodist Church and its role in the city of Gary, although not realized completely, shaped profoundly the way the congregation viewed itself and was viewed in the community. Inevitably it also influenced the standards by which the church was judged. Although it closed its doors in 1975 as a fairly conventional inner city Methodist church, conventional in both its program and its failure, City Church had once embodied progressive Protestantism in Gary, embodying as well the vision of William Grant Seaman. A church anniversary program in 1951 described Seaman's "great vision" this way: "he believed a church in the heart of a great city could set itself to a ministry designed for the purpose, and adapted to the problems, of such an industrial center as Gary has become. . . . The vision of Dr. Seaman is still true—'that Christ may dwell a living presence at the city's heart.'"[41]

Unfortunately Seaman, although a scholar as well as a pastor, did not write extensively on the role of the church in the city.[42] Fortunately the copious church records of City Methodist Church include numerous "working documents" undoubtedly prepared by Seaman, although not always signed by him, including correspondence, fund-raising pieces, and church newsletters. Taken together with his actions they provide considerable insight into his vision of the urban church and the urban minister. This vision was not altogether original, and it reflected both his denominational and educational context.[43] As we shall see, it reflected as well both the evangelical and the social gospel sides of his Protestant heritage. Seaman and his thirteen-year career in Gary illustrate the way in which these various influences worked themselves out in the life of one extraordinary minister in one distinctive urban milieu. In the words of William Switzer: "Doctor and Mrs. Seaman dreamed, planned, and were largely instrumental in bringing to completion as broad a program of institutional Church and social service activities, adapted to and woven into the growth and life of this modern industrial city, as has been the privilege or accomplishment of but few others in American life for a generation."[44] To understand William Grant Seaman and his vision for City Methodist Church, then, is to understand the heart of progressive Protestantism as it encountered the twentieth-century industrial city.

That vision was a multifaceted and yet unified ideal of the church's public presence in the city. The term, "presence" suggests not just the specific actions of a congregation but its entire stance toward the city and its relationship to other groups and organizations in it.[45] The term is an apt one for City Methodist Church. As we shall see, its physical presence in a particular type of building at the city center was of the utmost importance to Seaman and the congregation, embodying his ideal of what a city church should be and do. But he was not just a builder, and his vision of that urban presence included at least six elements that reflect his roots in evangelical Protestantism and his commitments to the progressive Protestantism represented by the social gospel. To Seaman, the church's public presence in the city should be Christian and evangelical, active and cooperative, comprehensive, mediating, uplifting, and modern and efficient.

Seaman was, first of all, a Methodist Christian. Though he was liberal theologically, he was by no means a theological radical. An heir to the Protestant evangelical tradition, he believed firmly that the urban church should be Christian and evangelical. Unlike his Presbyterian colleague, Frederick Backemeyer, there is little evidence that Seaman participated in traditional revival meetings. But although questioning the means of revivalism, he affirmed the ends and believed firmly that the urban church should evangelize, encouraging and assisting individuals to become Christians as part of its mission to bring in the Kingdom of God. Although the Kingdom entailed social transformation, it also involved individual faith, or, as Seaman put it, "that sense of the presence of Christ and that spirit of obedience to him which are necessary to make religion a real power in their lives." Christianizing the individual, for example, was one of the major goals of the weekday church schools. But in addition to reaching individuals outside the church, the urban church, Seaman felt, should train its own members as soldiers "for a war of conquest to take the whole society for Christ." In this respect, Seaman illustrates the continuing influence in the twentieth-century urban church of the social gospel's emphasis on the Kingdom of God.[46]

Second, Seaman felt that the church's presence in the city should be active and cooperative as well as Christian and evangelical. He distinguished here between what he called a neighborhood or family church and the city church. Although not exempt from social responsibility, the family church was a more traditional institution, serving mainly its own membership and neighborhood. By contrast the city church existed as much for the city at large as for its own members. It is almost as if Seaman were using Tönnies's concepts of *Gemeinschaft* and *Gesellschaft* to describe two kinds of church or congregation. The family church featured the face-to-face intimacy characteristic of the primary community; the city church by contrast was designed for the modern, anonymous urban society of the twentieth century. If it were to prosper, or even survive, downtown, the city church had to be active in a wide variety of areas, including traditional social services, religious education in the public schools, racial justice, labor issues, and so forth.[47] Since no individual congregation could solve all a city's problems or be equally effective in all areas of its ministry, cooperation was required. Consequently Seaman cooperated with all manner of institutions, including other Methodist organizations, other Protestant churches in Gary, the public school system, and the United States Steel Corporation. While aware of certain limits (for example, the schools could not encourage specifically denominational church schools), he sought allies where he could find them in his active thirteen years in Gary. Nor did he grant the possibility that the church and some of its secular partners might get in each other's way. As Seaman said to Norton: "It is doubtful if anywhere in America [a] case can be found where a church in the heart of our great cities is interfering with the other institutions at work there. When all the agencies there have done their best the field is still 'neglected.' "[48] It was clear to Seaman that the active, cooperative city church was a key figure in urban life, not a peripheral spectator.

Third, Seaman maintained that the urban church's presence in the city should be a comprehensive one, responding to the needs of all major groups making up the urban population.[49] From our perspective, that opinion seems incredibly naive; the complexity of contemporary urban society is such that a comprehensive approach to all city problems is beyond the grasp of any institution. But in the teens and twenties, even sophisticated observers of the urban scene believed it could be understood if approached with the right tools and resources. Neither urban reformers nor urban sociologists, for example, systematically despaired at the magnitude and complexity of their task. Their own work had, of course, convinced them and many thoughtful Americans that the modern industrial city presented new and complicated problems. But it also convinced them they could understand and address those very problems effectively.[50]

Seaman too felt that urban problems were many and serious. But they were not beyond solution, and he faced the city with confidence, not despair. As he analyzed Gary's urban society, he identified three major populations in need of ministry—immigrants, blacks, and native whites. Then, working with denominational home missions officials, he helped develop and implement a seven-part program to meet the needs in Gary, including a variety of church programs, a hospital, settlement houses, missions, weekday religious education, and so forth.[51]

Both his analysis and his strategy suggest that Gary, although a pluralistic city by any standard, illustrated a more manageable pluralism characteristic of the early twentieth century. Native, Protestant whites, although a minority of Gary's population, still held control. In his own study of the Calumet Region in 1921, Seaman described Gary as more of an industrial camp than a city. But his description of the area reveals, in fact, his own analysis of the modern city, anticipating in a striking manner Louis Wirth's classic analysis in "Urbanism as a Way of Life." To Seaman, as to Wirth, the modern city was plagued by a breakdown of traditional community and social control, resulting in an anonymous, mobile, materialistic, hedonistic population. The city church's role, he inferred, was to develop programs which would provide some of the support, guidance, and satisfaction characteristic of traditional communities. Although he did not think one could re-create a rural way of life in the city, it was necessary to provide various subcommunity groups that could substitute for some aspects of traditional culture which had been lost in the move to the city. Once one had identified the constituent groups in the city, Seaman felt it was possible to meet at least some of their needs with a comprehensive plan of church service.[52]

Fourth, Seaman maintained that the church's presence in the city should be a mediating one in areas of urban life characterized by social conflict.[53] In Gary, three major areas of social conflict were preeminent: conflict between labor and management, conflict between immigrant and native, and conflict between black and white. In each of these areas Seaman tried to make the congregation an agent of reconciliation, at least by the standards of the 1920s, and his contributions in these areas were significant.

But it is important to note that his emphasis was on mediation and reconciliation, not advocacy. Unlike some of his more radical Methodist colleagues, Seaman was politically moderate, not a social reconstructionist. This may reflect to some extent the makeup of the congregation he served, which was, as his secretary later recalled, "composed of American-born middle class who lived in the neighborhood around the church." Although perhaps slightly less prestigious than First Presbyterian Church, City Church was still a solidly white middle-class institution of skilled laborers, mill foremen, and middle management.[54] Such a congregation was not a likely source of social revolutionaries. Nor is there any evidence that Seaman himself was other than an evolutionary proponent of a more just social order. Although his vision of the just society was a limited one, emphasizing mediation and reconciliation, he was a consistent and conscientious laborer on its behalf.

Seaman also maintained, in the fifth place, that the church's urban presence should be an uplifting one. For example, his emphasis on high aesthetic standards in architecture, music, and liturgy was such that even Arthur Shumway had to acknowledge it, albeit grudgingly. For decades after Seaman's pastorate, City Church continued to nurture cultural life in Gary, especially music but also drama, and its building continued to be a source of pride.[55] But in a steel town like Gary, there was an inevitably elitist character to such activities, which were clearly the province of upper-middle-class, native whites. Elitism, moreover, is a neighbor of racism, and Seaman unfortunately shared in at least some of the racist presuppositions of his day, despite his strenuous efforts on behalf of racial justice. Seaman's concern with uplift had its negative as well as its more positive side.

Finally, Seaman's vision for the urban church held that its presence in the city should be modern and efficient. Theologically, Seaman was a liberal Protestant for whom modernity required both theological progressivism and the adoption of a scientific approach to the city. Consequently, such social scientific techniques as the social survey were essential to the urban church's assessment of urban needs. Seaman, for example, noted that in 1918 the church made an earnest attempt "to analyze the needs of the community as an engineer would analyze his problems, and to work out a program of institutions to meet these needs efficiently." In its publications, City Church emphasized that its church buildings reflected the latest scientific thought on the size of Sunday school rooms, curricular materials, and so forth. But Seaman thought that in addition to being modern (or perhaps as a part of being modern), the urban church should be "efficient." Throughout the church records the word "efficiency" reverberates. The entire program of the city church, the specific size and configuration of the building itself, and the "community plan" of weekday religious education were all justified on the grounds of their efficiency. Reflecting no doubt the business mentality of the day, Seaman's emphasis on modernity and efficiency was an important aspect of his vision for City Church.[56]

Although Seaman wrote no systematic treatise on the church and the city, his first five years illustrate vividly his activist vision of urban ministry, even before the construction of City Church's "Social Gospel Cathedral." He was already convinced when he arrived in October 1916, "that the Sunday School addition to the church ought to be built and a debt of approximately $15,000 taken care of at the earliest possible date." In a letter to Methodist executive D. D. Forsyth, in December 1916, he asked for help from the Board of Home Missions and Church Extension. Describing Gary's opportunities for ministering to the "foreign problem" and the "industrial problem," he sketched in embryonic form the outlines of the comprehensive program of urban ministry he envisioned and stated bluntly that local resources alone were inadequate to meet the need. "We feel," he said, "that we have here about the biggest job on the planet and we face it with only an auditorium, and there is a debt of $13,000 on that. . . . 'Come over into Macedonia and help us.'" Although there is no record of Forsyth's response, by the next spring the church had approved a financial campaign, the debt had been retired, and building plans for the addition were underway.[57]

Also facing him on his arrival was a crisis in the weekday church schools. Since their beginning in 1914, the various church schools, sponsored by individual congregations, had been plagued by financial difficulties, by the fact that most of the seven participating churches were in the vicinity of a single school, and by the difficulty of coordinating several individual church school programs with the program of the public schools. Several of the schools closed, and by 1917 "there was a feeling of uncertainty in the minds of the friends of week-day religious instruction." The answer, apparent to Seaman and several of the "enthusiastic friends" of the schools, was cooperation. Assuming that religious instruction was essential to the entire community, they concluded that the community should cooperate in providing it. They formed a Board of Religious Education to coordinate the work, and they selected Seaman as its president, a post he held until 1928.

By the fall of 1917, five Protestant churches and a settlement house had cooperated to provide three centers of religious instruction with eight hundred pupils enrolled, and the work grew steadily for the next several years, reaching an enrollment of five thousand in 1925.[58]

Clearly Seaman considered the weekday church schools to be a central aspect of his ministry at City Church. Not only did they illustrate the cooperative principle, they also were one of the major avenues of ministry to Gary's large immigrant population. In an article in *The Homiletic Review,* Seaman observed that many children in modern society live not in "our cultured Christian homes, but rather in the homes of the ignorant, the poor, the shiftless, and even the vicious." It was these largely immigrant children that Protestantism aspired to reach by means of the church schools. As noted in chapter 4, one major goal of the church schools was the Americanization and socialization of the immigrants, but another was to prepare them for evangelization. Although not a substitute for other church programs, the church schools were "a highly efficient supplement to all of them." Seaman and City Church thus were among the most enthusiastic supporters of the weekday church schools.[59]

Seaman and the Centenary

In addition to the cooperative reorganization of the weekday church schools in 1917, Seaman and City Church cooperated with other Methodists in the formation of the Calumet Missionary Society in order to minister more adequately to the needs of the Calumet Region.[60] It was soon, however, subsumed by a national Methodist effort in home and foreign missions known as the Centenary Campaign, launched in 1918 to celebrate the centennial of the Methodist Missionary Society. Seaman's heavy involvement in the Centenary Campaign illustrates his support of the social activist impetus within the Methodist denomination. It also illustrates the way he cooperated with both denominational and U.S. Steel officials in order to achieve his goals for Gary. Indeed Seaman's ministry in Gary after 1918 can be divided into two major and related periods, the first having to do with the Centenary Campaign's program for Gary and the second having to do with the construction of City Church.

One of the campaign's goals was to finance special mission projects in the Calumet Region, and the Northwest Indiana Conference sought to raise over $1 million by 1924 for this purpose. Although the financial goal was oversubscribed nationally, actual receipts amounted to only 46 percent of pledges.[61] Locally the Calumet Missionary Society oversaw the Centenary Campaign, and by 1923 DeBra reported that it had resulted in "strengthened churches, the development of week-day religious instruction, and the systematizing of the work on scientific lines." DeBra's report also illustrated the potent mixture of concern and loathing that often underlay such mission efforts. Speaking of the political threat represented by urban immigrants, he complained that, even with immigration restrictions in place, immigration of Mexicans and blacks was continuing and was "surely not much of an improvement over the Slav or the Italian." But he went on to note that "nothing will take care of any of these ignorant and dangerous elements like the practical Christian service that grows out of Bible instruction to the children, and through them to the parents, or like supervised play, regulated entertainment, social service, nurse visitation, day nursery, free and kindly help to employment, counsel in trouble, and the thousand other things that our community service makes a practical demonstration of Christian spirit and helpfulness."[62]

The Centenary also brought William Grant Seaman and the church he led to the attention of several influential Methodist leaders in home missions, as Seaman hitched his own vision for the church in Gary to the financial star of the Centenary Campaign. According to Beatrice Lewis the Centenary Campaign temporarily side-tracked Seaman's efforts for a downtown church by diverting his attention and that of Gary Methodists to several other projects. But, in fact, Seaman's eventual success depended in no small measure on his service to and alliance with the Centenary drive. On behalf of the Centenary, he worked closely with the leaders of the home missions movement in Methodism, men who in turn facilitated his access to Elbert Gary and his negotiations with United States Steel. In this effort, he was quick to give credit to the Centenary leaders for the success of the effort in Gary, understating his own considerable role in the process. They later returned the favor, as, for example, when D. D. Forsyth said at the opening service of City Church, "There is not another man in our denomination who could have accomplished this—with such spirit, perseverance, real devotion and skill in living effectively and efficiently in a community." Seaman described the Centenary's goal for Gary as "a program of ministry to the city of Gary based on its needs and carried out in cooperation with the other Christian churches." He identified its seven specific targets of ministry as Gary's peripheral areas, foreigners, blacks, the sick, school children, "down and outers," and "the downtown regions."[63]

Seaman and the church, like their Presbyterian neighbors, were already addressing several of these needs. Avann, for example, had begun a mission in Gary's outlying Glen Park region, and Seaman and the church had built a community house in the Ambridge neighborhood in 1919. Moreover Seaman and the church cooperated with the Presbyterians and others in support of the weekday church schools. In place of a rescue mission for street people, by 1925 plans were afoot to establish a Goodwill Industries in Gary, and "this work will doubtless develop with the city."[64] As for foreigners, the Campbell Friendship House, founded during Avann's pastorate, was strengthened still further under Seaman's pastorate. Centenary financial assistance during this period helped build needed facilities, and both Seaman and his wife, Laura Rice Seaman, served on its board of trustees. In fact, he chaired the board for a time.[65]

For Seaman, work with an immigrant population was one of Gary's premier challenges and attractions, and he committed himself to it enthusiastically. In effect, he took pride in the extent to which Gary represented in intensified form the challenge facing Protestants in many American cities to reach the foreign born. In a letter to D. D. Forsyth in 1916, Seaman observed that "from a Home Missionary standpoint our 'Foreign Problem' is at least 99 and 44/100% pure." He illustrated the problem several years later with an often-quoted remark that "the name of God is taken in vain in 43 different languages and dialects, and his praises are sung in only 16 languages in Gary."[66]

Finally, Seaman also was a central figure in the Methodist attempts to meet the needs of the sick by taking over a faltering Gary General Hospital. Founded in 1911, the Gary General Hospital's attempt to raise funds for a new building in 1917 foundered due to "the unattached nature of the organization without constituency." Attempts to find a sponsor were unsuccessful until W. G. Seaman became involved. Persuaded "that the Methodist church ought to have its ministry of healing activity at work in the Calumet district," Seaman helped convince the Board of Trustees of the Methodist Episcopal Hospital and Deaconess Home of the State of Indiana to take over the work in April 1919. Construction began in August and was completed in 1923 at a cost of $400,000, $95,000 of which was raised in Gary. Seaman himself was secretary of the board from 1923 to 1929. Seaman's strenuous efforts on behalf of the hospital undoubtedly delayed the new building for the church. But they also enhanced his reputation and status with Methodist Centenary officials and the community at large. Significantly, although "not one cent of Centenary money" went into the City Church building effort, Seaman generously credited the Centenary with important, nonmonetary contributions to the project.[67]

Seaman's and the Centenary's targets for Methodist work in Gary always included "a ministry to colored people,"[68] at that time the polite term to use in reference to African Americans. The relationship between blacks and whites was an important issue throughout Seaman's years in Gary and his own position on the matter was mixed. Although in some respects he was bound by the standards of his time in understanding persons of another race, in other respects he was ahead of his time and managed to cross the boundaries between the races in Gary, at least to a limited extent.[69]

As in other areas of Seaman's ministry, one must look at what he did in the area of race relations in addition to the quite meager record of what he said. His single greatest commitment in this area was to meet the Centenary goal of a combined African-American church and settlement house. Perhaps because of his conviction that black Methodist work in Gary should ultimately be answerable to white leadership, he was somewhat cool toward early black initiatives to establish a black Methodist church. But with or without Seaman's support, Trinity Church survived a succession of short pastorates and in 1918 the Reverend I. D. Smith renewed contacts with Seaman which "resulted in the writing of a program for Methodism in Gary." These conversations were no doubt connected with the Centenary Movement, under which "the Trinity Methodist Episcopal Church was put down for a new plant with equipment for social service work." Seaman, Holmes, DeBra, and other local Methodists encouraged Smith during his year in Gary and retained interest during the pastorate of the Reverend J. W. V. Hutchinson in 1919–20. Hutchinson, like Seaman a graduate of Boston University, supported the Centenary plans for the church and maintained close contact with Seaman and local Methodists. In the spring of 1920, the Reverend Frank S. Delaney was appointed to Trinity and remained one of Gary's leading black ministers until his death in 1939. It was his task to realize plans for an African-American Methodist church and settlement house in Gary.[70]

Working closely with Seaman, DeBra, and Holmes, Delaney approached both H. S. Norton of the Gary Land Company and the Methodist Board of Home Missions and Church Extension for help in relocating and improv-

Part of the segregated subdivision built by U.S. Steel for its black workers in 1918. These houses were on Carolina Street. Courtesy of Calumet Regional Archives, Indiana University Northwest.

ing the small Trinity Church building. This relocation occurred in September 1920, and the church began its work in earnest, "ministering to the social, moral and spiritual conditions in the community."[71]

But behind this seemingly simple move of a small building some six blocks lay considerable negotiation between Seaman and Norton concerning the role of Methodism in a small subdivision being built by United States Steel for its black workers. Unfortunately existing documents do not permit a complete reconstruction of this incident which perhaps would reveal a great deal about the nature of U.S. Steel's philanthropic involvements in Gary. But one long (three, single-spaced, typed pages) letter from Seaman to Norton suggests the following scenario, as well as affording the best insight we have into Seaman's attitudes toward African Americans.

At issue was which denomination should be assigned the responsibility of conducting religious work in U.S. Steel's black subdivision.[72] The Methodists, through the Centenary movement, were eager for the charge. Methodist officials had already discussed their plans for a comprehensive ministry in Gary with Judge Gary himself on several occasions, and on June 30, 1920, he requested more information about specific Methodist plans for working with Gary's rapidly growing black population. In response to Judge Gary's request, Seaman, M. P. Burns of the Methodist Department of City Work, and Ralph Diffendorfer of the Centenary movement met with H. S. Norton in his Gary home a few weeks later and outlined their plans. Seaman summarized the Methodist case in a letter to Norton on July 6.[73]

He began with the assumption that, although the black church was perhaps the central institution in the African-American community, it suffered from a low level of clerical leadership and reflected the generally low moral level of American blacks. But, he went on to argue, since the Methodists' centralized polity provided for white supervision of black clergy, Methodists should be granted the work. He bluntly stated two reasons for white supervision. First, white leaders could fire black clergy who fell short. Second, black denominations without white leadership "are cultivating in their people the sense of being wronged," thus undermining the national loyalty of American blacks. Moreover, the Centenary program would provide a balanced religious, educational, and social service ministry to Gary's blacks, thus giving their predominantly emotional religious life "a new and vastly better quality."[74]

The argument, racist though it was, carried the day. The Methodists, through Trinity Methodist Episcopal Church, assumed responsibility for the work, and two months later the church moved its building to Fifteenth Avenue and Massachusetts Street. On July 6, 1921, exactly one year after his letter to Norton, Seaman noted that "our church is now giving leadership to the organizing of a settlement work among colored people."[75]

The valuable work done by the John Stewart Memorial Settlement House during that economic slump in 1921 ensured its continuation, and a prestigious board of directors, including Holmes, DeBra, and Seaman along with Delaney and several black professional men and women, proceeded with plans for a more adequate building costing $75,000 on a site provided by the Gary Land Company. The new building, designed by black Gary architect William W. Cooke, was dedicated in November 1925, thus completing, with the exception of a downtown church, the Centenary's institutional goals for Gary.[76]

Despite the cooperation of black and white leaders in the establishment of Stewart House, the settlement did not illustrate unalloyed racial goodwill. Indeed, as Crocker has noted, Stewart House was one way in which Gary's "white church leaders sought to exert control over Gary's black churches and the Steel Corporation recognized some of the benefits of paternalistic control." Stewart House was, she said, "a cautionary tale, showing how a social work agency, born out of compassion and benevolence was, at the same time, an agency of social control in the black community." But given Gary's racial climate, the achievements of Stewart House were significant, and Delaney may have been "as versatile a 'race leader' as Gary's blacks could hope for in the 1920s and 1930s as he got what he could for his people from the Steel Corporation without disturbing the basic power relations in the town."[77] Like several other areas of race relations in Gary, Stewart House was a mixed picture. Mixed also were the motives of William Grant Seaman.

Seaman's 1920 letter to Norton both summarized the Methodist argument for work with African Americans and revealed that Seaman shared many of the racist views all too characteristic of his generation. According to the letter, Seaman thought African Americans were "very ignorant, and to a surprising degree morally undeveloped, and this fact is true of a very large number of their preachers." Although blacks "are perhaps not so viciously immoral as they are unmoral," said Seaman, still they illustrate a "looseness in social virtues and in respect for property rights." His views led him to support the Steel Company's plans for a black subdivision, in spite of some black church opposition to such racial segregation. According to Seaman, white leaders in Gary responded directly to that opposition, and "a very little effort lined up our colored people for the project." Based on this letter, Mohl and Betten concluded that Seaman was strongly prejudiced against blacks: "As minister of Gary's City Methodist church, the congregation of the city's elite, Seaman was articulating widely held attitudes among steel city opinion-shapers and decision makers. They wanted to segregate the blacks, but they wanted to control them too." That these racist views were mixed with more noble words and actions on the subject cannot explain them away.[78]

If this letter were all we knew about Seaman, the record would be very bleak indeed. But there is also evidence either that his views changed or that his public actions were more generous than his private opinions. First, given his long involvement with Stewart House, Seaman knew personally many of Gary's middle-class African Americans. Second, Seaman acknowledged that blacks had made significant progress in the face of serious obstacles. Although he could say they were "not far from the jungle" on one hand, he also claimed that "no race in the history of the world has made such remarkable progress as have the colored people in America since the signing of the Emancipation Proclamation." Elsewhere he observed that "their remarkable progress since the time of slavery gives promise of large results from whatever ministries are rendered them."[79]

Finally, he took a number of significant public stands against racial discrimination which, his son recalled years later, incurred the wrath of the Ku Klux Klan in the mid-1920s. According to historian James Lane, "Seaman tried hard to combat racism in Gary."[80] His efforts in this area were certainly more prominent than those of his Presbyterian colleagues. He held joint services with Trinity Methodist and other African-American congregations and participated actively in such city-wide programs as Race Relations Sundays. In 1927, for example, Seaman shared the pulpit with two of Gary's most prominent black pastors, F. S. Delaney of Trinity Methodist Church and Charles Hawkins of First Baptist Church, and proclaimed: "We shall make no progress toward race union until we view each other as God views us, children of the same Father and brothers all. There are indeed differences of culture and background that must not be overlooked, but the fact of basic equality is paramount. What we need in Gary is to pull together and to help each other in the solution of our mutual problems." Nor did he limit his actions to his own congregation. In 1924, he joined four other ministers and the NAACP in opposing the showing of the film *Birth of a Nation,* for fear it would "arouse racial prejudices." In addition he attempted unsuccessfully in 1923 to get the board of the Methodist Hospital to admit blacks. These efforts did not go unnoticed, and, on his departure from Gary, the *Post-Tribune* observed that "among his myriad interests was a keen conception, deep understanding and genuine sympathy with the problems of the colored population with particular cooperation centering in Stewart house." But, as Lane noted, Seaman was unable to overcome racial polarization either in Gary or in his own church.[81] Nor, perhaps, was he able to overcome it in himself.

Seaman and City Church

By 1925, then, Seaman and First Methodist Church had realized six of the seven Centenary goals for Gary and were on the verge of realizing the last and largest of them. On January 25, 1925, ground was broken, and on May 19 the cornerstone was laid for the new building which became known simply as "City Church.[82]

This downtown social gospel cathedral was, in turn, the cornerstone of

William Grant Seaman's vision for the urban church. It symbolized what he thought the church should and could do in Gary. The magnitude of the task, however, and the onset of the Depression insured that City Church would not fulfil his vision. Nor were his successors able to do so. As one of them acknowledged, City Church "was dreamed by a giant, and his successors never quite came up to that vision."[83] But that the dream was built at all and that it came to partial fruition confirms my thesis concerning the vitality of mainstream Protestantism in Gary. City Church illustrates that, at least until the 1940s, progressive Protestants were surprisingly at home in their city. William Grant Seaman certainly was.

When Seaman began to dream his dream is uncertain, but he apparently brought it to Gary with his baggage. Within three months of his arrival in 1916, for example, he wrote D. D. Forsyth of the denomination's Board of Home Missions and Church Extension, requesting the board's help in Gary. Citing its virtues as an ideal mission opportunity, Seaman asked for help in adding to the church building to make it more adequate "for social 'service' and Sunday School work."[84] Gradually he moved beyond this somewhat primitive notion and began to envision both a great downtown cathedral and an ambitious program of service to the entire city.

For Seaman, building the church downtown was the heart of the matter. While acknowledging that some people preferred a more traditional family church, Seaman outlined the distinctive service to be rendered by a downtown church on an appropriate site with an income-producing building alongside. Time and again, Seaman listed the same reasons for locating a church in the central part of the city.[85]

First, a central location placed the church on a par with other institutions located downtown whose influence extended throughout the city. As he said: "The whole city needs the 'Down-Town Church.' At the heart of the city are those institutions that stand for universal needs, the store, the bank, the professional office, the theatre. The Church should be there too, in a strong way sending out its healing influence to every part of the city." Consequently in his detailed discussion of three possible sites for City Church, he concluded that the central site at Sixth Avenue and Washington Street was virtually "an ideal location for a down-town church." Said Seaman, "We should have in Gary sufficient land to enable us to build a Churchly church, an adequate Social Service and recreational building for the needs of the city Gary is soon to be, and probably a business block." Although he did not say it quite this way, Seaman felt that to put the church on the periphery was to make it peripheral.[86] The 1920s were, of course, a premier period for America's central cities—the climax of the period that Goldfield and Brownell have called the "radiant center," in which the vital center of American urban culture was, in fact, downtown. To Seaman it was clear that the church must occupy that radiant center: "The downtown institutions dominate the city's life and largely determine its quality. Banks, department stores, theaters, office buildings are there. The church should be also." A central location was of strategic importance to the downtown church inasmuch as "we cannot save the world without saving the cities and we cannot save the cities without saving them at the heart."[87]

But for Seaman, this central location was not only strategic, it was also organic. The church's motto suggests this fact clearly: "That Christ may dwell, a Living Presence, at the city's heart." As Christ should be in the heart of the Christian, so the church should be at the heart of the city. "Out from the city's heart go those forces that mould its life—the church should be there and from that vantage point send its healing influence to the city's every part." The downtown church had to be placed at the city's heart if its influence were to radiate *from* the center *to* the periphery.[88]

But to Seaman it was equally necessary that the church be located downtown in order to fulfil its mission to the center. On the one hand, many of the evils to be fought, including "the strongholds of ignorance, immorality, crime, disease," as well as "debasing amusements, low theatres, immoral dance halls," were located there.[89] On the other hand, many of the groups to which the church needed to minister were located there as well—businessmen and other downtown workers, foreigners, transients, newcomers, and young people rooming away from home, among others. And yet, Seaman said, echoing Josiah Strong, Paul Strayer, and other social gospel advocates, Protestants had been fleeing the downtown regions in droves. Nonetheless such a church would appeal to "those who prefer a church on the firing line, or with a special civic spirit."[90] The program Seaman outlined illustrates just how pivotal the central location was in his vision of the city church.

Seaman connected the downtown location and the church's program as follows: "From the heart of a city radiates its life and influence. That is why our church was put where it is. Then came the plan of service, a plan for a church open seven days a week, a church presenting the beautiful in music and architecture, a church providing Christian educational features, healthful recreation, appealing and clean entertainment for youth and age, and above all, a church spreading by deed and word the spirit of Christian friendliness."[91] The fact that Seaman used this description almost verbatim on several different occasions confirms that it accurately, if briefly, articulated his vision of the program City Church should launch. Seaman insisted that the effective city church must render a comprehensive ministry to its community, which required a more complex staff than the traditional one or two ministers and a secretary. Very early on, for example, Seaman insisted that the church needed at least two male pastors, a woman assistant, and a secretary. He later enlarged his ideal staff to include a minister of music (one of only three in the country according to the *Post-Tribune*), a minister of recreation, and another secretary.[92] Financing such a staff, however, proved to be impossible once the Depression had begun.

A comprehensive ministry required a suitable building. By the early twenties, Seaman said such a building should include four large rooms (a sanctuary, a gym, a dining room, and an assembly hall), eight medium-sized rooms (for Sunday school, music classes, and so forth), smaller rooms for Sunday school classes and community organization offices, and a roof garden. Floor plans confirm that he got what he wanted. The roof garden, alas, was a mistake. The *Epworth Herald* predicted it would "prove wonderfully attractive on a hot summer night, for it is high enough to catch refreshing breezes from the lake, blowing over the roofs of neighboring buildings." Unfortunately the refreshing breezes blew first over the massive steel mills, and the smoke and smell made the roof garden virtually unusable.[93]

From the outset, an essential element in the building plans was an income-producing unit. Repeatedly, Seaman hammered away at the fact that Gary, as a mission situation, could not provide the resources locally to address the magnitude of the needs. "The down-town church," he said, "cannot hope to raise from its constituency sufficient funds to carry on its work." His case was a good one, given the nature of Gary, and its largely non-Protestant, young, working- and middle-class, highly mobile population. Consequently Seaman concluded that, as other downtown churches had done, City Church would have to build an income-producing unit. In 1921 he estimated that such a unit would produce $18,000 annually. Inasmuch as the church's total receipts in 1920 amounted to only $12,000, the importance of rental income to the church's mission as he envisioned it was obvious.[94]

With an adequate staff and building, the church could render a program of service every day of the week. As Seaman observed: "The sturdy maker of iron and steel, the active man of commercial life, the busy woman and the growing youth are best convinced of the Christ by seeing His influence every hour of the week-day as well as an hour on Sunday." The church was to illustrate Christ's influence through a comprehensive ministry—"religious, educational, evangelistic, musical, social, recreational, missionary, social service, civic." Since such a ministry would seek to address a whole range of daily human needs, "Christ will minister every day of the week."[95]

One way of meeting this variety of human needs was to cooperate in meeting them, not only with other congregations but with a variety of secular community organizations. City Church was already working with First Presbyterian Church and other Protestant congregations in a number of ways, including most notably the weekday church schools. In addition the congregation was a member of the Calumet Church and Home Missionary Federation, which coordinated regional Protestant mission efforts. Such cooperation, Seaman claimed, was particularly effective in "making religion a factor in the community and the lives of the people." He also thought it was important that a downtown church take the lead in ecumenical cooperation, among other reasons to avoid an unnecessary duplication of services.[96] But, even when cooperating, the churches alone could not (and probably should not) meet all human needs. They could, however, cooperate with a whole range of organizations devoted to human betterment and civic welfare. Among such organizations Seaman included the city government, YMCA, Boy Scout Council, Salvation Army, Anti-Saloon League, Municipal Voters League, Associated Charities, Committee on Child Welfare, and the police. According to Seaman, the city church could assist these organizations by being a community center, providing rooms for various welfare offices, the weekday church schools, "a social clinic and a People's Lawyer."[97] Seaman's vision for social service, then, was a cooperative one and an integral part of the program of the city church.

Such a program required that the membership be educated appropriately. Part of the church's educational responsibility, of course, was traditional religious education, which should strive to make children "efficient members of an organization that shall bring the kingdom of God on earth." "Every congregation," Seaman said, "should train its children for a war of conquest to take the whole of society for Christ." Such a task required at least a full-time director of religious education, vacation Bible schools, a children's church service, and support of the weekday church schools. But it was also the congregation's responsibility to educate both its children and adults about social problems. For example, in a document outlining the proposed program of a downtown church, Seaman listed in three parallel columns the needs to be met, the cooperative approach to meeting the needs, and the approach of the individual church. The primary role of the church was to instruct its members concerning human needs such as the need for better living conditions and the "lifting of amusements to a scientific basis."[98]

Seaman's concern with amusements in the city was not merely related to the church's educational task. If not as important as the sanctuary, the gymnasium was still integral to all of Seaman's plans for the downtown church. Nor was it to be simply a playground for the church's children. Rather the church's recreational ministry should help instil in the residents of the city an appreciation for the "joys of clean play." Recreation for Seaman had a moral value and was a God-given impulse: "this church believes in the gospel of play and will furnish quiet game rooms, bowling alleys and a romp room and gymnasium, where both young and old will be invited to share in the joys of clean play."[99] It is clear that, in a city known more for its brothels than its basketball teams, Seaman's emphasis on the "gospel of play" was a central strategy in the church's ministry of friendliness to its neighbors.

Precisely because the downtown church was downtown, Seaman emphasized its responsibility to be "a church spreading by deed and word the spirit of Christian friendliness." But his admonition was not to some anachronistic, small-town gregariousness. To the contrary, the friendliness of the city church reflected urban life in both specific and more general ways. The specific friendliness of the church Seaman illustrated with two metaphors. The church was both a "reception hall" and a "Mother Church." At a banquet of civic and business leaders in 1926, Seaman said: "This church is a downtown reception hall. Strangers always come to the downtown section of a city and we are here to receive them. We are now in the center of great activities of the city and all who come downtown are welcome here." Among these "strangers" were groups to whom the church should act like a mother, including young people rooming in the city, transients of all sorts, and foreigners. But in a more general sense friendliness should characterize all the ministries of a city church. In the new building, for example, Seaman built a tastefully appointed "Friendship

Room" rather than the more traditional small chapel, reflecting his concern with establishing a sense of community in the church.[100]

As noted above, Seaman, like his contemporary Louis Wirth, was conscious of the anonymity and rootlessness of modern urban life. Unlike the rural and small-town environment from which Seaman himself had come, the city provided no overall sense of community and social control, and yet the need for community was nowhere more evident. Though he did not use the term "subcommunity," Seaman in effect proposed that the city church should both be a subcommunity and facilitate still others. In this respect, both First Presbyterian Church and City Methodist Church were much alike. To Seaman such a task reflected both the nature of the city's population and the genius of Christianity. Since the downtown church was surrounded by persons "outside of any social group," it must work to "tie them into such groups and provide group socials and pasttimes for them." In fact the entire ministry of the church should reflect the fact that "Christianity is a social religion. This church will try to show, by the friendly spirit of all its services, that Christ lives at the corner of Sixth Avenue and Washington Street. Wholesome social gatherings for people of all ages will be included in its program." The city church should be both friendly and urban.[101]

In Seaman's eyes, the city church should also be "a church presenting the beautiful in music and architecture." Notwithstanding that the church was to minister to persons of all social classes, no compromises were to be made in aesthetic standards. Indeed, given Seaman's conviction that the church's ministry involved uplifting persons from where they were, it was especially important that aesthetic standards be maintained. Three words recur in Seaman's references to the building—"beautiful," "commanding," and "monument." Christianity, to Seaman, was both true and beautiful, and truth and beauty were enduring. Consequently it was no accident that a *Post-Tribune* reporter thought that City Church reflected both the old and the new, looking like an "old English church," but "with a sense of the progressive, forward-moving spirit of Gary." Seaman and the architects consciously selected medieval motifs for the numerous carvings throughout the building, thus illustrating symbolically Christianity's ancient truths. For Seaman, architecture itself was one way of bringing the ancient truths of Christianity into the heart of the modern city. "This church will be an imposing edifice, chaste, sincere, beautiful in all its lines, a fitting experience of the God of holiness, truth, and beauty."[102]

The city church should also be "commanding." His triumphalist tone reflects Seaman's conviction that the downtown church should be not only geographically central, but also *important*. Its building should be "commanding," and its services of "prophetic" preaching and rich sacred music should be "dynamic, inspiring, triumphant." It should not only be analogous to the banks, theaters, department stores, and so forth; it should be their equal.[103]

It should not, however, be confused with them but should clearly be a "monument to the spiritual life." This was evident to Seaman fairly early in the planning process for City Church. In a letter to H. S. Norton in February 1920, Seaman affirmed that

> . . . it is my conviction that such a church as we plan should have a churchly auditorium devoted exclusively to religious purposes, that its architecture and that of the building without should be such that it would be immediately recognized as a church, and not taken for a fine bank building, a court house, Christian Science temple, or any other possible building. Our enterprise is a religious one and the religious note should be dominant in architecture as well as in programs. Such a building would stand continually in the midst of the rush of the city streets as a monument to the religious life. It would also deepen the religious message of the stated religious services, and would therefore be one of the factors in that efficiency we seek.

The building, as well as the program, should thus be profoundly religious as well as efficient, comprehensive, and beautiful.[104] Even architecture, and the sacred space it created, was a means of proclaiming the gospel for the city church.

To build such an edifice and implement such a ministry was Seaman's greatest challenge in Gary. He met it with energy, enthusiasm, and perseverance, and by 1926 the dream became, at least for a few brief years, a reality. The story is a remarkable tale of a visionary urban pastor who used every means at his disposal to lead, inspire, and cajole not only his own congregation but also his denominational superiors and some of the country's leading industrialists on behalf of his dream. It is thus a tale blending congregational history with the broader history of religion in America and even with American industrial and philanthropic history. But most of all it is a tale of human beings serving a cause in which they believed. Although their perception of the cause was often flawed and their service of it often mixed with other motives, their actions revealed their conviction that the church should be a prominent force for good, even in the modern city.

Although Seaman may well have come to Gary with much of his dream for a downtown church in place, congregational historian Beatrice Lewis suggested that his vision developed "as his knowledge of the growing city's needs enlarged."[105] If so, that maturation occurred fairly rapidly in 1917–18. During a period of some eighteen months, Seaman and the church participated in the formation of two local missionary organizations—the Methodist Calumet Missionary Society and the ecumenical Calumet Home and Missionary Federation.[106] Moreover the beginning of the Centenary campaign in 1917 broadened considerably the range of possibilities that might be accomplished. The original Centenary survey proposed relocating First Methodist Church on the city's residential west side. But Seaman arranged for a group from the Board of Home Missions to visit Gary and persuaded them of the desirability of creating a downtown Methodist Church, preferably on "the open tract at the corner of Sixth Avenue and Washington Street." The matter apparently had already been discussed as well by certain "leaders of our local congregation." At this time, "it was thought that we might secure the above tract and build a block with stores on the ground floor to provide resources in part for such a program as should be conducted, and place the auditorium and necessary rooms on the floors above." The Board of Home Missions, however, probably in conjunction with Seaman, recommended a larger plant in which the religious portion of the building would dominate, although that plan required the purchase of two additional lots. By mid-1918, Seaman confirmed that the Methodist seven-part program in Gary, including a downtown church, had been approved by Centenary officials.[107]

In 1919 Ralph Diffendorfer, a Centenary official who had visited Gary and consulted with Seaman and other local leaders about Methodism's program there, was placed next to Judge Gary at a Centenary dinner in New York and discussed with him Methodist plans for the city. It was to prove the most important meal in the history of the congregation. The Judge expressed to Diffendorfer some interest in the project and initiated a series of meetings between Methodist officials and local representatives of United States Steel, especially Eugene Buffington, the corporate head of the Gary Works. These meetings, occurring over several months, resulted in a proposal that United States Steel and the Methodist Church contribute equally to the establishment in Gary of a comprehensive social service program, including a foreign settlement house, an African-American church and settlement house, and a downtown church, at a total cost of one and one-half million dollars.[108]

On the first Saturday in February 1920, Seaman met with Gary Land Company head, H. S. Norton, to enlist his assistance on the downtown church project. In a letter to Norton on February 6, 1920, he summarized the results of their conversation and attempted to describe the project in a way that would be persuasive to U.S. Steel. Seaman emphasized that the type of comprehensive ministry envisioned would serve all of Gary and would neither compete with other institutions nor simply serve Methodist interests. It would, however, require a substantial building and the entire site at Sixth and Washington. By this time Seaman had in hand preliminary plans and had visited similar churches in other cities, which convinced him that an architecturally impressive sanctuary seating at least one thousand was required in addition to an income-producing unit. Finally Seaman concluded that none of this would be possible unless "it should appeal to the makers of Gary and its industries as worthy of their assistance." Norton and his colleagues were persuaded.[109]

After their approval by Norton and other local steel officials, plans for the downtown church were delivered to Judge Gary by a delegation including Diffendorfer, Nicholson, DeBra, and Seaman. At Judge Gary's request they were presented in April 1920 to the Finance Committee of U.S. Steel by a delegation including Bishop Nicholson, Diffendorfer, Seaman, Mayor William Hodges, and local steel officials.[110]

In June 1920, the Finance Committee approved a commitment of up to $325,000 for the project plus the site (six of the eight lots) at Sixth and Washington, with the Methodists to supply an additional $325,000.[111] A word should be said concerning U.S. Steel's generosity toward City Church. No doubt relatively pure philanthropic, and perhaps sentimental, motives were mixed with less honorable social control intentions in the minds of Judge Gary and the Finance Committee. Inasmuch as U.S. Steel made many contributions to a wide variety of Gary institutions during the teens and twenties, the City Church grant was an extreme example of a well-established pattern. It may also have reflected Judge Gary's well-known vanity. According to James Lane, the Methodist Judge Gary silenced Finance Committee opponents to the grant by exclaiming, "hell, men, they want to build a church in *our* town." Although Seaman intended the church to be a monument to the religious life, Judge Gary may well have intended it to be a monument to something else.[112] On June 30, Gary met with Buffington and Diffendorfer and indicated U.S. Steel's willingness to proceed with the downtown church. He also raised several questions concerning the proposed work with African Americans and foreigners in Gary.

Seaman wrote to Judge Gary on July 1, expressing his "appreciation of your careful consideration of our appeal."[113] The first battle was over, but the war had just begun.

Seaman had to fight on three fronts for the next four and a half years. He had to remain in favor both with Judge Gary and with Methodist officials and on occasion had to mediate disputes between them concerning City Church. But he also had to convince his congregation that they *should* become the church he envisioned, and that they *could* become such a church. Although the story must be reconstructed from a variety of sources, it is clear that fighting the battle on these three fronts was a major challenge to Seaman, but he won at least qualified victories on all three.

After the approval by U.S. Steel's Finance Committee in June 1920, Seaman had to secure the congregation's support for the downtown church concept. Although a number of leaders had been involved from the beginning, the congregation had as yet taken no formal action concerning Seaman's plan. So on July 11, 1920, the issue was discussed at the Fourth Quarterly Conference of the Official Board, and a committee was elected "to consider and report on the future policy of our congregation, as to the type of church ours should be." Predictably, C. O. Holmes was on the committee along with prominent laymen Richard Hotchkiss, A. M. Fisher, A. N Hirons, and C. R. Kuss.[114]

After meeting during the summer, the committee reported back to the Official Board at a dinner meeting on September 23, 1920. Seaman and the assistant pastor reported on the background of the project, and the board examined blueprints of the proposed building. Then the committee read its report recommending that First Methodist Church undertake the task of "maintaining a downtown church, as defined by the Board of Home Missions," including "religious, educational, and social service activities," provided that U.S. Steel and the Methodist board provide the site and all but fifty thousand dollars of construction funds. The report was adopted unanimously and referred to the congregation. Congregational life is often a mixture of the grand and the trivial. After approving this mammoth undertaking that would dominate the life of the church for the next six years, the board "collected a free will offering for the washing of the dishes and . . . thanked the ladies for their services in preparing the dinner of the evening."[115]

On the following Sunday, September 26, Seaman "presented to the morning congregation the need for a down-town church, the desire of the

City Methodist Church under construction, 1925, looking northeast. The old Hotel Gary is in the background. Courtesy of DePauw University Archives.

Board of Home Missions that we should make our church that type, and the action of the Quarterly Conference last Thursday night that we should do so." The congregation approved the proposal and elected a building committee.[116]

But this was not, of course, the end of the matter. When the building was completed in October 1926, the *Post-Tribune* candidly acknowledged that "the congregation has many times been dubious about the matter, partly because of the size of the task, and partly because of the new and difficult nature of the undertaking in a rapidly growing city," but "one obstacle after another melted away due to the insistent hammering of Dr. Seaman and his wife." The obstacles were usually financial ones, and Seaman's hammering took the form of a financial campaign in late 1923 and massive borrowing in 1924.[117] After getting the congregation's basic approval, Seaman visited similar churches around the country, including Fourth Presbyterian in Chicago, Central Methodist in Detroit, and congregations in New York, Boston, Pittsburgh, and Cleveland, and initial architectural plans were prepared.[118]

But the agreement of the congregation and the approval of architectural plans merely laid the groundwork for a four-year, three-way struggle

City Methodist Church cornerstone-laying ceremony, May 10, 1925, looking north up Washington Street. Courtesy of DePauw University Archives.

among Seaman, Methodist denominational officials, and U.S. Steel to negotiate the financing of the project.[119] After his long battle, Seaman broke ground at the conclusion of the morning service on January 25, 1925, and construction was completed in October 1926. A week of services and programs during October 3–10 celebrated concurrently the completion of the building, Seaman's tenth anniversary in Gary, and the church's twentieth anniversary. The selection of the week's speakers suggested the broad ministry Seaman envisioned for City Church. For example, issues they addressed included religion and education, the church and the immigrant, religion and music, religion and business, and the church's worldwide ministry. Speakers included, among others, D. D. Forsyth of the Board of Home Missions and Church Extension, Bishops Nicholson and Leete, James Thomas, a Detroit pastor popular with labor, and T. G. Soares, the chaplain of the University of Chicago. Throughout the week, they emphasized the activist, comprehensive, and progressive ministry needed if the city in America were to become the city of God. On the cover of the church bulletin were both a photograph of the new building and the motto of City Church, "That Christ may dwell, a Living Presence, at the city's heart."

City Methodist Church cornerstone-laying ceremony, May 10, 1925. Left to
right: Clarence Kuss (in light hat), C. Oliver Holmes (bareheaded), Rev. O. E.
Tomes (in dark hat, pastor of Central Christian Church), Dr. William Grant
Seaman (in light hat, pastor of City Methodist Church), Dr. William Switzer (in
back row, long-time assistant minister of City Methodist Church), H. S. Norton
(with arm on chair and wearing hat), and Bishop Frederick D. Leete (speaking).
Courtesy of DePauw University Archives.

Interracial meeting at Seaman Hall in October 1926. This auditorium in City Methodist Church (named Seaman Hall upon W. G. Seaman's departure in 1929) provided space for many public meetings in Gary, as a part of the church's ministry to the wider city. Present at this meeting were the Reverends Frank S. Delaney of Trinity Methodist Church and Stewart Settlement House (second from left), William Grant Seaman (third from left), and Willard Crosby Lyon of First Congregational Church (fifth from left). Courtesy of Calumet Regional Archives, Indiana University Northwest.

City Methodist Church, with the new Hotel Gary in the background. Courtesy of DePauw University Archives.

After the dedication of the building, the church was always referred to as simply "City Church." The dream had become a reality.[120]

After two weeks of cool, wet autumn weather, October 3, 1926, dawned fair and warm for the opening service at City Church. Taking advantage of a high temperature of eighty-six degrees, many Gary residents took a Sunday afternoon drive in the country. By Monday, however, cool, wet weather had returned, and "the familiar cloudbank underlaid with the usual pall of smoke covered the city."[121]

Like the weather that October, City Church seemed to warm briefly to the vision of its leader, before relapsing toward an ecclesiastical normality more characteristic of its time. For three brief years, Seaman attempted to lead the congregation to become the church he had envisioned—a church at home in the very heart of the industrial city. To a certain extent he succeeded. The grand new building hosted a wide variety of activities. For example, in 1927 Seaman reported: "Our Community Hall is rendering a real service to our city and to different groups of our city. Within the last few days there has been held in it an oratorical contest on the Constitution under the auspices of the colored Elks for the purpose of providing college scholarships to worthy colored high school graduates, a concert by the Mexican band, and a concert by a Swedish male chorus, and next week, in it will be held the services of the G.A.R. encampment. One could hardly think of a more varied ministry than this."[122]

Seaman took special care to sponsor joint services with foreign churches and interracial services with African-American ones. A particular favorite was the Roumanian Orthodox Church led by Reverend John Trutia which visited City Church shortly after it opened. Trutia later addressed a Church Family Night and ". . . pointed out how difficult it is for the better foreigners to cultivate the acquaintance of the better American citizens. The better Americans seldom cultivate the foreigners. That is left for those who wish to exploit the foreigners. Their church in Gary is 20 years old, and never has any Christian church in Gary sought their acquaintance or friendship until within the last year." The congregation even sent lilies to the Orthodox churches in Gary on the Orthodox Easter in 1927. Race Relations services occurred annually in February, usually in conjunction with other Gary churches. Of one such meeting that was well attended, Seaman said it "ought to be helpful in our community life," by helping the respective races to understand each other.[123]

In the pulpit Seaman urged the congregation to fulfil its ministry in the city. For example in January 1927, he spoke on "Making a New City." Two weeks later, as part of the Chamber of Commerce Civic Week program, Seaman preached on "The Challenge of the City" to a large audience which included Mayor Floyd Williams and other city officials. Citing the home, school, and church as the central institutions in making cities "a good place in which to produce good men and women," Seaman urged the church to inspire the other two institutions to make urban life what it should be. As part of his agenda for the city he supported the prohibition efforts of the Anti-Saloon League, preaching on "Prohibition—A Social Reform."[124] Seaman also supported the congregation's extensive music program, its religious drama program in the new community hall, and a range of other activities.[125]

Like his Presbyterian colleagues Walton and Backemeyer, Seaman also devoted himself to church membership efforts as well as financial efforts to support the church's multifaceted program and to pay off its large indebtedness. Church attendance did, in fact, increase rapidly after the completion of the building. By April 1927, some 205 new members had joined the

Dedication service for new chancel window, December 18, 1927. Courtesy of DePauw University Archives.

church, and on Easter Sunday that year 1,100 worshippers crowded into the new sanctuary. By 1927, the 500-member church Seaman had inherited in 1916 had grown to over 1,200 members with an annual budget of $33,000, and the pastor's salary had increased from $2,000 to $5,000. The 1927 budget, which projected congregational giving of $20,000 and a rental income of $10,500, indicates that Seaman's earlier estimates of $15,000–$18,000 in rental income were already falling short. Realizing that rental income and weekly giving were inadequate by themselves, Seaman attempted to cultivate systematically several major donor prospects in Gary, including the Snyder family, who owned the *Post-Tribune*. He conceded, however, that U.S. Steel "might be hard boiled when it came to giving any more to this church."[126]

All in all, for three years Seaman and the congregation were busy with a complex, ambitious church program, "very much as Dr. Seaman had so long planned."[127] Then came the Depression, bringing to an end much of the dream.

But shortly before the stock market crash, Gary had its own bombshell: "With the information coming as a complete surprise to Gary church, social, business and welfare circles, announcement was made today that Rev. William Grant Seaman, for nearly 13 years pastor of the First Methodist Episcopal church of Gary, has been transferred to the pastorate of the First Methodist Church of Lancaster, Ohio."[128]

The transfer did not, however, come as a complete surprise to C. Oliver Holmes and others on the church's Pastoral Relations Committee, which had, in a split decision, voted to ask Bishop Edgar Blake for Seaman's transfer. Their reasons for doing so are not altogether clear. Years later Seaman's son contended that Holmes and other allies of U.S. Steel management wanted him out on account of his opposition to certain labor practices, especially concerning Mexican immigrants. William Clark, however, said he had heard not a word about this during his fourteen years in Gary, despite numerous private conversations with both Seaman and Holmes. James Lane plausibly suggested that those responsible for Seaman's transfer "rationalized that Seaman had done his part, and now what was needed was an efficient man, not a liberal visionary." But whatever the reasons, Seaman left Gary reluctantly and, according to William Clark, "his heart always remained there."[129]

The *Post-Tribune* announced Seaman's departure on its front page and praised him lavishly in an editorial. Citing his work with City Church, the

Methodist Hospital, and Stewart House, the *Post-Tribune* observed that "one of the biggest accomplishments in the history of Gary is the work of Dr. W. G. Seaman," and went on to add: "Any one of these jobs would have been considered sufficient for most individuals but Dr. Seaman not only handled them all ably but at the same time he participated in all civic endeavors. His has been a service not merely to one organization but his broad sympathies and intellect have been given freely to this community. Gary has needed such a man. The best years of his life have been given that Gary might be a more complete and better city. . . . We know of no man whose going would be a greater civic loss than Dr. Seaman." Echoing the editorial praise, prominent Roman Catholic priest John DeVille wrote the *Post-Tribune* two days later, describing Seaman as "an enlightened leader in religious and civic work, a gentleman of refinement and culture, a man of the broadest human sympathies, and last, but not least—a loyal, devoted friend." At a farewell luncheon, the church presented Seaman with a gift of a thousand dollars and voted unanimously "to change the name of community hall in the church edifice to Seaman hall."[130]

Although he left against his will, Seaman did so with characteristic generosity, remarking: "I like Gary—I love the city; I have had more fun here than I ever had before in my life and I regret exceedingly that I am called to another city, but my memories of the City of Steel will be cherished ones and many of my contacts here undoubtedly will be retained in the spirit in which they were made—that of friendship and mutual understanding, both of which I have found to a marked degree in this city with a truly western spirit of progress and hospitality." He did, in fact, remain in contact with the city, subscribing to the *Post-Tribune* and returning to City Church on at least two occasions to assist William Clark in fund-raising efforts. After his death in an automobile accident in 1942, his ashes were interred in the chancel of City Church.[131]

In assessing William Grant Seaman and City Church, historians Quillen, Meister, and Lane have concluded that they failed to achieve their goals in Gary. Quillen, basing his conclusions on an interview with Seaman, blamed the excessive financial burden of the big building, internal dissension in the congregation, and a lack of support and cooperation from other churches. Meister, dealing more with the congregation's failure than with Seaman's, blamed the location of the building, the Methodist policies against such activities as card playing and dancing, and the financial crisis of the Depression. Lane's more detailed critique cited criticism of the ornate building, poor financial planning that failed to provide adequate funds for maintenance, the preference of workers for saloons over churches, and the reluctance of the congregation to open itself sufficiently to immigrants and African Americans. He also observed that "too many members regarded the opening of their new building as the culmination rather than the beginning of their mission." City Church failed, he concluded, because "the crusade had too few resources, and Seaman had too few allies." But although telling in many respects, their evaluations do not give us the whole story.[132]

Clearly Seaman did not succeed in his desire to create for the long term a congregation committed to active, innovative urban ministry. As we shall see, after Seaman the congregation began to turn inward somewhat like its Presbyterian neighbor and became more like the traditional family church that Seaman had tried to avoid by remaining downtown. But in at least a few respects he was successful in realizing his goals for Gary. He was a moderating influence in labor-management relations and certain other local conflicts, and, principally through the hospital and the settlement houses, he did realize some of his hopes for Gary's immigrants and African-American citizens. Although blacks and immigrants "did not participate in the religious thrust of City Church in the way he had hoped," some of the congregation's programs, especially the recreational programs, did have some appeal. Moreover, Seaman promoted the community hall "as a religiously neutral ground for artistic and civic events" and was "reasonably successful" in this, although foreign and black groups tended to use it independently, and there was little mixing of cultures. Finally the successful conclusion of the building project was in itself a major accomplishment.[133]

But, as William Clark observed, Seaman, like all of us, was limited by his own times. A "pragmatic thinker" as well as a dreamer, he did what he could, given the realities of his day. Clark concluded: "Seaman was a leader with a great dream, and he led City Church into a broader sense of mission. I would not call his efforts at that time and place a failure in any sense of that word. Indeed he laid foundations on which I was later to build as did the whole city. Although present day events have engulfed much of his efforts and mine as well we were serving the people of our day and that must be the final judgment."[134] Although he was unable to build for all time, in his day William Grant Seaman's articulation and partial implementation of a vision for City Church proclaimed that even in a diverse, pluralistic urban environment like Gary, the church should and could minister effectively to the city.

THE VISION FADES

Seaman's vision survived in the collective memory of City Church, but it never inspired the church's ministry in the comprehensive way Seaman had hoped.[135] Although City Church survived the Depression and war period and flourished under the leadership of William Clark, the church's active commitment to the city became ever more tentative during the 1950s and 1960s, despite a brief resurgence during the pastorate of Elbert Cole. By the 1970s, the bleak future of the church became painfully clear to all, and it closed in October 1975, just one year short of its seventieth anniversary. In the end, it succumbed to rapid and massive social change, challenges to which it did not, and perhaps could not, respond in time. But the dream did not die all at once. Indeed it informed the church to a greater or lesser degree for at least three decades after Seaman's departure.

After the brief, uninspiring pastorate of Seaman's successor, Richard Millard, the bishop transferred William Clark from Fort Wayne to City Church in 1932. (If Millard's stolid sermon titles are any indication, he must have been an uninspiring successor to William Grant Seaman; it is difficult to imagine the eleven hundred seats filled with worshipers eager to hear "How to be Christian in a Sub-Christian World" or "Quest for Dynamic Leadership, part V—Keeping Life Winsome".)[136] Born in Scotland, Clark had served Methodist churches in Minnesota prior to moving to Indiana. His immediate challenge was the Depression. As was the case in churches everywhere, individual contributions to City Church dropped along with individual income, and rent from the commercial unit dried up as well. Although the budget was "trimmed to a minimum," it was difficult to raise even that amount as Clark attempted to meet both current expenses and the substantial indebtedness from the construction period.[137]

Creditors, including both banks and the Board of Home Missions and Church Extension, regularly dunned the congregation for payments that it simply could not make. In September 1934, for example, the chairman of the church's Finance Committee responded to the Board of Home Missions as follows: "I regret very much to advise that at the present time, the economic situation in Gary has gone from bad to worse. Practically all the mills are on materially reduced bases, and as you well know, so goes the mills, so goes the City Church."[138]

Although little more than financial survival was possible during the Depression, the church's economic picture brightened when the steel industry improved, and Clark undertook a financial drive during World War

Table 6. Pastors, City Methodist
Church, 1907–1975

George Deuel	1907–11
Joseph Avann	1911–16
William Grant Seaman	1916–29
Richard Millard	1929–32
William E. Clark	1932–46
Allen Rice	1946–53
Samuel Carruth	1953–55
Elbert Cole	1955–59
Richard Thistle	1959–64
S. Walton Cole	1964–70
Charles R. Ellinwood	1970–72
Floyd Blake	1972–73
Edward Boase	1973–75

Source: Lewis, "At Home in the City."

II that left the congregation debt free by Christmas 1945. It was one of his proudest accomplishments in Gary.[139]

But it was not his only one. As Seaman had done before him, Clark tried to serve as a mediating influence between management and labor in the steel city. In Clark's time the congregation remained a mainly white, middle-class institution, but included a number of second-generation immigrants as well as a significant number of laborers. It was not, that is, simply a management church.[140] Clark, of course, maintained a cordial relationship with U.S. Steel executives, but he prided himself on maintaining relationships with labor representatives as well, even during times of industrial strife. One observer referred, perhaps simplistically, to a "refreshing comradeship" between management and labor in the church, but a relatively amicable relationship existed at least between management and white employees. Clark himself was sympathetic to the labor cause and approved the strong pro-labor stance of his friend (and Seaman's), Bishop Francis McConnell.[141]

On the issue of race, Clark noted that "we were heavily involved in securing racial equality long before the nation took note of it." Although a number of African Americans attended services at City Church and even sang in the choir, few if any actually joined the church, "although they were free to do so." But Clark's service as president of the Urban League and member of the board of Stewart House and his participation in a campaign to open the membership of the chamber of commerce to blacks reflected his generally progressive views on the subject. Occasionally the congregation took fairly safe public stands on the issue, as when it held a reception for noted black singer Marian Anderson, when the Hotel Gary refused to do so. Clark also worked behind the scenes on behalf of racial tranquility as, for example, during the Froebel School Strike in 1945. Although journalist Thomas Chilcote's opinion that "if interracial crisis comes, City Church is going to have its membership ready to meet it," was tragically off the mark, Clark did regard race relations as an important issue during his years at City Church and, by the standards of the 1940s, worked responsibly at it.[142]

Like Seaman before him, Clark thought City Church should fill an important artistic role in Gary, and he was active in sponsorship of the South Shore Music Festival and in the church's religious drama program. He also continued Seaman's policy of opening the building to a wide variety of musical, ethnic, and political programs, even some that were quite controversial, such as an appearance by Socialist Norman Thomas.[143]

Finally, Clark also maintained, as had Seaman before him, that the pastor of City Church should maintain a prominent public role in the life of the city as an integral part of his ministry, inasmuch as the public arena was the place where the gospel of Sunday morning was put into practice. Consequently he served as president of the Gary Ministerial Association, the Urban League, and the Rotary Club, was a member of the chamber of commerce, and served on the boards of the Methodist Hospital and Goodwill Industries. As the *Post-Tribune* observed: "Reverend Clark's interests have long extended beyond his own parish and denomination, and . . . he was a prominent leader in numerous civic and patriotic endeavors."[144]

Church membership, which had leveled off under Millard, actually declined during the late 1930s to 1,236 but then rose sharply, virtually doubling during Clark's last few years in Gary and exceeding 2,500 by the time he left Gary in 1946.[145] Clark left City Church, then, considerably stronger than he had found it, in terms of both finances and membership.

Clark's talents were different from Seaman's. According to his parishioner and good friend Herschel Davis, "Seaman was a visionary, a missionary," but Clark was "a businessman" and "an administrator rather than a theologian." Given the success of the church during his fourteen years,

Clark's style of leadership may well have been what City Church needed in the 1930s and 1940s. For his part, Clark was following Seaman's invigorating dream: "I tried to keep the dream of City Church alive and well in the day that then was and under the prevailing conditions. History will have to be the judge of that. It was a great day to be alive!" Although he was more managerial than visionary, Clark's mission was still informed by Seaman's dream for City Church. If the widespread social commitments of Herschel Davis are at all characteristic of his more active parishioners, he was supported in his efforts by at least some in the congregation. But Clark later described the church membership as "generally conservative" and "a bit brow beaten by the depression." He served during a time that was hard on dreams but maintained all the same a vision of a responsible urban church.[146]

Despite congregational opposition to his transfer, Clark was replaced in 1946 by Allen Rice, the first of several men who held the Gary pulpit for rather brief periods in the next twenty-five years, years of decline and eventually defeat.[147] Although the founder's dream for City Church was remembered periodically, it was not enough to stem the decline. In fact, the magnitude and pace of social change during those years exceeded anything Gary had seen since, perhaps, its first decade. This tidal wave of change swept away much of Gary's traditional social structure, including churches, replacing it with a new and unfamiliar one. As Gary's ethnic Democratic political machine failed to respond in time to avoid its own demise, so also did City Church.

Rice's pastorate (1946–53) is remembered for still another campaign to clean up vice and crime in Gary. Reminding his congregation that City Church had been founded as "a living evidence of the place Christian faith must play in urban life," he urged the establishment of a laymen's campaign to clean up Gary, in cooperation with the Gary Ministerial Association. Although Rice disclaimed any partisan intent, the campaign against "drunkenness, gambling, and immorality" turned political when the Ministerial Association decided to support Republican Clarence Smith in his 1947 mayoral campaign against Democrat Eugene Swartz. Despite pulpit pleas on Smith's behalf, Swartz won the election. In addition to fighting vice, Rice worked to increase Methodism's presence in Gary and supported in 1947 the establishment of churches in the suburban neighborhoods of Ambridge and Miller. Eventually, however, these two churches drew members away from City Church in the next decade as suburbanization took hold in the Calumet Region.[148]

The Reverend Elbert Cole, minister at City Methodist Church, 1955–1959. Courtesy of DePauw University Archives.

Rice's successor, Samuel Carruth (1953–55), pastored City Church only briefly, leaving a reputation as a "wonderful individual" and an "excellent pulpit man." But he was not strong physically, and his emphases on prayer and the spiritual life never took root in Gary's sandy soil.[149]

Membership during Rice's eight years (1946–53) continued the increase begun under Clark, and City Church shared in the general post–World War II Protestant success. In fact, as table 5 indicates, church membership peaked at 3,185 about the time Carruth came to Gary, and then began a precipitous collapse to 1,769 in the next two years.[150] It was the not inconsiderable accomplishment of Elbert C. Cole to halt the slide and even reverse it slightly during his four years in Gary.

Cole assumed the Gary pulpit in 1955 at the age of thirty-seven. After graduating from the University of Chicago Divinity School in 1942, Cole had served in campus ministry, as a navy chaplain during World War II, and for six years in the parish ministry in the small town of Farmington, Missouri. Although he came to Gary with little previous experience in urban ministry, he remained in urban pastorates for the next thirty years.[151] Perhaps because he was pastor during the congregation's (and Gary's) fiftieth anniversary, Cole appeared more sensitive than any pastor since Clark to the vision of William Grant Seaman, "who made City Church a living evidence of God in the heart of a city of steel." But his anniversary sermon in 1956, "Unfinished Journey," focused not on the church's past achievements but on its future ministry, the comprehensive nature of which echoed Seaman's vision. Like Seaman, Cole believed that the church's ministry must be a seven-day-a-week ministry and affirmed the importance of lay leadership and responsibility in the church. His vision of the church's ministry to an industrial population was reminiscent of Seaman's famous survey of the Calumet Region, with a few modern wrinkles. Cole emphasized, as did Seaman, the youth and transience of a mill town population and the necessity of the church serving as a conscience both to management and to labor. For example, he once arranged for fifteen major labor leaders, including I. W. Abel, to attend a Rotary Club meeting in Gary. But Cole also noted genuine disagreement as to whether steel corporation profits should go principally to higher wages or to capital investment. The *Post-Tribune* stated that, under Cole's leadership, "the church again is beginning to function as a center of city life, the religious hub in the center of a still growing city."[152]

That evaluation may have been unduly optimistic, and Cole subsequently judged his years in Gary as only partially successful. Despite the presence in the church of good young leadership, Cole felt the church had, by and large, lost its vision and sense of common purpose. They had "a beautiful facility" but "no idea how it should be used," a problem Cole did not feel he solved.[153]

Cole's assessment of his time in Gary emphasized its transitional character. In the late 1950s in Gary, racial confrontation and fear of the city were still in the future, although there was a vague sense that something should be done for the youth in the neighborhood. Although Methodist churches in suburban Hobart and Merrillville were thriving, there was little sense yet of "white flight" from Gary's Northside to the suburbs or, for that matter, of Gary's decline. Employment in the mills remained high, and Gary remained to all appearances prosperous.[154]

But, as indicated by table 5, membership had declined dramatically, and the building was in serious need of repair. As Cole summarized the situation years later, ". . . hope had already been lost, and I found myself restoring hope, giving a sense of vision to the congregation, a sense of confidence, a sense of purpose. They had lost all that, even in '55. It had

Aerial view of Gary in 1962. City Methodist Church and the adjoining Hotel Gary are visible at lower right and Christ Church Episcopal at lower center. Courtesy of Calumet Regional Archives, Indiana University Northwest.

been going down and down and down." His success in reversing that decline, even briefly, reflects Cole's leadership abilities during difficult times. He was, said one of the congregation's leaders, Herschel Davis, the "finest personification of what we think a minister should be." Whether his continuing presence at City Church could have reversed permanently the church's slide is doubtful. But his success in the late 1950s was the church's only glimmer of hope during a generally bleak period.[155]

Cole's successor, Richard Thistle (1959–64), saw the resumption of the membership slide, although at a more modest pace. Thistle, like Rice earlier, took an active reformist role in Gary politics, working with the Lake County Churchmen for Good Government on behalf of Republican reform candidates for prosecutor and sheriff. Their campaign included a "Good Government Sunday" featuring sermons on the topic. His brief period in the pastorate at City Church, however, left little permanent imprint, and he was transferred to South Bend in 1964.[156]

The year of Thistle's departure, the Indiana Council of Churches studied the plight of Gary's downtown churches, including City Methodist. The report, not surprisingly, described an increasingly ineffective Protestant presence on Gary's changing Northside. Although Gary's growing African-American population was not yet a major factor in the area of the study, the population there was older and less stable than in previous years. Virtually all the churches in the area, including First Presbyterian Church and City Church, were losing members, were failing to reach substantial numbers in their immediate area, and were relying on members from outside the Northside. The report concluded that City Church would have to retain its middle-class suburban support as well as minister to its immediate neighborhood if it were "to become the voice of protestantism in the city."[157]

The former proved nearly as difficult as the latter, and by the mid-1960s it was becoming obvious that changes underway in downtown Gary blunted the appeal of a downtown church for many people. Among those changes was a rapid increase in Gary's African-American population. The Census reported only two blacks in 1960 in the census tract containing City Church, compared with 3,253 whites. The situation changed dramatically, however, in the next decade. By 1970 the census tract numbered 544 blacks and 2,218 whites; by 1980, there were 1,634 blacks there and only 496 whites.[158]

In light of this change in racial balance, the Reverend S. Walton Cole (1964–70) devoted considerable attention to the issue of race relations, earning an award from the local NAACP in recognition of his work. Church mission projects also included a program for Spanish-speaking residents, and Cole led the congregation to participate with other downtown churches in discussions of common problems faced by city churches. As was not the case earlier in the 1960s, City Church's continuing membership decline was now accompanied by rapid decline in attendance as well. Whereas church attendance averaged 395 in 1964, it dropped to 221 by 1970, a 44 percent decline. Despite the precipitous membership decline after 1968, donations increased. But considering the massive maintenance needs of the large building, even this increased level of giving was inadequate.[159]

When Charles R. Ellinwood assumed the pastorate of City Church in 1970, it was clear that drastic action, particularly in the area of its relationship to Gary's African-American population, was necessary if the church were to survive. Consequently in 1971 he urged, unsuccessfully as it turned out, that City Church appoint a representative to a community organization called the Calumet Community Congress, notwithstanding charges that some of its leaders were communists.[160]

Later that year he delivered a "State of the Church" report outlining three alternatives for the church: to continue on its present course, to appoint an African-American senior minister, or to move out and relinquish the building to a black congregation. The latter two alternatives were rejected by a congregational vote in December. Early in 1972, the administrative board voted to balance the budget by trimming expenses and selling both parsonages and to begin discussions on January 30 with the First Presbyterian Church concerning a possible merger. As noted in chapter 6, however, these merger discussions foundered, apparently over the question of which building would be retained.[161]

Ellinwood may well have felt that the congregation had not yet faced up to its future with respect to African-Americans, and he suggested that the administrative board continue to think about the future of City Church. "Consideration should be given that City Church is a church in a predominantly Black community; consideration should be given to membership to all people regardless of race." Although the failure of the merger talks with the Presbyterians after six months of discussion must have disappointed Ellinwood, as late as May 1972 he intended to stay at City Church and asked the church for a loan to assist in the purchase of a home. But by June 1972 he was gone, and Floyd Blake had been appointed in his stead.[162]

CLOSING CITY CHURCH

Some members of the congregation assumed Blake had been sent by the bishop for the express purpose of closing the church, a charge Blake denied. But attending to the future of the church clearly was his main agenda, to which he devoted 70 to 80 percent of his time in his first six months. To assist in this effort, in August he retained a church planning consultant from Garrett Theological Seminary, and a series of planning sessions began in September 1972. In addition, between July and December he visited a number of other inner-city churches throughout the country—a rather sad repetition of William Grant Seaman's visits to similar churches in a happier time fifty years before. Finally, Blake interviewed over one hundred community residents before delivering his sobering report to the administrative board in February 1973. It was not a report he wanted to make. "I have prayed, struggled, rolled awake in agony night after sleepless night in trying to determine in my own mind what and how we could redeem our beloved church." But he concluded it could not be saved.[163]

Blake's conclusions were based on two major realities—the church's weak membership and financial situation and its reputation in the community. Membership had declined to a realistic figure of only 451 by 1973, with attendance in worship running from 109 to 140. Even the music program had declined, and financial projections indicated the church would fall at least $21,000 short of its $81,000 budget for 1973. Finally, and to Blake this seemed to be the most discouraging factor, "our image is not good in this community." In his study of other inner city churches, Blake had concluded that timing was of the essence in a city church's response to its changing community. Said Blake, in a way not even Seaman could have improved upon: "you must serve the changing community as it changes and you must serve it with flexible changing methods or there comes a time when it is too late! This is best done cooperatively and ecumenically." Like other churches before it, Blake observed, City Church had not properly discerned the nature and direction of social change. "Circumstances over which we had no control have engulfed us," and the church had run out of time. Given this analysis, Blake concluded: "We have waited too long. It is too late to do our dreams."[164]

He presented the administrative board with a series of options for closing the church or merging with another church, warning that "if we cannot find a way to become inclusive with Blacks or this church building and facilities be used predominantly by Blacks, we will have to close." After hearing his report, the board decided to discuss the situation with the bishop and solicit his recommendation. In its March meeting, the board adopted draconian budget cuts as a "holding action" while a final decision was made. One of these was a drastic salary cut for the pastor which meant a reduced level of pastoral leadership after June 1973. In April the board met with the bishop, who echoed Blake's conclusion that the church would have to include African Americans on a substantial level or die.[165]

In June 1973, Ed Boase, a minister within eighteen months of retirement, took over the pulpit to lead the church toward the inevitable. A Task Force on the Future of City Church reported in February 1974, echoing many of Blake's conclusions about the impossibility of continuing much longer. Discussions with several smaller congregations concerning a possible merger were fruitless, and the Charge Conference voted on December 8, 1974, to close the church during the next year.[166] On May 31, 1975, the North Indiana Annual Conference of the United Methodist Church approved a resolution that City Church "be discontinued as of October 5, 1975."[167]

On October 5, with the district superintendent in the pulpit, members of City Church celebrated their last communion. Methodists had been invited from all over the area, and 201 were in attendance, making it one of the largest services in several years. Shortly after noon, to the strains of Bach's Fugue in C, City Church closed its doors forever. It had been sixty-nine years to the day since "the people called Methodists came together . . . and formed the society, First Methodist Episcopal Church of Gary."[168] The dream was over.

But in its day, the dream of City Church had filled the heart and mind of a pastor, had motivated a congregation, and, to a considerable extent, had caught the imagination of a city. The reality of a social gospel cathedral in the very heart of Gary witnessed to the continuing significance of progressive Protestantism in the industrial city. For a time, City Church was Gary's premier example of a church at home in the city.

Epilogue

AT HOME IN THE CITY

The histories of First Presbyterian Church and City Methodist Church remind us that, despite their differences, both traditional and progressive downtown Protestant congregations were prominent actors on the wider Gary stage. As these mainstream Protestant congregations confronted the industrial city in the early decades of the twentieth century, they did so not with despair and resignation but with energy and enthusiasm, reflecting their conviction that the church could be and should be at home in the city.

In one sense the congregations themselves constituted subcommunities in the bustling new city, as indicated by the persistent denominational loyalties of Gary's citizens. But they wove an even richer subcommunal pattern through such organizations as Tri Mu and Alpha Class in First Presbyterian Church, the Epworth League and Wesleyan Service Guild in City Methodist Church, and the various women's missionary organizations in both. In these groups, generations of Gary Protestants found, among other things, an outlet for philanthropic sensibilities and a sense of belonging in the midst of the city. These groups in turn mediated between individual members and the wider congregational community and often became involved directly in the more explicit public outreach of their respective congregations to Gary's diverse society.

Throughout their history, to a varying extent, both First Presbyterian Church and City Church acknowledged and attempted to address Gary's ethnic and racial diversity. Although they did so from the limited perspective of white, native-born, middle-class Americans, they generously invested time, money, and institutional energies in settlement houses and weekday church schools, among other things, in an attempt to Americanize and, if possible, to convert the foreign-born residents of their city. By the standards of our day, and even by the standards of Gary's own International Institute, their efforts were tainted by paternalism at best and xenophobic nativism at worst.[1] But though we may not be able to endorse all their motives wholeheartedly, their efforts to address their city's pluralism were impressive and important for their time. The settlement houses and weekday church schools were two of the institutions that contributed to greater understanding between native and foreign born, an understanding that had eliminated much of the major tension between these two groups by the end of the 1930s. That the same degree of understanding was not reached between Gary's white and black citizens reflects the sad reality that Gary shared fully in the racial animosities characteristic of broader American society.

These attempts to address Gary's social diversity were a significant part of the active public role played by both congregations. Despite their differences, both First Presbyterian Church and City Church saw the church at the center of the city at least into the 1950s. Admittedly the traditional, inward-looking Presbyterian congregation was not quite as prominent in the public eye. But it too thought the church should be a force for civic righteousness by means of its various subcommunities, its outreach to Gary's diverse peoples, and its somewhat reluctant public role. Unlike their Methodist colleagues, Walton and Backemeyer said little explicitly about the church's role in the city, but their efforts on behalf of the Assyrian Presbyterian church, Neighborhood House, and political reform reflected a more activist conception of the church's public role than they perhaps would have acknowledged.

The Methodists, of course, repeatedly espoused and at least on occasion fulfilled their mission to be a "city church." By their work on behalf of the weekday church schools, their creation of a downtown "cathedral," their efforts to build the Methodist Hospital, their leadership in the ministerial associations and Council of Churches, their sponsorship of interracial and interethnic worship services, their sometime involvement in labor issues, and their persistent witness against political corruption, Avann, Seaman, Clark, and Cole sought to make their church a city church. In so doing, they made City Methodist Church the premier advocate in Gary of the progressive Protestant tradition of urban activism associated with the social gospel at the turn of the century. The City Church experience thus confirms that the legacy of the social gospel extended at least to the eve of the Depression if not beyond. For Seaman and at least some of his successors the church was not placed physically at the center of the city just in order to be prominently located. Rather it was only from the center that the church's influence might extend to the rest of the city. Indeed its nourishment of subcommunities, both within and outside the congregation, its various efforts to reach out to Gary's diverse population, and its active public role represented the impressive attempt of City Methodist Church to realize its motto "that Christ may dwell a living presence at the city's heart."

But slowly during the 1950s, and more rapidly thereafter, Gary's social, economic, and political scene began to change, and the Protestant congregations moved increasingly from Gary's center to its periphery. As Congregational, Christian, and Baptist churches moved to Gary's growing suburbs, the Protestant presence at the center faded. Even those churches that remained geographically at the center, like First Presbyterian and City Methodist, became increasingly peripheral to the life of the city. Despite their tradition of involvement in the broader community they became preoccupied with their own institutional survival as their membership declined and their financial condition disintegrated in the 1960s and 1970s. To be sure, some attempts were made to remain engaged with the city even then. Individuals and groups in City Methodist Church to 1975 and in First Presbyterian Church to at least 1991 insisted that the congregation must minister to the city if it was to remain faithful to its mission as the church. But in their depleted condition, First Presbyterian Church and City Church were a less commanding voice in the city than they once had been, even if anyone had been listening.

Few, of course, were listening. Not only did the churches' decline push them to the periphery of the city's consciousness, but so too did the changing place of American Protestantism on the national scene. As chronicled by William Hutchison, Wade Clark Roof, and William McKinney, among others, the decline of the Protestant establishment mainstream was well underway by the 1960s, affecting particularly such groups as Presbyterians and Methodists. Clearly the traditional place of honor for Protestantism in the American mind and public order was no more. An acknowledged Protestant hegemony gave way first to Will Herberg's celebrated triumvirate of Protestant-Catholic-Jew, followed by the broader religious pluralism of the 1970s and 1980s. As Hutchison has summarized, between

1920 and 1960, the Protestant establishment was facing "a transition from Protestant America to pluralist America."[2]

Moreover the decline of Protestantism in the central city was only one facet of the decline of many institutions in the central city, from the economic infrastructure to the family. It was a decline documented by the movement of mainstream Protestant congregations from the central city altogether, both by moving to the suburbs and by closing.[3] In Gary as of this writing it is documented by the small, courageous Presbyterian congregation still worshipping in the grand sanctuary at Sixth and Monroe and, more graphically, by the physical devastation of the formerly grand Methodist cathedral at Sixth and Washington. Gary's mainstream Protestants thus shared in a broader urban Protestant decline. But in Gary we can isolate several aspects of that period of decline, contrasting them with a more prosperous period in the churches' history.

Thriving subcommunities helped support and enliven the congregations in Gary's first half-century. But as the congregations declined the subcommunities sometimes became their own *raison d'être*. In both churches the choir and music program, for example, survived long after religious education had withered away, partly because the subcommunal loyalties to the music program were so strong. As for pluralism, First Presbyterian Church and City Methodist Church had been leaders in their day in responding to Gary's ethnic diversity. But they were unable to adapt to the racial diversity of the 1960s and 1970s, which resulted in a black majority in the city. Finally the congregation's public role appeared in the late 1950s and 1960s to be limited to ministerial pronouncements on political corruption. The congregation's public role, that is, became little more than the pastor's public role. In these respects First Presbyterian Church and City Church were quite similar during these decades, as indicated by the accounts of their decline. The merger enabled First Presbyterian Church to survive, but it did so as a congregation quite different from what it once had been.

To chronicle the decline of these congregations and their movement to the periphery of Gary life, however, is not to deny the importance of their years at the center. Indeed First Presbyterian Church and City Methodist Church illustrate an impressive mainstream Protestant response to the American industrial city. It was no doubt a major challenge. But in Gary, at least, Protestants were energized by the challenge, not immobilized by it. Despite their own differences in style and approach to the city, both First Presbyterian Church and City Church made an important contribution to their city as they sought to minister to its people and its institutions. If one important function of a religious institution in a culture is to serve as a source of meaning in the midst of a confusing world, then the churches and synagogues of Gary, including First Presbyterian Church and City Methodist Church, were very important indeed. Their ministry, even apart from its important public implications, was of intrinsic value to many of Gary's citizens, a value not diminished by their subsequent decline.

On October 29, 1983 (fifty-six years almost to the day after City Church opened its grand new building), I attended the seventy-fifth anniversary service of Christ Episcopal Church in Gary, Indiana, just a few blocks down the street from First Presbyterian Church and the former City Methodist Church. It was also Christ Church's final service. The sanctuary was filled with people on that warm, autumn day. Many of them were white but many others were black. All ages were there, the older of them perhaps recalling the days when Christ Church, Central Christian, First Presbyterian, and City Church all flourished in Gary, but the younger ones remembering only years of urban and ecclesiastical decline. It was a moving occasion of mixed sadness and joy. Clearly people had come both to remember and to celebrate the past—the past of their church, but the past also of their city and of themselves. As I looked for the first time at the church's lovely interior, heard the Scripture readings, sang the hymns, and received communion, I knew that, even on this its final day, Christ Episcopal Church, like its neighbors down the block, had not ministered for seventy-five years in vain. These congregations, despite their flaws and failures, filled a central place in the lives of thousands of men and women and in the public life of the city they called home.

Notes

CHAPTER I

1. *Gary Post-Tribune Golden Jubilee Edition,* May 20, 1956, p. 9, and May 27, 1956, p. 105. This edition was published in four installments in 1956—May 20, 27, June 3, and 10. The Indiana Room of the Gary Public Library (hereafter "Gary Public Library") includes the issues paginated by hand as follows: May 20 (pp. 1–72), May 27 (pp. 73–144), June 3 (pp. 145–216), June 10 (pp. 217–80). See also James B. Lane, *"City of the Century"* (Bloomington: Indiana Univ. Press, 1978), 28.

2. Chamber of Commerce of Gary, Indiana, *Gary at a Glance* (n.p., [1928]); U.S., Department of Commerce, Bureau of the Census (hereafter, "Bureau of the Census"), *Fifteenth Census of the United States: 1930, Population,* 3:715.

3. Lane, *"City of the Century,"* 28.

4. Eric H. Monkonnen, *America Becomes Urban* (Berkeley: Univ. of California Press, 1988), 69.

5. Winthrop is cited in "John Winthrop's Model of Charity," in *American Christianity: An Historical Interpretation with Representative Documents,* ed. H. Shelton Smith, Robert T. Handy, and Lefferts A. Loetscher, 2 vols. (New York: Charles Scribner's Sons, 1960), 1:102. Alan Trachtenberg, *The Incorporation of America* (New York: Hill & Wang, 1982), 101–2.

6. On the relationship between these Protestant thinkers and their reform context, see James W. Lewis, "At Home in the City" (Ph.D. diss., Univ. of Chicago, 1987), 12–18.

7. Andrew Lees, *Cities Perceived* (New York: Columbia Univ. Press, 1985), 306–7.

8. Samuel Lane Loomis was a Protestant minister whose lectures at Andover Theological Seminary were published as the influential *Modern Cities and Their Religious Problems* (New York: Baker & Taylor Co., 1887). Strong was a prominent author and ecumenical leader at the turn of the century. See Martin E. Marty,

Pilgrims In Their Own Land (Boston: Little, Brown & Company, 1984), 337–43. Graham Taylor was a prominent settlement house leader and professor in the late nineteenth and early twentieth centuries. Both he and his son, Graham R. Taylor, visited and wrote on the new city of Gary. See Louise Wade, *Graham Taylor* (Chicago: Univ. of Chicago Press, 1964). Charles Stelzle was a Presbyterian minister in New York City especially known for his ministry to workingmen. His *Christianity's Storm Centre* (New York: Fleming H. Revell, 1907) was among the most important early Protestant discussions of the city. See Sydney E. Ahlstrom, *A Religious History of the American People* (New Haven: Yale Univ. Press, 1972), 802–3.) Paul Moore Strayer was an Episcopal priest in Rochester, New York, and a colleague of Walter Rauschenbusch. His 1915 *The Reconstruction of the Church with Regard to its Message and Program* (New York: Macmillan, 1915) is an excellent example of Protestant reflection on the city and was cited by one of Gary's religious leaders, William Grant Seaman, as a rationale for a downtown ministry. Finally, Harlan Paul Douglass was the major figure in Protestant social research in the 1920s and 1930s. As head of the Institute of Social and Religious Research he participated in vast amounts of research on the church in modern America. See his *The City's Church* (New York: Friendship Press, 1929) among other works and Jeffrey K. Hadden, "H. Paul Douglass: His Perspective and His Work," *Review of Religious Research* 22 (September 1980):66–88.

9. For Stelzle, see Jerald C. Brauer, ed., *The Westminster Dictionary of Church History* (Philadelphia: Westminster Press, 1971), 788; for Taylor, see Wade, *Graham Taylor,* 4–5; for Strong and Strayer, see *National Cyclopaedia of American Biography* (New York: James T. White & Co, 1931), vols. 9 and 21; for Loomis and Douglass, see *Who Was Who in America* (Chicago: A. N. Marquis Co., 1942 and 1960), vols. 1, 3.

10. Arthur Meier Schlesinger, *Rise of the City* (New York: Macmillan Co., 1933; reprint ed., Chicago: Quadrangle Books, 1971), 58, 62; Loomis, *Modern Cities,* 30–31.

11. On Strong, See Ahlstrom, *Religious History,* 798–99, and Marty, *Pilgrims,* 338–41. Josiah Strong, *The Twentieth Century City* (New York: Baker & Taylor Co., 1898), 181, cited in Richard Hofstadter, *The Age of Reform: From Bryan to F. D. R.* (New York: Random House, Vintage Books, 1955), 176.

12. Strong, *The Challenge of the City* (New York: Young People's Missionary Movement, 1907), v, 199.

13. Carl Douglas Wells, *The Changing City Church* (Los Angeles: Univ. of Southern California Press, 1934).

14. Strayer, *Reconstruction of the Church,* 139; Charles Stelzle, "Decline of American Protestantism," *Current History* 33 (October 1930):24.

15. Douglass, *City's Church,* 51, 53; Harlan Paul Douglass, "Religion—The

Protestant Faiths," in *America Now: An Inquiry into Civilization in the United States,* ed. Harold E. Stearns (New York: Charles Scribner's Sons, 1938), 515.

16. Truman B. Douglass, "The Job the Protestants Shirk," in *Cities and Churches,* ed. Robert Lee (Philadelphia: Westminster Press, 1962), 87; William Petersen, "The Protestant Ethos and the Anti-Urban Animus," in *The Church and the Exploding Metropolis,* ed. Robert Lee (Richmond: John Knox Press, 1965), 63, 75.

17. Robert Handy, "The City and the Church: Historical Interlockings," in *Will the Church Lose the City?,* ed. Kendig B. Cully and F. Nils Harper (New York: World Publishing Co., 1969), 90.

18. Ibid., 94. See also Paul Peachey, *Church in the City* (Newton, Kans.: Faith & Life Press, 1963), 51.

19. Ahlstrom, *Religious History,* 736, 846.

20. Marty, *Pilgrims,* 339. Between 1890 and World War I, Protestant church growth outstripped population growth, even in the cities. See Martin E. Marty, *Modern American Religion,* vol. 1: *The Irony of it All, 1893–1919* (Chicago: Univ. of Chicago Press, 1986), 153.

21. Catherine L. Albanese, *America, Religions and Religion* (Belmont, Calif.: Wadsworth Publishing Co, 1981), 107.

22. A surprising counter-example of this rural bias were the antebellum southern, urban theologians who took great pains to be *urban* pastors and professors. See E. Brooks Holifield, *The Gentlemen Theologians* (Durham: Duke Univ. Press, 1978), 6–8, 13–23.

23. See, for example, Charles N. Glaab and A. Theodore Brown, *A History of Urban America* (New York: Macmillan Publishing Co., 1967), p. 236, and Schlesinger, *Rise of the City,* 330, 332.

24. Robert D. Cross, "The Changing Image of the City Among American Catholics," *Catholic Historical Review* 48 (April 1962):36. See also Petersen, "The Protestant Ethos and the Anti-Urban Animus," 62.

25. Gutman, rejecting the assumption that nineteenth-century workers "wandered from the fold, and the churches lost touch with the laboring classes," maintains that Christianity legitimized their struggle against rapacious Gilded Age capitalism. See Herbert G. Gutman, *Work, Culture and Society in Industrializing America* (New York: Random House, 1977), 83, 109. See Raymond B. Williams, *Religions of Immigrants from India and Pakistan* (New York: Cambridge Univ. Press, 1988), 38. See also David Thelen, "Memory and American History," *Journal of American History* 75 (March 1989):1123, 1125.

26. Charles Howard Hopkins, *The Rise of the Social Gospel in American Protestantism, 1865–1915* (New Haven: Yale Univ. Press, 1940; reprint ed., New York: AMS Press, n.d.). Eldon G. Ernst, *Moment of Truth for Protestant America* (Missoula, Mont.: Scholars Press, 1974); Robert T. Handy, *A History of the Churches in*

the United States and Canada (New York: Oxford Univ. Press, 1977), 377–427; Ahlstrom, *Religious History,* 905, 909; George M. Marsden, *Fundamentalism and American Culture* (New York: Oxford Univ. Press, 1980).

27. Martin E. Marty, "In Praise of the Civil Congregation," *Currents in Theology and Mission* 15 (December 1988):545.

28. The history of religious congregations in America contributes to social history, ethnic history, and women's history. See, for example, Joan R. Gunderson, *"Before the World Confessed"* (Northfield, Minn.: Northfield Historical Society, 1987).

29. James P. Wind explores both the reasons for scholarly inattention to congregational history as well as its great promise in his *Places of Worship* (Nashville: American Assn. for State and Local History, 1990), 101–17.

30. Ernest Sandeen, "Congregational Histories as History," in *The Church and History,* ed. Glenn W. Offerman (St. Paul: Concordia College, 1981), 2–13.

31. As Wind notes (*Places of Worship,* 114), historian Oscar Handlin deplored this situation more than thirty years ago. Two excellent recent histories, however, confirm the significant contribution to scholarship of congregational history. Rima Lunin Schultz's *The Church in the City* (Chicago: Cathedral of Saint James, 1986) is an excellent account of one urban congregation. Joan R. Gunderson's very fine *"Before the World Confessed"* emphasizes the leadership role of women in churches on the Minnesota frontier. But even these fine works illustrate the marginal role of congregational history in American religious historiography. Prepared for congregational anniversaries, both were published locally, virtually guaranteeing a narrow distribution and small readership.

32. Alexandra Shecket Korros and Jonathan Sarna, *American Synagogue History* (New York: Markus Wiener Publishing, 1988), 2.

33. Marty, "In Praise of the Civil Congregation," 543. See Bureau of the Census, *Religious Bodies: 1926,* 1:426–27.

34. In Gary, as in other industrial cities, however, the working classes participated at a lower level. See Henry F. May, *Protestant Churches and Industrial America,* 2nd ed. (New York: Farrar, Straus & Giroux, 1977), 119.

35. James M. Gustafson discusses the congregation's role in both individual and social life in his *Treasure in Earthen Vessels* (New York: Harper & Brothers, 1961; Midway Reprint ed., Chicago: Univ. of Chicago Press, 1976), 14–28. See also James Hopewell, *Congregation,* ed. Barbara Wheeler (Philadelphia: Fortress Press, 1987), 198, for reference to the congregation as a mediating structure.

36. Martin E. Marty, "Public and Private: The Congregation as a Meeting Place," essay prepared for the Congregational History Project at the Univ. of Chicago; copy courtesy of the author. See also Wind, *Places of Worship,* 109–10.

37. Liston Pope, *Millhands and Preachers* (New Haven: Yale Univ. Press, 1942); Stephan Thernstrom, *Poverty and Progress* (Cambridge: Harvard Univ. Press,

1964; reprint ed., New York: Atheneum, 1975); Michael H. Frisch, *Town Into City* (Cambridge: Harvard Univ. Press, 1972).

38. Hugh McLeod notes that there is "not only a general history of religion in the modern city, but a local history, with features peculiar to particular countries, or even to particular cities." See his "Religion in the City," *Urban History Yearbook* (1978):11.

39. Raymond A. Mohl and Neil Betten, *Steel City* (New York: Holmes & Meier, 1986), 3.

40. Marshall Frady, "Gary, Indiana," *Harper's* 239 (August 1969):38; Edward Greer, *Big Steel* (New York: Monthly Review Press, 1979), 108.

41. McLeod, "Religion in the City," 16.

42. See Mohl and Betten, *Steel City*, 161–78, on the immigrant church in Gary. For a discussion of the cultural hegemony of mainstream Protestantism in the twentieth century, see William R. Hutchison, ed., *Between the Times* (Cambridge: Cambridge Univ. Press, 1989), viii. On the decline of mainstream Protestantism in America since the 1960s, see also Wade Clark Roof and William McKinney, *American Religion* (New Brunswick, N.J.: Rutgers Univ. Press, 1987), 16–29, 36–39. As these and other recent works have indicated, the very shape of American religion, including the role of the Protestant mainstream, has changed dramatically since World War II. See especially Robert Wuthnow's *Restructuring American Religion* (Princeton: Princeton Univ. Press, 1988). Wuthnow emphasizes the response of American religion to the expanding role of the national government and the increased importance of higher education and technology. Denominations have declined in importance as a broad division between liberal and conservative (within as well as between denominations) has come to characterize American religion (9, 113, 163–64, 218, 244).

43. See, for example, Hopkins, *Rise of the Social Gospel*, 245–56, and May, *Protestant Churches and Industrial America*, 112–24, 182–203.

44. See, for example, George Marsden, *Fundamentalism and American Culture* (New York: Oxford Univ. Press, 1980), 11–14, 127–32.

45. Ahlstrom, *Religious History*, 845; George Marsden, *Reforming Fundamentalism* (Grand Rapids: William B. Eerdmans Publishing Co, 1987), 1–11, 153–71; Harry S. Stout, "Soundings from New England," *Reformed Journal* 37 (August 1987):12.

CHAPTER 2

1. *Gary Post-Tribune*, January 5, 1927; Isaac James Quillen, "Industrial City" (Ph.D. diss., Yale Univ., 1942), 138, 150, 153–54, 163–68; Garry J. August, reply to Arthur Shumway in *Gary Post-Tribune*, January 29, 1929; interview with Garry August, Gary, Ind., March 8, 1984.

2. Gary Chamber of Commerce, "Gary at a Glance" (n.p., [1928]). Other booster publications were even less modest: "Gary, Indiana America's Magic City 1906–1912," "Gary, Indiana, the Coming Steel & Iron Manufacturing Center of the World," "Gary, the Magic City," "An Industrial Utopia" (pamphlets located in Gary Public Library).

3. *Gary Post-Tribune*, March 12, 1926.

4. Lane, "*City of the Century,*" 37–39; Quillen, "Industrial City," 7, 13–21, 23–24, 27–28; Robert H. Wiebe, *Businessmen and Reform* (Cambridge: Harvard Univ. Press, 1962), 45–46; Arundel Cotter, *The Gary I Knew* (Boston: Stratford Co., 1928), 45–51, 62, 111, 116; David Brody, *Steelworkers in America* (Cambridge: Harvard Univ. Press, 1960), 152, 157; Ida Tarbell, *The Life of Elbert H. Gary* (New York: Appleton, 1925), 206, 345.

5. Judge Gary's quotation from U.S. Steel Corporation Bureau of Safety, Sanitation and Welfare, *Bulletin Number Eight* (New York, 1920), 3, cited in Quillen, "Industrial City," 228. See also Brody, *Steelworkers in America*, 165, and Tarbell, *Life of Elbert H. Gary*, 339.

6. Tarbell, *Life of Elbert H. Gary*, 63, 206; Frederick D. Leete, *Adventures of a Traveling Preacher* (Boston: W. A. Wilde Co., 1952), 392–93. But Arundel Cotter "never heard Gary talk religion and it was not until after his death that I learned he was a professing Methodist." See Cotter, *The Gary I Knew*, 55, 97.

7. Brody, *Steelworkers in America*, 149, 275; Lane, "*City of the Century,*" 38. See Cotter, *The Gary I Knew*, 40–42; Lane, "*City of the Century,*" 105; James Weinstein, *The Corporate Ideal in the Liberal State* (Boston: Beacon Press, 1968), 230.

8. Lane, "*City of the Century,*" 39. See also Cotter, *The Gary I Knew*, 41.

9. Thomas H. Cannon, Hannibal H. Loring, and Charles J. Robb, eds., *History of the Lake and Calumet Region of Indiana Embracing the Counties of Lake, Porter and LaPorte*, 2 vols. (Indianapolis: Historians Association, 1927), 1:769; Cotter, *The Gary I Knew*, 45; Lane, "*City of the Century,*" 38–39; William Dale Fisher, "Steel City's Culture: An Interpretation of the History of Gary, Indiana" (B.A. thesis, Yale Univ., 1941), 36.

10. Powell A. Moore, *The Calumet Region* (Indianapolis: Indiana Historical Bureau, 1959), 331; Quillen, "Industrial City," 228, 319; Fisher, "Steel City's Culture," 37; Weinstein, *Corporate Ideal*, x; *Gary Post-Tribune, Golden Jubilee Edition*, 96. James Weinstein, Robert Wiebe, and David Brody, among others, emphasize the mixed motives underlying such corporate philanthropy in the early twentieth century. See Weinstein, *The Corporate Ideal*, Wiebe, *Businessmen and Reform*, and Brody, *Steelworkers in America*.

11. David R. Goldfield and Blaine A. Brownell, *Urban America* (Boston: Houghton Mifflin Co., 1979), 223; Raymond A. Mohl and Neil Betten, "The Failure of Industrial City Planning: Gary, Indiana, 1906–1910," *Journal of the*

American Institute of Planners 38 (July 1972):203–4; Brody, *Steelworkers in America*, 26, 71–77; Cotter, *The Gary I Knew*, 111; Tarbell, *Life of Elbert H. Gary*, 162; Wiebe, *Businessmen and Reform*, 45–46, 165; Lane, "*City of the Century*," 38.

12. Queen Cheadle, "Gary—A Planned City" (M.A. thesis, Univ. of Chicago, 1938), 6–9; Anthony Brook, "Gary, Indiana: Steel Town Extraordinary," *Journal of American Studies* 9 (April 1975):38; Quillen, "Industrial City," 48, 50, 121, 131.

13. Quillen, "Industrial City," 83; Cheadle, "Gary—A Planned City," 9; Cannon, Loring, and Robb, *Lake and Calumet Region*, 2:11–12; Lane, "*City of the Century*," 12.

14. Moore, *Calumet Region*, 261; Mohl and Betten, "Failure of Industrial City Planning," 205. Quillen reports that twelve thousand acres were purchased. See Quillen, "Industrial City," 84.

15. Moore, *Calumet Region*, 259; Lane, "*City of the Century*," 14.

16. Cheadle, "Gary—A Planned City," 11; Lane, "*City of the Century*," 11–12.

17. Ed Brennan, "A Diary Revives Gary's First Days," *Gary Post-Tribune*, March 12, 1947. This article was based on the diary Ralph Rowley kept during Gary's early days. See also Quillen, "Industrial City," 98, 100–1.

18. Mohl and Betten, "Failure of Industrial City Planning," 213; Lane, "*City of the Century*," 28; *Gary Post-Tribune, Golden Jubilee Edition*, 6.

19. Graham R. Taylor (the son of Chicago settlement pioneer, Graham Taylor) reported that U.S. Steel planned to spend approximately $75 million to build the plant, harbor, and town. Taylor called Gary "the greatest single calculated achievement of America's master industry"; see his *Satellite Cities* (New York: D. Appleton & Co., 1915), 165, 168.)

20. Quillen, "Industrial City," 103–6, 148; Cheadle, "Gary—A Planned City," 34.

21. Edward G. Smith, *Great Gary* (Gary: n.p., 1908), cited in Quillen, "Industrial City," 148. For photographs see Cheadle, "Gary—A Planned City," 27–30; Cannon, Loring, and Robb, *Lake and Calumet Region* (see, for example, opposite 1:743); Lane, "*City of the Century*," between 116 and 117.

22. Moore, *Calumet Region*, 261; Brook, "Gary, Indiana: Steel Town Extraordinary," 40. See also Richard J. Meister, "A History of Gary, Indiana," (Ph.D. diss., Univ. of Notre Dame, 1966), 10; Taylor, *Satellite Cities*, 172, 174; and Charles P. Burton, "Gary—A Creation," *The Independent* 70 (February 1911):345.

23. Quillen, "Industrial City," 116–19, 191; Meister, "History of Gary," 5; Cannon, Loring, and Robb, eds., *Lake and Calumet Region*, 1:740; Eugene J. Buffington, "Making Cities for Workmen," *Harper's Weekly* 53 (May 8, 1909):15.

24. Pullman, a company town south of Chicago, was the site of a major strike in 1894. See Stanley Buder, *Pullman: An Experiment in Industrial Order and Com-*

munity Planning 1880–1930 (New York: Oxford Univ. Press, 1967). See also Mohl and Betten, "Failure of Industrial City Planning," 206, and Quillen, "Industrial City," 116–20.

25. Quillen, "Industrial City," 191; Christopher Tunnard and Henry Hope Reed, *American Skyline* (Boston: Houghton Mifflin Co., 1955), 169; Taylor, *Satellite Cities,* 28; Mohl and Betten, "Failure of Industrial City Planning," 206.

26. Wiebe, *Businessmen and Reform,* 9, 211–12; Weinstein, *Corporate Ideal in the Liberal State,* xiii, xv; Edward Greer, *Big Steel* (New York: Monthly Review Press, 1979), 66.

27. Quillen, "Industrial City," 125–27, 145; Buffington, "Making Cities for Workmen," 17; Meister, "History of Gary," 14, 22.

28. Taylor, *Satellite Cities,* 25.

29. See, for example, Lane, *"City of the Century,"* ix; James Henry Maloney, "To Strike at Steel: Gary, Indiana, and the Great Steel Strike of 1919" (B.A. thesis, Harvard Univ., 1972), 20, 87; Quillen, "Industrial City," 149.

30. Henry B. Fuller, "An Industrial Utopia: Building Gary, Indiana, to Order," *Harper's Weekly* 51 (October 12, 1907):1482, 1495. See also Moore, *Calumet Region,* 306; Lane, *"City of the Century,"* 34; and Meister, "History of Gary," 16.

31. Fuller, "Industrial Utopia," 1495.

32. Taylor, *Satellite Cities,* 217, 228; Moore, *Calumet Region,* 326; Fisher, "Steel City's Culture," 37; Mohl and Betten, "Failure of Industrial City Planning," 206, 208.

33. Mohl and Betten, "Failure of Industrial City Planning," 213.

34. Brook, "Gary, Indiana: Steel Town Extraordinary," 51. See also Mohl and Betten, "Failure of Industrial City Planning," 203.

35. Taylor, *Satellite Cities,* 174, 182–84; Mohl and Betten, "Failure of Industrial City Planning," 208; Burton, "Gary—A Creation," 339; Buffington, "Making Cities for Workmen," 17. Eventually U.S. Steel built 1,476 houses including 100 reserved for foreign and black workers. See *Gary Post-Tribune, Golden Jubilee Edition,* 96.

36. Taylor, *Satellite Cities,* 190–92; John K. Mumford, "This Land of Opportunity: Gary, the City that Rose from a Sandy Waste," *Harper's Weekly* 52 (July 4, 1908):23; Quillen, "Industrial City," 127–28, 146, 232; Mohl and Betten, "Failure of Industrial City Planning," 209, 212; Brook, "Gary, Indiana: Steel Town Extraordinary," 45–46; Quillen, "Industrial City," 145. For excellent photographs contrasting housing in the First Subdivision and the Patch, see Mohl and Betten, *Steel City,* between pages 118 and 119, and Calumet Regional Archives, *Steelmaker-Steeltown: Building Gary, 1906–1930, A Photographic Exhibit* (Gary: Calumet Regional Archives, Indiana Univ. Northwest, 1990).

37. Quillen, "Industrial City," 138–43, 192, 215; Cannon, Loring, and Robb, *Lake and Calumet Region,* 1:764; William F. Howat, ed., *A Standard History of*

Lake County, Indiana and the Calumet Region, 2 vols. (Chicago: Lewis Publishing Co., 1915), 1:406–11.

38. Warner, *Urban Wilderness,* 105, 107, 110, 171. Warner describes the Chicago of 1870–1920, for example, as "a highly fragmented society tightly structured along economic lines" (110). Eric Monkonnen, on the other hand, has a more benign view of urban America's diversity, asserting that the development of what he calls the "service city" created a "tolerant system without requiring individual tolerance." See Monkonnen, *America Becomes Urban,* 232–33.

39. Warner, *Urban Wilderness,* 171; see also Quillen, "Industrial City," 96.

40. Quillen, "Industrial City," 192, 217, 262; Bureau of the Census, *Fourteenth Census of the United States, 1920: Population,* 3:307; Burton, "Gary—A Creation"; Mumford, "Land of Opportunity"; Fuller, "An Industrial Utopia"; Buffington, "Making Cities for Workmen."

41. Mumford, "Land of Opportunity," 23; Bessie B. Ross, "Early Women Risked Much to Establish Gary Homes," undated clipping from *Gary Post-Tribune,* [1931], in Gary Public Library; *Biographical Sketches of Gary and Lake County Residents,* (Scrapbook, 11 vols., Gary, Indiana, n.p., 1950), Gary Public Library; Burton, "Gary—A Creation," 344. The Ross article is a fascinating account of early Gary history through women's eyes.

42. Quillen, "Industrial City," 151, 163; Taylor, *Satellite Cities,* 196.

43. Arthur Mann, *The One and the Many: Reflections on the American Identity* (Chicago: Univ. of Chicago Press, 1979), 71.

44. David Ward, *Cities and Immigrants: A Geography of Change in Nineteenth-Century America* (New York: Oxford Univ. Press, 1971), 53.

45. Ibid., 75–76.

46. Less than half of the population in nonindustrial cities, immigrants were comparatively rare in such midwestern cities as Indianapolis. See Ward, *Cities and Immigrants,* 51; Glaab and Brown, *History of Urban America,* 95, 140; and table 1, this volume.

47. Taylor, *Satellite Cities,* 196; Buffington, "Making Cities for Workmen," 17; Meister, "History of Gary," 52; Mumford, "This Land of Opportunity," 29; Howat, *Standard History of Lake County,* 405.

48. Quillen, "Industrial City," 218.

49. Elizabeth Balanoff, "A History of the Black Community of Gary, Indiana 1906–1940" (Ph.D. diss., Univ. of Chicago, 1974), 158; Greer, *Big Steel,* 96; Bureau of the Census, *1980 Census of Population,* vol. 1, ch. B:16–8; Lane, "*City of the Century,*" 270–71. Mohl and Betten claim that one aspect of the Americanization process for Gary's immigrants was the development of racist attitudes toward blacks. They discuss Gary racism in schools, employment, and housing in their *Steel City,* 48–90.

50. The censuses of 1940 and 1950 did not distinguish between native white

citizens of native parents and those of foreign or mixed parents in the main reports. See Bureau of the Census, *Census of Population, 1950* 2:Part 14, p. xvi. They did, however, report on the nativity and parentage of the white population in separate, sample-based reports for cities with more than 50,000 foreign-born whites. Neither Gary nor Indianapolis had that many. See Bureau of the Census, *Sixteenth Census of the U.S.: 1940, Population,* 4:Part 2, p. 2, and *Census of Population, 1950* 2:Part 14, p. xvi. In 1960 the census resumed the distinction based on parentage. In 1960, Gary's native whites of native parentage numbered only 69,451 out of a total population of 178,312. See Bureau of the Census, *Census of Population: 1960,* 1:Part 16, p. 204. In 1970 they numbered 53,007 out of 175,415. See Bureau of the Census, *1970 Census of Population,* 1:Part 16, pp. 104, 283.

51. Quillen, "Industrial City," 117–27; Meister, "History of Gary," 13–14; Burton, "Gary—A Creation," 339–44.

52. Meister refers only to "Northside" and "Southside." See Quillen, "Industrial City," 145; Meister, "History of Gary," 14–15.

53. Quillen, "Industrial City," 128; Meister, "History of Gary," 14–15. Gary's physical segregation was common, of course, in urban America. See Warner, *Urban Wilderness,* 101–5, 111.

54. Shumway, "Gary, Shrine of the Steel God," 28.

55. Lane, "*City of the Century,*" 268, 290; Balanoff, "History of Black Community," 49.

56. Quillen, "Industrial City," 151–52, 156; Moore, *Calumet Region,* 290.

57. Ora L. Wildermuth, "Early Days in Gary," in "Vesper Service, Congregational Church, Gary, Indiana, Sunday, November 27, 1927," Gary Public Library; Cannon, Loring, and Robb, *Lake and Calumet Region,* 2:800; Citizens Historical Association, Indianapolis, Indiana, *Biographical Sketches of Gary, Indiana Residents* (Indianapolis: n.p., 1943), s.v. "Wildermuth, Ora."

58. Many skilled mill employees and professional men came to Gary from western Pennsylvania, northern Ohio, Michigan, Iowa, Minnesota, and Indiana. Quillen, "Industrial City," 159–60; Wildermuth, "Early Days in Gary"; and various biographies in Cannon, Loring, and Robb, *Lake and Calumet Region,* vol. 2.

59. Ross, "Early Women Risked Much"; Quillen, "Industrial City," 159–60; Moore, *Calumet Region,* 290.

60. Cited in Ross, "Early Women Risked Much."

61. Quillen, "Industrial City," 168–69.

62. Quillen, "Industrial City," 125, 165, 169, 248; Taylor, *Satellite Cities,* 166.

CHAPTER 3

1. On American urban politics, see Jon C. Teaford, *Unheralded Triumph* (Baltimore: Johns Hopkins Univ. Press, 1984). On Gary's educational system, see

Ronald D. Cohen and Raymond A. Mohl, *The Paradox of Progressive Education* (Port Washington, N.Y.: Kennikat Press, 1979), and Ronald D. Cohen, *Children of the Mill* (Bloomington: Indiana Univ. Press, 1990). On Gary's settlement houses, see Ruth Hutchinson Crocker, "Sympathy and Science: The Settlement Movement in Gary and Indianapolis, to 1930" (Ph.D. diss., Purdue Univ., 1982).

2. Cited in Meister, "History of Gary," 21, and Lane, "*City of the Century*," 45. They cite only the first of four verses of the poem "Going to Vote." The entire poem was reprinted in "Gary's Golden Jubilee 1906–1956," Historical Souvenir Program, June 9–17, 1956, courtesy of Herschel Davis.

3. Lane, "*City of the Century*," 29, 34; Meister, "History of Gary," 45.

4. Tom Knotts moved to Gary on April 18, 1906, soon after his brother, A. F. Knotts, helped select the site for U.S. Steel's mill. His wife Ella and their five children followed him from Hammond, Indiana, on May 4, 1906. The Knotts brothers soon began to sell real estate south of the Wabash tracks. Indeed a suspicion that A. F. Knotts was more interested in selling his own lots than the corporation's lots led to his replacement as head of the Gary Land Company by Horace S. Norton in April 1907. In addition to his real estate activities, Tom Knotts became Gary's first postmaster and sold insurance as well. See Quillen, "Industrial City," 103, 108, 121; Lane, "*City of the Century*," 43.

5. Quillen, "Industrial City," 109–10; Cannon, Loring, and Robb, *Lake and Calumet Region*, 1:765–66.

6. Howat, *Standard History of Lake County*, 384; Quillen, "Industrial City," 111–12; Buffington, "Making Cities for Workmen," 17.

7. Howat, *Standard History of Lake County*, 388; Quillen, "Industrial City," 138, 140, 142–43; Meister, "History of Gary," 9; Mohl and Betten, "Failure of Industrial City Planning," 210–12; *Northern Indianan*, July 12, 1907. In his 1909 article, "Making Cities for Workmen," Buffington referred to water, gas, and electric franchises but said not a word about trolley service (17).

8. Howat, *Standard History of Lake County*, 384; Quillen, "Industrial City," 204, 214; Meister, "History of Gary," 19–22. This election inspired W. A. Woodruff's poem cited above.

9. Quillen, "Industrial City," 201–3; Meister, "History of Gary," 202; Ross, "Early Women Risked Much"; Moore, *Calumet Region*, 314.

10. Lane, "*City of the Century*," 47–48; Quillen, "Industrial City," 251.

11. Quillen, "Industrial City," 305–6, 465, 480; Meister, "History of Gary," 23–24, 38; Lane, "*City of the Century*," 47, 127.

12. Quillen, "Industrial City," 216–17, 265, 268, 273; Meister, "History of Gary," 25.

13. Quillen, "Industrial City," 28, 271, 295–301; Cannon, Loring, and Robb, *Lake and Calumet Region*, 1:229–32. Ora Wildermuth, for example, was the chairman of the Four Minute Men in Lake County. See Cannon, Loring, and Robb, *Lake and Calumet Region*, 2:800.

14. See Quillen, "Industrial City," 297, 300, 305; Lane, "City of the Century," 88. Cannon's seventeen-page list of those from Gary who served in the war testified to the patriotism of Gary's immigrant population. See Cannon, Loring, and Robb, Lake and Calumet Region, 1:270, 301–18.

15. Quillen, "Industrial City," 288, 304–5, 309. See also Brody, Steelworkers in America, 197–98.

16. Quillen, "Industrial City," 300; Lane, "City of the Century," 89.

17. Maloney, "To Strike at Steel," 2; Moore, Calumet Region, 497; Brody, Steelworkers in America, 71, 73, 77; Quillen, "Industrial City," 315.

18. Brody, Steelworkers in America, 80, 90, 96; Quillen, "Industrial City," 319. Daniel Rodgers maintained that "these highly mobile and uncommitted workers . . . provided what the factories sorely needed—a reserve army of workers able to iron out the fluctuations of an expanding economy." See Daniel T. Rodgers, "Tradition, Modernity, and the American Industrial Worker: Reflections and Critique," in Industrialization and Urbanization, ed. Theodore K. Rabb and Robert I. Rotberg (Princeton: Princeton Univ. Press, 1981), 229. In his Businessmen and Reform, Robert Wiebe described U.S. Steel's labor policy as a "showcase of open shop paternalism," which "carefully blended coercion, inducement, and public relations" (165).

19. Brody, Steelworkers in America, 116–24; Maloney, "To Strike at Steel," 24. A celebrated report on the steel strike concluded that the church provided little support for the strike, at least in Pittsburgh, and that "the great mass of steel workers paid no heed to the church as a social organization." See Commission of Inquiry, Interchurch World Movement, Report on the Steel Strike of 1919 (New York: Harcourt, Brace & Howe, 1920), 243.

20. Brody, Steelworkers in America, 146; Interchurch World Movement, Report on the Steel Strike of 1919; Quillen, "Industrial City," 313, 319, 322–29, 335–42; Lane, "City of the Century," 39.

21. Lane, "City of the Century," 91; Brody, Steelworkers in America: the Non-Union Era, 246, 248.

22. Cannon, Loring, and Robb, Lake and Calumet Region, 1:834; Quillen, "Industrial City," 331, 347–48; Mohl and Betten, Steel City, 30–31; Maloney, "To Strike at Steel," 61–63; Graham Taylor, "At Gary: Some Impressions and Interviews," Survey 43 (November 8, 1919):65–66.

23. Quillen, "Industrial City," 354, 361, 364, 370, 378; Lane, "City of the Century," 92–93; Taylor, "At Gary: Some Impressions and Interviews," 65–66; Maloney, "To Strike At Steel," 3; Mohl and Betten, Steel City, 32–33, 38–39; Meister, "History of Gary," 248. Finally in 1937 U.S. Steel accepted union organization of the industry. See Brody, Steelworkers in America, 252, 271; Lane, "City of the Century," 93.

24. Shumway, "Gary, Shrine of the Steel God." Shumway, twenty-three years old

at the time his article appeared, subsequently became a columnist for a paper in Evanston, Illinois, wrote short stories and one novel, and joined the staff of *Esquire* magazine before committing suicide in April 1934. See Lane, *"City of the Century,"* 124.

25. Lane, *"City of the Century,"* 105; Quillen, "Industrial City," 384–85; Meister, "History of Gary," 37.

26. *Gary Post-Tribune,* December 15, 1926; Quillen, "Industrial City," 386–87. See also *Gary Post-Tribune,* January 5, 1927, and January 7, 1927.

27. *Gary Post-Tribune,* December 15, 1926; Quillen, "Industrial City," 388; Shumway, "Gary, Shrine of the Steel God," 24.

28. Quillen, "Industrial City," 389–91, 394, 397–406; Gary Chamber of Commerce, "Gary at a Glance"; *Gary Post-Tribune,* December 14 and 22, 1926; Greer, *Big Steel,* 84; Lane, *"City of the Century,"* 106,108.

29. Fisher, "Steel City's Culture," 126; Shumway, "Gary, Shrine of the Steel God," 23; Gary Chamber of Commerce, "Gary at a Glance"; Quillen, "Industrial City," 394.

30. *Gary City Directory (1927)* (Indianapolis: R. L. Polk & Co., 1927), 7.

31. Gary Chamber of Commerce, "Gary at a Glance." Of Rotary, the *Post-Tribune* (December 30, 1926) said, "it is doing a large part in making Gary a city in which it is well worth while to live and be counted a good citizen." See also *Gary Post-Tribune,* December 31, 1926, on the Commercial Club and Gary Chamber of Commerce. For the YMCA and other organizations see *Gary Post-Tribune,* January 6 and 7, 1927. See also Fisher, "Steel City's Culture," 73, 130.

32. Quillen, "Industrial City," 411, 422; Balanoff, "History of Black Community in Gary," 161, 163; Lane, *"City of the Century,"* 130.

33. Kenneth T. Jackson, *The Ku Klux Klan in the City, 1915–1930* (New York: Oxford Univ. Press, 1967); Goldfield and Brownell, *Urban America,* 314–15; Lane, *"City of the Century,"* 93; Neil Betten, "Nativism and the Klan in Town and City: Valparaiso and Gary, Indiana," *Studies in History and Society* 4 (Spring 1973):6.

34. Meister, "History of Gary," 43; Lane, *"City of the Century,"* 95; Quillen, "Industrial City," 475–77; Betten, "Nativism and the Klan in Town and City," 7.

35. Lane, *"City of the Century,"* 96; interview with William R. Seaman, Cincinnati, Ohio, November 23, 1983; interview with Herschel B. Davis, Greenwood, Ind., October 11, 1984. Both Seaman and Davis reported opposition to the Klan by some Gary clergymen.

36. Meister, "History of Gary," 44–45; Neil Betten and Raymond A. Mohl, "The Evolution of Racism in an Industrial City, 1906–1940: A Case Study of Gary, Indiana," *Journal of Negro History* 59 (January 1974):54; Lane, *"City of the Century,"* 144, 147; "The Gary Strike," *The Christian Century* 44 (October 1927):1192–93.

37. Lane, "*City of the Century,*" 92; Quillen, "Industrial City," 305, 352; Taylor, "At Gary: Some Impressions and Interviews," 65–66; Meister, "History of Gary," 23. In their *Steel City,* Mohl and Betten are particularly critical of Hodges's activity during the steel strike of 1919 (31, 38).

38. Meister, "History of Gary," 38.

39. W. A. Forbis to R. O. Johnson, April 22, 1922, Church Records, First Presbyterian Church, Gary, Ind. (hereafter, "First Presbyterian Church Records").

40. Quillen, "Industrial City," 467, 474; Meister, "History of Gary," 38.

41. William Fulton presided over a brief caretaker government after R. O. Johnson went to jail. But he lost his own bid for the job later that year to the Klan-backed Floyd Williams (1926–30), who ran as a reform candidate. Williams's administration was charged by Southsiders with "police brutality, racism, and municipal indifference to the plight of the poor," and he failed to win reelection in the Republican primary of 1929. See Quillen, "Industrial City," 475–78; Lane, "*City of the Century,*" 96. Herschel Davis acknowledged that Williams benefitted from Klan support, but he denied that Williams was a Klansman. See Davis Interview, and Meister, "History of Gary," 39.

42. Lane, "*City of the Century,*" 127, 173–74. Johnson had been paroled in 1925 after serving seven months of his eighteen-month sentence and returned to Gary.

43. Shumway, "Gary, Shrine of the Steel God;" Garry J. August in *Gary Post-Tribune,* January 29, 1929.

44. Quillen, "Industrial City," 501, 504; Garry August in the *Gary Post-Tribune,* January 29, 1929.

45. Meister, "History of Gary," 147, 167, 176; Greer, *Big Steel,* 88–89, 92.

46. Meister, "History of Gary," 172, 175, 199; Lane, "*City of the Century,*" 185; Neil Betten and Raymond A. Mohl, "From Discrimination to Repatriation: Mexican Life in Gary, Indiana, during the Great Depression," *Pacific Historical Review* 42 (August 1973):370–88.

47. Meister, "History of Gary," 141, 143, 158; Greer, *Big Steel,* 88.

48. Meister, "History of Gary," 97.

49. Ibid., 77, 96, 97, 317; Fisher, "Steel City's Culture," 165.

50. Meister, "History of Gary," 287–88; Lane, "*City of the Century,*" 182, 190.

51. Meister, "History of Gary," 303, 305; Lane, "*City of the Century,*" 191–93.

52. Cannon, Loring, Robb, *Lake and Calumet Region,* 2:42–43; Mohl and Betten, *Steel City,* 4; Lane, "*City of the Century,*" 39–42, 201.

53. Lane, "*City of the Century,*" 41, 202; Citizens Historical Association, *Biographical Sketches of Gary, Indiana residents, 1943,* s.v. "Capt. H. S. Norton, Retired."

54. Meister, "History of Gary," 330.

55. Ibid., 331–34; Lane, "*City of the Century,*" 201–2; *Gary Post-Tribune,*

Golden Jubilee Edition, 7. Greer strongly disagrees that U.S. Steel exercised less control in Gary. See Greer, *Big Steel,* 19–20.

56. Meister, "History of Gary," 332, 334.

57. Lane, "*City of the Century,*" 208; Greer, *Big Steel,* 94–95.

58. Lane, "*City of the Century,*" 232–39. See also Mohl and Betten, *Steel City,* 55–59, for a discussion of Gary's systematic and pervasive pattern of school segregation.

59. Lane, "*City of the Century,*" 239–41.

60. Ibid., 274, 251; *Presbyterian Life,* October 15, 1949; *Gary Post-Tribune,* March 7, 1949.

61. Lane, "*City of the Century,*" 259–69.

62. Bureau of the Census, *Sixteenth Census of the U.S.: 1940, Population,* 2:Part 2, p. 806; *Census of Population:1950,* 2:14–153; *Census of Population:1960,* 1:16–324; *1970 Census of Population,* 1:16–104; *1980 Census of Population,* 1, Chapter B:16–8; Greer, *Big Steel,* 95–96.

63. Greer, *Big Steel,* 96, 102, 103, 108; Lane, "*City of the Century,*" 270–71, 277–79, 282; Marshall Frady, "Gary, Indiana," *Harper's* 239 (August 1969):35–45.

64. Lane, "*City of the Century,*" 282.

65. Lane, "*City of the Century,*" 293, 295, 302–3; Greer, *Big Steel,* 98; Frady, "Gary, Indiana," 35–45. Hatcher lost his bid for a sixth term in the 1987 Democratic primary, "ending his tenure as dean of northern black mayors." See *Chicago Tribune,* May 6, 1987.

66. Greer, *Big Steel,* 99; Lane, "*City of the Century,*" 304. Frady, "Gary, Indiana," 38.

67. Frady, "Gary, Indiana," 45; Greer, *Big Steel,* 111; Lane, "*City of the Century,*" 305.

CHAPTER 4

1. William Grant Seaman (compiler), "The Calumet Region," Gary—City United Methodist Collection, Archives of DePauw University and Indiana United Methodism, Greencastle, Ind. (hereafter "DePauw University Archives"). All materials cited from DePauw University Archives are from the Gary—City United Methodist Collection.

2. *Gary Evening Post,* May 21, 1914.

3. Balanoff, "History of Black Community," 48–49, 163, 504; Betten and Mohl, "Evolution of Racism," 64; Mohl and Betten, *Steel City,* 90.

4. See Lees, *Cities Perceived,* 224–27; Arthur J. Vidich and Stanford M. Lyman, *American Sociology: Worldly Rejections of Religion and Their Directions* (New

Haven: Yale Univ. Press, 1985), 61. In their *Steel City* (127), Mohl and Betten distinguish between the professionally run settlements and the much larger number of "religious missions" in American cities.

5. See, for example, Raymond A. Mohl and Neil Betten, "Paternalism and Pluralism: Immigrants and Social Welfare in Gary, Indiana, 1906–1940," *American Studies* 15 (Spring 1974):11, and their chapter on settlement houses in their *Steel City,* 108–28.

6. *Gary Daily Tribune,* September 2 and 4, 1913.

7. Lois W. Banner, "Religious Benevolence as Social Control: A Critique of an Interpretation," *Journal of American History* 60 (June 1973):23, 41.

8. See, for example, Crocker, "Sympathy and Science."

9. Lane, *"City of the Century,"* 56; Balanoff, "History of Black Community," 387.

10. Cannon, Loring, and Robb, *Lake and Calumet Region,* 1:596; Lane, *"City of the Century,"* 56; William Switzer, "Notes for Gary First Methodist Church History," 16, DePauw University Archives.

11. Mohl and Betten, "Paternalism and Pluralism," 11; F. S. Delaney, "History of Trinity Methodist Episcopal Church and the John Stewart Memorial Settlement House by Reverend F. S. Delaney," Mimeograph, [1931], p. 4, Gary Area Churches Box, Calumet Regional Archives, Indiana University Northwest, Gary, Ind. (hereafter "Calumet Regional Archives").

12. Mohl and Betten, "Paternalism and Pluralism," 11, 15; see also their *Steel City,* 109, and Cannon, Loring, and Robb, *Lake and Calumet Region,* 1:596.

13. Crocker, "Sympathy and Science," 274.

14. Ibid., 270.

15. Ibid., 271.

16. Ibid., 321.

17. Ibid., 344–52.

18. Ibid., 323.

19. *Gary Post-Tribune,* February 1, 1935; Delaney, "History of Trinity Methodist Episcopal Church," 6; Balanoff, "History of Black Community," 447; Crocker, "Sympathy and Science," 490. Neighborhood House, which gradually lost Presbyterian support during the Depression, relied on Gary's new Community Chest drive for support after 1937. See Meister, "History of Gary," 126, 133. Mohl and Betten are more skeptical of the racial harmony evident in the settlement houses, noting that "until the late 1930s, Gary's three white settlement houses either excluded blacks or segregated them in separate activities and groups." See their *Steel City,* 63.

20. *Gary Post-Tribune,* February 1, 1935; Fisher, "Steel City's Culture," 110; Brook, "Gary, Indiana," 50; Mohl and Betten, "Paternalism and Pluralism," 26. On the International Institute, see also Mohl and Betten, "Steel City, 117–28.

21. The International Institutes were founded in association with the YWCA in more than sixty cities after the end of World War I; the relationship with the YWCA ended in 1933. The Gary Institute was founded in 1919. See Mohl and Betten, "Paternalism and Pluralism," 13, 21, 23; Raymond A. Mohl and Neil Betten, "Ethnic Adjustment in the Industrial City: the International Institute of Gary, 1919–1940," *International Migration Review* 6 (Winter 1972):361, 373; Mohl and Betten, "From Discrimination to Repatriation," 384–85. For a description of the "Know Your City Tours" see Mohl and Betten, *Steel City,* 123.

22. Meister, "History of Gary," 97–98; Lane, *"City of the Century,"* 233, 279; Balanoff, "History of Black Community," 279.

23. Shumway, "Gary, Shrine of the Steel God," 29; Taylor, *Satellite Cities,* 218; Lane, *"City of the Century,"* 64; Moore, *Calumet Region,* 471; Meister, "History of Gary," 113.

24. A disciple of John Dewey, Wirt, who had studied at DePauw University and the University of Chicago, came to Gary from a similar post in Bluffton, Indiana. See Meister, "History of Gary," 113; *Gary Post-Tribune, Golden Jubilee Edition,* 146; Lane, *"City of the Century,"* 203; Moore, *Calumet Region,* 472; Mohl and Betten, *Steel City,* 132.

25. Lane, *"City of the Century,"* 63; Howat, *Standard History of Lake County,* 397; *Gary Post-Tribune,* January 13, 1927, and October 9, 1934; Quillen, "Industrial City," 169.

26. Lane, *"City of the Century,"* 63; Moore, *Calumet Region,* 472.

27. Howat, *Standard History of Lake County,* 403–4; Moore, *Calumet Region,* 476. Wirt wrote the section in Howat on the Gary schools.

28. Moore, *Calumet Region,* 475.

29. Cohen and Mohl, *Paradox of Progressive Education,* 11; Lane, *"City of the Century,"* 62; William Wirt, *The Great Lockout in America's Citizenship Plants* (Gary: Horace Mann School, 1937), 9. Wirt was born in 1874 near Markle, Indiana. Wirt's *Great Lockout* was an apologia for the Gary schools, published only a year before his death.

30. Wirt, *Great Lockout,* 10, 12–13, 21; Howat, *Standard History of Lake County,* 400.

31. William Wirt, "The Gary Public Schools and the Churches," *Religious Education* 11 (June 1916):222.

32. Wirt, *Great Lockout,* 15–16; Howat, *Standard History of Lake County,* 401.

33. Wirt, *Great Lockout,* 11, 17–20, 112; Howat, *Standard History of Lake County,* 399.

34. Wirt, *Great Lockout,* 38–40, 114; Howat, *Standard History of Lake County,* 405.

35. Wirt, *Great Lockout,* 37; Lane, *"City of the Century,"* 674; *Gary Post-Tribune,* January 18, 1926; Howat, *Standard History of Lake County,* 397.

36. Cohen and Mohl, *Paradox of Progressive Education*, 159, 175. See Wirt's pamphlet *America Must Lose—by a planned economy, the stepping stone to a regimented state* (New York: Committee for the Nation, 1934). See also *Gary Post-Tribune*, October 11, 1934.

37. Lane, *"City of the Century,"* 64; Cohen and Mohl, *Paradox of Progressive Education*, 94, 141.

38. Cohen and Mohl, *Paradox of Progressive Education*, 29, 94, 112. But Brook claimed to the contrary that, like the International Institute, Wirt rejected the melting pot model and "saw great strength and validity in the immigrants' own culture and heritage." See Brook, "Gary, Indiana: Steel Town Extraordinary," 50.

39. Mohl and Betten emphasize that Americanization was often a two-way street and that "strong ethnic identification and adoption of American patriotism and other values were not mutually exclusive characteristics." Many immigrant parents used the schools for their own purposes and were not simply passive consumers. See their *Steel City*, 134, 152.

40. Ibid., 7; Cohen cited in Lane, *"City of the Century,"* 65.

41. *Gary Post-Tribune*, November 9, 1926.

42. Cohen and Mohl, *Paradox of Progressive Education*, 94; Ronald D. Cohen, *Children of the Mill*, 60–61, 100–1, 206–7; Donald Boles, *Bible, Religion, and the Public Schools* (Ames: Iowa State Univ Press, 1965), 174, 179. According to William Clayton Bower and Percy Roy Hayward, by 1948 there were weekday church schools in 3,000 communities in 46 states with 2 million enrolled; see their *Protestantism Faces its Educational Task Together* (Appleton, Wisc.: C. C. Nelson Publishing Co., 1949), 175.

43. Bower and Hayward, *Protestantism Faces its Educational Task*, 175.

44. *Gary Post-Tribune*, June 4, 1931; William Grant Seaman and Mary Elizabeth Abernethy, *Community Schools for Week-Day Religious Instruction, Gary, Indiana* (Gary: Board of Religious Education, 1921), 3–4. Wirt's address apparently was a response to clerical discontent with the way the Wirt schools "monopolized the time and energy" of the children. See James E. Foster, *Christ Church, Gary, Indiana: A Sketch Book of Parish History* (Gary: n.p., 1940), 27; Wirt, "Gary Public Schools and the Churches," 221.

45. Joseph M. Avann, "The Church School," *The Church Promoter* 4 (October 1915):1. Wirt acknowledged the Jewish precedent in his February 28,1916, address to the Thirteenth Annual Convention of the Religious Education Association. See William Wirt, "The Gary Public Schools and the Churches," *Religious Education* 11 (June 1916):221, 225. See "Thirteenth Annual Convention, Report of the Recording Secretary," *Religious Education* 11 (April 1916):184. Avann's account of the origin of the schools is confirmed in Arlo A. Brown, "The Week-Day Church Schools of Gary, Indiana," *Religious Education* 11 (February 1916):5.

46. Howat, *Standard History of Lake County*, 112; Seaman and Abernethy, *Community Schools*, 4.

47. The number of church schools in the very early days is somewhat unclear. Seaman and Abernethy identify work in eight Protestant churches; Arlo Brown claims that in 1914–15 there were nine churches in addition to the synagogue. See Seaman and Abernethy, *Community Schools,* 4, and Brown, "Week-day Church Schools of Gary," 5. See also Walter A. Squires, *The Gary Plan of Church Schools* (Philadelphia: Presbyterian Board of Publication and Sabbath School Work, 1919), 11. Some of the churches received assistance from their denominations, enabling them to hire their own director of religious education, such as Myron Settle at Central Christian Church and H. W. Farrington at First Methodist Church. See Avann, "The Church School"; *Gary Evening Post,* September 22, 1914; and letter from Monroe G. Schuster to James W. Lewis, March 3, 1984.

48. *Gary Post-Tribune,* June 4, 1931; Brown, "Week-Day Church Schools of Gary," 12; Squires, *Gary Plan of Church Schools,* 11.

49. Mary Abernethy, "Facts About Gary's Community Church Schools; Steel City Is First in This Form of Study," *Gary Post-Tribune,* January 21, 1924. Arlo Brown had proposed in his 1916 "Week-Day Church Schools of Gary" that a cooperative approach would reach more children (13). Actual discussions of an interdenominational, cooperative program started as early as June 1916 in a committee chaired by Methodist laywoman, Mrs. C. E. Kendrick. See *Gary Daily Tribune,* June 15, 1916. An ecumenical board of religious education became an important characteristic of weekday church schools around the country. Such a board both reflected the cooperative nature of the enterprise by including persons from different Protestant groups and constituted the independence of the weekday church schools from the public schools. See Bower and Hayward, *Protestantism Faces its Educational Task.*

50. Abernethy, "Facts About Gary's Community Church Schools"; Seaman and Abernethy, *Community Schools,* 7; Cohen, *Children of the Mill,* 60.

51. Abernethy, "Facts About Gary's Community Church Schools," *Gary Post-Tribune,* January 21, 1924; *Gary Post-Tribune,* December 11, 1930; Abernethy and Seaman, *Community Schools,* 7–8; report from Mary Abernethy to donors in form of a letter, October 1, 1923, in Gary School Scrapbook, Gary Public Library.

52. John Wolever, "U.S. Studies Church School Developed Here Since 1914," *Gary Post-Tribune,* June 4, 1931; *Gary Post-Tribune,* April 18, 1921.

53. Seaman and Abernethy, *Community Schools,* 15; interview with Lillian Call, Gary, Ind., June 22, 1984.

54. Seaman and Abernethy, *Community Schools,* 9–10; Brown, "Week-Day Church Schools of Gary", 12. See Wirt to Barondess, October 23, 1915; Wirt to Blakely, June 19, 1916 (both letters in Wirt Papers, Lilly Library, Indiana University, Bloomington, Ind.; copies courtesy of Ron Cohen). Wolever, "U.S. Studies Church School," *Gary Post-Tribune,* June 4, 1931.

55. Seaman and Abernethy, *Community Schools,* 19, 24; *Gary Post-Tribune,* April 9, 1926.

56. *Gary Post-Tribune*, April 9, 1926, January 21, 1924, and March 18, 1927; report from Abernethy to donors, October 1, 1923; Seaman and Abernethy, *Community Schools*, 24. See also Bower and Hayward, *Protestantism Faces its Educational Task Together*, 177.

57. Seaman and Abernethy, *Community Schools*, 25–27 and cover.

58. Ibid., 29; *Gary Post-Tribune*, October 24, 1921.

59. *Gary Post-Tribune*, April 26, 1927; Cohen and Mohl, *Paradox of Progressive Education*, 94; Cohen, *Children of the Mill*, 61; Seaman and Abernethy, *Community Schools*, 12. Lillian Call confirmed that few Roman Catholic children attended the church schools. See interview with Lillian Call, Gary, Ind., June 22, 1984.

60. Seaman and Abernethy, *Community Schools*, 12; *Gary Post-Tribune*, August 3, 1920, and December 11, 1930; Wolever, "U.S. Studies Church Schools," *Gary Post-Tribune*, June 4, 1931.

61. Abernethy, "Facts About Gary's Community Church Schools," *Gary Post-Tribune*, January 21, 1924.

62. Seaman and Abernethy, *Community Schools*, 12–13; *Gary Post-Tribune*, October 24, 1921, January 21, 1924, January 4 and April 26, 1927, and October 3 and December 11, 1929; Abernethy, "Facts About Gary's Community Church Schools"; Meister, "History of Gary," 111.

63. Cohen, *Children of the Mill*, 206–7.

64. Mohl and Betten claim that "Gary's Protestant educators in the public schools and in the churches conceived of the weekday religious schools as an additional means of promoting Americanization, cultural conformity, and a uniform Protestant morality." See their *Steel City*, 143.

65. Seaman and Abernethy, *Community Schools*, 5–6; Squires, *Gary Plan of Church Schools*, 12. Cohen emphasizes the consensus among schools and churches in a "religious-secular educational alliance." See his *Children of the Mill*, 207.

66. Seaman and Abernethy, *Community Schools*, 6.

67. Ibid., 8; *Gary Post-Tribune*, April 11, 1921; William Grant Seaman, "Report of the Opening of the Community Church School, Gary, Indiana," Mimeograph, in Wirt Papers, Lilly Library, Indiana University, Bloomington, Ind.; Abernethy, "Facts About Gary's Community Church Schools," *Gary Post-Tribune*, January 21, 1924.

CHAPTER 5

1. On the notion of "presence," see Milton J Coalter, John M. Mulder, and Louis B. Weeks, eds., *The Presbyterian Predicament* (Louisville: Westminster/John Knox Press, 1990), 10.

2. Wind, *Places of Worship*, 109–10. For a discussion of congregations as medi-

ating structures, see Peter L. Berger and Richard J. Neuhaus, *To Empower People* (Washington: American Enterprise Institute for Public Policy Research, 1977), 2–3, 26–33. Marty, "Public and Private," 16–21, 34–52; Martin E. Marty, *The Public Church* (New York: Crossroad Publishing Co., 1981), p. 54.

3. James E. Foster, *Christ Church, Gary, Indiana: A Sketch Book of Parish History* (Gary, Ind.; n.p., 1940), 28.

4. Ross, "Early Women Risked Much to Establish Gary Homes."

5. Ora L. Wildermuth, "Early Days in Gary"; *Gary Post-Tribune*, March 2, 1946.

6. *Gary Post-Tribune, Golden Jubilee Edition*, 56; *Gary Post-Tribune*, June 22, 1957; Wildermuth, "Early Days in Gary," 6–7. On July 12, 1907, the *Northern Indianan* quoted H. S. Norton of the Gary Land Company: "I have tried lately to interest the various denominations in establishing churches here. Several protestant denominations are considering sites, but just where they will locate I do not know yet."

7. Wildermuth, "Early Days in Gary," 7; Mrs. Frank Kemp, *From Sand to Service* (Gary, Ind.: n.p., 1943), 11.

8. C. A. DeLong, "Beginnings of Our Church," in First Congregational Church, "Vesper Service, Congregational Church, Gary, Indiana," Mimeograph (Gary, Ind.: 1927), 20.

9. *Gary Post-Tribune*, March 2, 1946; DeLong, "Beginnings of Our Church," 20.

10. Foster, *Christ Church*, 6; First Congregational Church, "Vesper Service," 31.

11. *Gary Tribune*, September 23, 1910; *Gary Post-Tribune*, March 2, 1946, and June 22, 1957; *Gary Post-Tribune, Golden Jubilee Edition*, 56; *Northern Indianan*, July 12, 1907.

12. Foster, *Christ Church*, 5–6.

13. Ibid.; see also *Gary Tribune*, September 23, 1910.

14. Foster, *Christ Church*, 6, 9; Mumford, "This Land of Opportunity," 23.

15. Foster, *Christ Church*, 12–13.

16. Ibid., 14–16.

17. Ibid., 11, 13, 28, 35; *Gary Post-Tribune*, December 13, 1947.

18. Kemp, *Sand to Service*, 11–12; *Gary Tribune*, September 23, 1910; *Gary Post-Tribune*, July 17, 1942; Claude V. Ridgely, "History of the Church," in *A Decennial of Central Christian Church in Christian Fellowship and Enterprise* (Gary: n.p., 1938), 3, Gary Public Library.

19. Kemp, *Sand to Service*, 12, 42; *Gary Tribune*, September 23, 1910; Ridgely, "History of the Church," 3; O. F. Jordan, "Chicago," *The Christian Century* 26 (March, 1909):283.

20. *Gary Tribune*, September 23, 1910; Kemp, *Sand to Service*, 12, 29; *Gary Post-Tribune*, September 3, 1961; Ridgely, "History of the Church," 3.

21. Designed by A. F. Wickes, a local architect and member of the church, the

building cost approximately $150,000. Ridgely, "History of the Church," 3–4; Kemp, *Sand to Service,* 30–31.

22. Monroe G. Schuster to James Lewis, March 3, 1984; Kemp, *Sand to Service,* 38, 45; *Gary Post-Tribune,* November 29, 1940. Schuster, who came to Gary in 1928 fresh from Yale Divinity School, was described shortly after his 1941 departure as "a scholarly, eloquent preacher and community leader." See George K. Tomes, "Central Christian—An Historical Note." On Settle, see Bower and Hayward, *Protestantism Faces its Educational Task,* 169.

23. *Gary Post-Tribune,* November 29, 1940; Central Christian Church, "Community Vespers 1959," copy courtesy of the Reverend Fred Perry; Central Christian Church, "1944 Series, Gary Community Vespers," in "Churches-Protestant" folder, Gary Public Library.

24. Ross, "Early Women Risked Much to Establish Gary Homes."

25. Quillen, "Industrial City," 175; Ross, "Early Women Risked Much to Establish Gary Homes."

26. *Gary Post-Tribune,* March 2, 1946.

27. "Laying of Corner Stone," *Gary Daily Tribune,* December 7, 1908, and September 23, 1910.

28. Foster, *Christ Church,* 6, 11; Kemp, *Sand to Service,* 12; *Gary Post-Tribune,* March 2, 1946.

29. Quillen, "Industrial City," 394; Foster, *Christ Church,* 14–15; *Gary Post-Tribune,* December 28, 1926.

30. Meister, "History of Gary," 83; Foster, *Christ Church,* 15–16.

31. *Gary Post-Tribune,* February 5, 1935.

32. See, for example, Robert Handy, *A History of the Churches in the United States and Canada,* 396, for a discussion of "this heady period of affluence and revival."

33. Balanoff, "History of Black Community," 49.

34. Ibid.; Howat, *Standard History of Lake County,* 410; *Gary Post-Tribune, Golden Jubilee Edition,* 66.

35. Balanoff, "History of Black Community," 372, 377, 382; Lane, *"City of the Century,"* 174; Frank S. Delaney, "History of Trinity"; Meister, "History of Gary," 89.

36. Balanoff, "History of Black Community," 371, 378, 382–84.

37. Ibid., 225; *Gary Tribune,* October 1, 1919; Greer, *Big Steel,* 35.

38. Balanoff, "History of Black Community," 50, 188, 382; "Statement of Significance," Typescript, Calumet Regional Archives; Delaney, "History of Trinity," 7.

39. Balanoff, "History of Black Community," 128, 279; Delaney, "History of Trinity," 5.

40. Balanoff, "History of Black Community," 104, 390–91.

41. Martin E. Carlson, "A Study of the Eastern Orthodox Churches in Gary, Indiana" (M.A. thesis, Univ. of Chicago, 1942), 61; Fisher, "Steel City's Culture," 65. Although there were a few immigrant Protestant churches, most were either Roman Catholic or Orthodox. See Howat, *Standard History of Lake County,* 411; Writers' Program of the Works Progress Administration, *The Calumet Region Historical Guide* (East Chicago, Ind.: Garman Printing Co., 1939), 159; Cohen and Mohl, *Paradox of Progressive Education,* 107.

42. Raymond A. Mohl and Neil Betten, "The Immigrant Church in Gary, Indiana: Religious Adjustment and Cultural Defense," *Ethnicity* 8 (March 1981): 2, 14. See also their updated version of this article in their *Steel City,* 161–78. Oddly enough, only about 14 percent of Gary's immigrant children attended parochial schools in the mid-1920s, a considerably lower figure than in comparable cities. But several of the churches held Saturday classes in native language and culture, several of which survived into the 1960s. These schools were not, however, part of the Gary community church schools. See Cohen and Mohl, *Paradox of Progressive Education,* 106–7; Carlson, "Eastern Orthodox Churches," 55.

43. Mohl and Betten, "Immigrant Church in Gary," 12; Betten and Mohl, "From Discrimination to Repatriation," 375.

44. Meister, "History of Gary," 81; see also Mohl and Betten, "Immigrant Church in Gary," 12.

45. *Gary Post-Tribune, Golden Jubilee Edition,* 230, 235, 241; Carlson, "Eastern Orthodox Churches," 11, 17, 21. Mohl and Betten emphasize that Gary's ethnic parishes reflected strong lay initiative from the very beginning, unlike those in larger cities with well-established hierarchies. See Mohl and Betten, *Steel City,* 163–65.

46. Meister, "History of Gary," 80; Bureau of the Census, *Religious Bodies: 1936,* 1:528.

47. Meister, "History of Gary," 88.

48. *Polk's City Directory of Gary, 1922;* Howat, *Standard History of Lake County,* 411; Bureau of the Census, *Religious Bodies:1926,* 1:426.

49. Thomas Stebbins Pierce, "The Curious Individual and the Churches," undated clipping from 1930s, copy courtesy of Rabbi Garry August; August Interview. Rabbi August died on September 11, 1985, at the age of 91. See *Gary Post-Tribune,* September 12, 1985.

50. Meister, "History of Gary," 96; Shumway, "Gary, Shrine of the Steel God," 29; Lane, *"City of the Century,"* 126; *Gary Post-Tribune,* November 10, 1926, January 22, and February 5 and 28, 1927.

51. Kevin J. Christiano, *Religious Diversity and Social Change* (Cambridge: Cambridge Univ. Press, 1987), 49. Christiano discusses the four censuses of religious bodies produced by the United States Bureau of the Census between 1906 and 1936. He acknowledged that religious statistics in general have often been

problematic and that the U.S. Census in particular "has maintained a long and conflict-ridden relationship with religious matters" (24). The 1936 Census of Religious Bodies was particularly flawed as a result of "organized resistance to reporting" by religious libertarians and conservative clergy. Despite these problems Christiano concluded that "the Census statistics adequately represent the main historical contours of organized religion in the United States" (38). The four religious censuses are also problematic in the case of Gary. The 1906 census, based on the 1900 census data, preceded Gary; the 1916 census omitted specific reference to all cities of less than 25,000; the 1936 census was systematically flawed. Consequently my statistical snapshot of Gary's religious landscape relies heavily on the 1926 Census of Religious Bodies, occasionally supplemented by other information as noted.

52. Gary experienced a much sharper drop in religious identification during the decade than did Indianapolis (from 49 percent to 48 percent), Pittsburgh (from 73 percent to 67 percent), and Youngstown (from 68 percent to 65 percent). Bureau of the Census, *Religious Bodies:1926,* 1:426, 436–37, 511–12, 575–76, and *Religious Bodies:1936,* 1:527, 542–44, 635–36, 716–17.

53. Bureau of the Census, *Religious Bodies:1926,* 1:426, 436–37, 511–12, 575–76, and *Religious Bodies:1936,* 1:527, 542–44, 635–36, 716–17. Gary's heavy percentage of Roman Catholics was similar to that in other industrial cities like Pittsburgh (50 percent in 1926 and 53 percent in 1936) and Youngstown (43 percent in 1926 and 49 percent in 1936). But it was much larger than that in less industrialized Indianapolis (25 percent in 1926 and 23 percent in 1936). The three industrial cities also had similar patterns of little or no growth in mainstream Protestant groups such as Presbyterians and Methodists.

54. Bureau of the Census, *Religious Bodies:1926,* 1:426, 436–37, 511–12, 575–76, and *Religious Bodies:1936,* 1:527, 542–44, 635–36, 716–17. Gary's similarities with its industrial siblings are striking. In Pittsburgh these mainstream groups represented 34 percent of its religious membership in 1926 and 32 percent in 1936; in Youngstown the figures were 39 percent and 34 percent, respectively. By contrast, mainstream Protestants in Indianapolis constituted a majority of the city's religious members (55 percent in 1926 and 58 percent in 1936).

55. Writers' Program of the Works Progress Administration, *Calumet Region Historical Guide,* 162; Foster, *Christ Church,* 14; Quillen, "Industrial City," 459.

56. Quillen, "Industrial City," 459. See also Mohl and Betten, *Steel City,* 181.

57. Meister, "History of Gary," 81; Greer, *Big Steel,* 35. See also Balanoff, "History of Black Community," 225.

58. *Gary Tribune,* October 1, 1919. See also *Gary Tribune,* October 3, 1919. Dennis C. Dickerson describes a similar pattern of cooperation between employers and black churches in Pittsburgh in the teens and twenties. See his "The Black Church in Industrializing Western Pennsylvania, 1870–1950," *Western Pennsylvania Historical Magazine* 64 (October 1981):329–44.

59. Foster, *Christ Church,* 13; Balanoff, "History of Black Community," 225; Quillen, "Industrial City," 460. The Gary churches resembled those in Gastonia, North Carolina, studied by Liston Pope, which "contributed unqualified and effective sanction to their economic culture." See Pope, *Millhands and Preachers,* 330. Although Fisher ("Steel City Culture," 113) claimed that the Christ Church rector, William Dean Elliott, was dismissed for his support of the strikers, Foster's candid account of Christ Church says nothing of the kind. Nor did the *Gary Daily Tribune* when it announced on June 29, 1920, the conclusion of his "highly successful" pastorate.

60. Betten and Mohl, "Evolution of Racism in an Industrial City," 54; Lane, "*City of the Century,*" 112; Mohl and Betten, *Steel City,* 64.

61. Meister, "History of Gary," 97; Balanoff, "History of Black Community," 390; *Gary Post-Tribune,* April 26, 1938.

62. Betten and Mohl, "Evolution of Racism in an Industrial City," 64.

63. On Ayer, see *Gary Post-Tribune,* February 21, 1927; on Ketcham, see *Gary Post-Tribune,* January 12, 1935.

64. Ibid., November 26, 1926.

65. Ibid., November 10, 1926; undated clipping in Gary Public Library, *Biographical Sketches,* s.v. "August."

66. Quillen, "Industrial City," 450.

67. Meister failed to indicate how many of these leaders were Jewish in his "History of Gary," 91–92. He compiled his figures from Citizens Historical Association, *Biographical Sketches of Gary, Indiana Residents, 1943,* Gary Public Library; Bureau of the Census, *Religious Bodies:1936,* 1:527.

68. Meister, "History of Gary," 92.

69. Greer, *Big Steel,* 35; Citizens Historical Association, *Biographical Sketches of Gary, Indiana residents, 1943,* s.v. "Norton" and "Hall"; Foster, *Christ Church,* 28.

70. First Congregational Church, "Vesper Service," 2; Citizens Historical Association, *Biographical Sketches of Gary, Indiana residents, 1943,* s.v. "Hodges"; Davis Interview; Kemp, *Sand to Service,* 49.

71. *Gary Post-Tribune,* January 25, 26, and 28, 1935.

72. Stanley S. Jacobs, "Brotherhood Solves Gary's Problems," *Coronet* 27 (November 1949):81; Anselm Forum, "Anselm Forum, First Decade," Mimeograph, Gary, Ind., 1943, Gary Public Library.

73. Meister, "History of Gary," 98; Margaret Frakes, "They Put Meaning into Brotherhood," *The Christian Century* 66 (February 16, 1949):204.

74. In fact, a 1943 account of the Forum noted that the first subject discussed by the eight founding members in February 1932 was religion. That same document also includes a list of forty-six members, representing almost forty separate congregations and religious groups, including Spiritualist, Rosicrucianist, and

"Albanian Mohammedan," along with Presbyterians, Methodists, and Episcopalians. See "Anselm Forum, First Decade" and Frakes, "They Put Meaning into Brotherhood," 204.

75. "Anselm Forum, First Decade"; Jacobs, "Brotherhood Solves Gary's Problems," 80–83; Frakes, "They Put Meaning into Brotherhood," 204–6.

76. Frakes, "They Put Meaning into Brotherhood," 205; Fisher, "Steel City's Culture," 177. Although the Anselm Forum had an all-male membership, a women's auxiliary was formed which included twenty nationalities, fifteen religions, and three races. See Jacobs, "Brotherhood Solves Gary's Problems," 83. The Anselm Forum formally dissolved October 1, 1972. See letter of Paul Huang, Frank Urban, and E. T. Mitchell to Mrs. Janet Manis of the Internal Revenue Service in "The President's Book," a collection of papers from Anselm Forum presidents from 1932 to 1962, in Gary Public Library.

77. Lane, "*City of the Century*," 56; Cannon, Loring, and Robb, *Lake and Calumet Region*, 1:596; Balanoff, "History of Black Community," 446–47. See also Crocker, "Sympathy and Science," 299, 335, 443. According to Crocker (335), Neighborhood House served blacks in the main building by 1925 and had black social workers by 1929; Friendship House served blacks by 1929 (299).

78. Foster, *Christ Church*, 27.

79. Lane, "*City of the Century*," 70.

80. Balanoff, "History of Black Community," 268, 279; *Gary Post-Tribune*, November 17, 1926, and January 4, 1927.

81. Lane, "*City of the Century*," 114.

82. *Gary Post-Tribune*, February 9, 14, 15, and 21, 1927. Calls for racial understanding and equality were proclaimed from Protestant pulpits on other occasions as well. See, for example, *Gary Post-Tribune*, November 5, 1926 (Westminster Presbyterian Church), and December 20, 1926 (First Congregational Church).

83. *Gary Post-Tribune*, October 2, 1945.

84. Fisher, "Steel City's Culture," 178. See, for example, the yearbooks of the Gary Council of Church Women for 1947–48 and 1948–49 in the "Church Organizations-Protestant" folder, Gary Public Library. The Gary Council of Churches, established April 25, 1938, included both white and black churches from the beginning. In February 1939, it sponsored its first Race Relations Sunday, which included a discussion of race relations at many Gary churches. See *Gary Post-Tribune*, April 26, 1938, and February 13, 1939.

85. *Gary Post-Tribune*, June 1, 1940. The Fireside Forum idea apparently originated with Reuben Olson, founder of the Anselm Forum, when he was serving as president of the Gary Council of Churches. The steering committee for the Fireside Forum included Rabbi Julius Siegel and the Reverend Monroe Schuster of Central Christian Church. See brochure entitled, "The Fireside Forum," in "Church Organization-Protestant" folder, Gary Public Library. See also *Gary Post-Tribune*,

March 11 and 12 and June 1, 1940, and Harold E. Schmidt, "Democracy at the Fireside," *The Christian Century* 57 (May 29, 1940):701–3.

86. *Gary Post-Tribune,* September 10, 1946.

87. *Gary Post-Tribune,* December 9, 1926, January 20, 1927, October 24, 1934.

88. *Gary Post-Tribune,* October 1 and 7, 1926. On one celebrated occasion the *Post-Tribune* attacked a visiting evangelist at Central Baptist Church for his scandalous charges about immorality in Gary. See Lane, *"City of the Century,"* 108–12.

89. *Gary Post-Tribune,* February 5, 1935, and October 16, 1934.

90. Ibid., February 5, 1935, October 4 and 17, 1938, and October 22 and 26, 1962; Lane, *"City of the Century,"* 250.

91. For example, the churches made it clear that a "United Protestant Church Loyalty Crusade" in 1932 was not an old-fashioned revival. See pamphlet entitled, "United Protestant Church Loyalty Crusade" in "Church Organizations-Protestant" folder, Gary Public Library. See Northwest Indiana Conference, *Minutes,* 286.

92. Schuster to Lewis, March 3, 1984. See, for example, *Gary Post-Tribune,* November 6 and 26, 1926, and November 28, 1934.

93. *Gary Post-Tribune,* October 4, 12, 18, and 21, November 5, and December 28, 1926.

94. *Gary Post-Tribune,* November 13 and December 27 and 28, 1926.

95. Ibid., November 13, 1926.

96. Ibid., February 3, 7, and 8, 1927.

97. *Gary Post-Tribune,* February 3, 4, 8, and 12, 1927.

CHAPTER 6

1. For a succinct, insightful discussion of the American evangelical mainstream, see Ahlstrom, *Religious History,* 470–71. For a humorous, thoughtful discussion of the terms "mainline" and "mainstream," see Martin Marty's MEMO columns in *The Christian Century* 106 (November 8, December 6, December 13, 1989):131, 1159, 1183. In his *Between the Times* (p. x) William Hutchison proposes that such terms as "establishment" and "hegemony" avoid any suggestion of Protestant triumphalism.

2. On Methodism (324–29 and 436–39) and Presbyterianism (267–72 and 455–71) in the United States, see Sydney Ahlstrom, *Religious History.*

3. The Presbyterian denomination was one of the major battlegrounds of the fundamentalist-modernist debate. See George Marsden, *Fundamentalism and American Culture* (New York: Oxford Univ. Press, 1980), 109–18, 164–84. The

Methodist liberal-conservative struggle included a struggle over orthodoxy at Vanderbilt University and the establishment of Emory University as a conservative counterweight. See Hunter Dickinson Farish, *The Circuit Rider Dismounts* (Richmond: The Dietz Press, 1938), 294–304; Ahlstrom, *Religious History*, 718–19; Marty, *Righteous Empire*, 225. On the liberal side, both denominations were important in the development of the social gospel and in the establishment of the Federal Council of the Churches of Christ in America in 1908. See Hopkins, *Rise of the Social Gospel*, 280–83, 289–92, 302–17; and William McGuire King, "The Emergence of Social Gospel Radicalism: The Methodist Case," *Church History* 50 (December 1981):436–49.

4. *Gary-Tribune*, September 23, 1910; Gary Chamber of Commerce, *Gary at a Glance* (n.p., [1928]); Foster, *Christ Church*, 5–6; Frederick W. Backemeyer, "The Symbols in First Presbyterian Church, Gary, Indiana" (n.p.: original date unknown, reissued 1968), First Presbyterian Church Records; "Romance of City Church Architecture" (Gary: n.p., original date unknown, reissued 1970), DePauw University Archives.

5. Martin Marty underscores the significance for the congregation's civic role of its ordinary round of congregational life in his "In Praise of the Civil Congregation," 546.

6. Thomas Bender, *Community and Social Change in America* (New Brunswick, N.J.: Rutgers Univ. Press, 1978), 148. Bender's study refutes scholars who, based on their reading of the works of Ferdinand Tönnies and Louis Wirth, conclude that the modern city hinders the development of community. Bender insists (42) rather that Tönnies's *Gemeinschaft* (community) and *Gesellschaft* (society) denote two types of social interaction which coexist in the city and that the distinction between them does not document the collapse of community in the modern city. This move frees the historian from the myth of inevitable decline and allows him or her to assess the ways in which the meaning of community has changed in urban America (11). Central to Bender's position is Claude Fischer's article, "Toward a Subcultural Theory of Urbanism," *American Journal of Sociology* 80 (1975):1319–41. See also William H. Anderson, "The Local Congregation as a Subculture," *Social Compass* 18 (1971):287–91. Louis Wirth's "Urbanism as a Way of Life" is reprinted in Richard Sennett, ed., *Classic Essays on the Culture of Cities* (New York: Appleton-Century-Crofts, 1969), 143–64.

7. For a discussion of the cultural significance of denominations in the pluralistic American situation, see William H. Swatos, Jr., "Beyond Denominationalism? Community and Culture in American Religion," *Journal for the Scientific Study of Religion* 20 (1981):217–27.

8. William Joder, "Lights and Shadows: A Resume of First Church Records," Mimeograph (1933), 11–12, First Presbyterian Church Records; Frederick E. Wal-

ton, addendum to historical sketch of First Presbyterian Church by I. M. Houser, written in Walton's hand in Session Records, after meeting of February 11, 1911, First Presbyterian Church Records.

9. I. M. Houser, "History by Rev. I. M. Houser," [1908], both a typescript and a handwritten version (in Frederick Walton's hand) in First Presbyterian Church, Session Minutes, after meeting of February 11, 1911, in First Presbyterian Church Records.

10. Houser, "History"; Lane, "*City of the Century*," 13, 45. In any case, the Gary Land Company did donate 40 percent ($960) of the purchase price of the three lots on which the Presbyterians built their first building in 1908. See Foster, *Christ Church*, 6, and Eugene J. Buffington to George Knox, July 28, 1909, First Presbyterian Church Records.

11. Houser, "History." The Logansport Presbytery had only recently approved the purchase of a lot in Gary for a church. See *Northern Indianan*, September 21, 1906.

12. Joder, "Lights and Shadows," 6; Houser, "History"; "A Brief History of the Presbyterian Church, Corner of Sixth Avenue & Monroe St., Gary, Indiana," Typescript (probably 1931), First Presbyterian Church Records (hereafter cited as "Brief History").

13. Houser to ?, February 18, 1908, J. B. Donaldson to John C. Vanatta, September 4, 1908, and Board of Trustees of First Presbyterian Church to Vanatta, December 31, 1908; Joder, "Lights and Shadows," 7. All letters cited in this chapter, except where noted otherwise, are located in First Presbyterian Church Records.

14. Joder, "Lights and Shadows," 7–8; J. B. Donaldson to "Fellow Presbyter," November 11, 1908; Henry Webb Johnson to J. B. Donaldson, May 5, 1908; I. M. Houser to J. B. Donaldson, October 3, 1908; Albany Presbytery, fund-raising letter. Although the latter is undated, its reference to Gary's being a dry city indicates a date in early 1909 during Gary's brief experience with local prohibition, discussed in ch. 3.

15. See "Brief History"; First Presbyterian Church, Session Minutes, April 1909; Joder, "Lights and Shadows," 12; "First Presbyterian Church" (1955), three-page typed historical sketch (hereafter cited as "1955 Historical Sketch") in First Presbyterian Church Records. The theater's very existence was connected with the churches. E. J. Buffington and Elbert Gary, neither of whom had ever seen a motion picture, were reluctant to permit the construction of a theater until H. S. Norton suggested that a theater could also be used by Gary's infant churches. See Quillen, "Industrial City," 172; *Gary Post-Tribune*, November 18, 1939.

16. William Fulton to John C. Vanatta, October 9, 1908.

17. According to a much later account, this site "was selected because of the

development of Jefferson park, the proximity of 5th Avenue, and the central location." See "Golden Jubilee Pageant or First Presbyterian Church Through the Years," Typescript (1958), 3, First Presbyterian Church Records.

18. Donaldson to Vanatta, September 4, 1908; Fulton to Vanatta, October 9, 1908; Houser to (Vanatta), August 6, 1908; George Knox to John Vanatta, July 23, 1908; Joder, "Lights and Shadows," 9–11.

19. Houser, "History," and Walton addendum thereto. Houser indicated in a letter that the Gary Presbyterians "say Presbytery selected Hamilton for us." See Houser to (Vanatta), August 6, 1908.

20. *Northern Indianan*, July 3 and August 7, 1908. Despite the newspaper's apparent surprise over the charges, at least one Indiana minister referred in a 1908 letter to "the old charge of a year ago, of drinking ale in a buffet car." See Henry Webb Johnson to John Vanatta, July 7, 1908.

21. Houser to (Vanatta), August 6, 1908.

22. *Northern Indianan*, August 7, 1908.

23. Houser, "History" and Walton addendum thereto; Houser to (Vanatta), August 6, 1908; William Fulton to J. B. Donaldson, July 13, 1908; Knox to Vanatta, July 23, 1908; Henry Webb Johnson to Vanatta, July 29, 1908; I. M. Houser to George Knox, July 28, 1908; I. M. Houser to John Vanatta, September 8, 1908.

24. Houser to Knox, July 28, 1908; George Knox to ?, July 9, 1908; Johnson to Vanatta, July 29, 1908.

25. Fulton to Donaldson, July 13, 1908; I. M. Houser to John Vanatta, July 8, 1908; Houser to Knox, July 28, 1908; First Presbyterian Church, Fiftieth Anniversary Booklet, 1958, p. 2, First Presbyterian Church Records; Cannon, Loring, and Robb, *History of Lake and Calumet Region*, 1:469.

26. Johnson to Vanatta, July 29, 1908; A. M. Smith to John Vanatta, July 29, 1908; Knox to Vanatta, July 23, 1908.

27. Houser to Knox, July 28, 1908; Donaldson to Vanatta, September 4, 1908.

28. I. M. Houser to John Vanatta, July 29, 1908; Fulton to Donaldson, July 13, 1908; Houser to (Vanatta), August 6, 1908; A. M. Smith to John Vanatta, July 29, 1908, August 7, 1908, and August 11, 1908. William Joder's twenty-fifth anniversary history, written in 1933, relied heavily on some of the same correspondence I have used but said nothing about the "old ladies." See also a two-page Handwritten Historical Sketch of Walton Years, c. 1930 (hereafter cited as "Handwritten Historical Sketch"), and church bulletins for January 23, 1946, and January 22, 1950, all in First Presbyterian Church Records.

29. *Gary Post-Tribune*, January 2, 1925; Frederick W. Backemeyer, "In Loving Remembrance: Memorial and Founders' Day Service of First Presbyterian Church, Gary, Indiana," May 25, 1930, 13–16, First Presbyterian Church Records; "Brief History," 1–2; Walton, addendum to Houser's "History."

30. "Brief History," 2; Frederick Walton to John Vanatta, June 23, 1909; Backemeyer, "In Loving Remembrance," 14; Frederick Walton to George Knox, January 22, 1909.

31. *Gary Post-Tribune*, March 12, 1929.

32. Synod minutes cited in a letter from Stewart to Backemeyer, September 4, 1933. See also the membership list in "Report of the Board of Trustees, January 1, 1920, to April 1, 1920," First Presbyterian Church Records. Call's father, Mark Sandler, came to Gary from Pittsburgh in 1911 and brought the rest of his family in 1912. He served as a trustee of the Presbyterian church in the 1920s. See interview with Lillian Call, Gary, Indiana, June 22, 1984, Chart of Elders and Trustees, First Presbyterian Church Records. See also Roderic P. Frohman, "Pastoral Hospitality with Worship Visitors in a Multi-Racial Setting" (D.Mn. thesis, Princeton Theological Seminary, 1983), 4, for brief sketches of William Fulton, John McFadden, and Thomas Cutler, prominent Presbyterians in Gary's early history.

33. Session Minutes, Meetings of March 27, 1910, July 6, 1913, July 27, 1913, and October 24, 1917; "Church Register, 1908–1918," First Presbyterian Church Records.

34. Session Minutes, various meetings in 1908–1909 and January 16, 1910.

35. Walton to Knox, January 22, 1909; Backemeyer, "In Loving Remembrance"; Session Minutes, April 1910–1913 and 1920; First Presbyterian Church, Walton Installation Service Program, June 27, 1917, First Presbyterian Church Records; *Gary Daily Tribune*, October 7, 1918.

36. Walton Installation Service Program, June 27, 1917, First Presbyterian Church Records.

37. "Alpha History," (1941), "Church Organizations-Protestant" folder, Gary Public Library.

38. *Tri Mu Tattler*, May 6, 1934 (all copies in First Presbyterian Church Records); Backemeyer, "In Loving Remembrance," 15; "Organization of the First Presbyterian Church of Gary"; Session Minutes, Meeting of July 21, 1918; Program for 1934 Tri Mu banquet; all from First Presbyterian Church Records. See also Frohman, "Pastoral Hospitality," 6; *Gary Post-Tribune*, May 6, 1934, and May 5, 1941; "Golden Jubilee Pageant," 5. Tri Mu's minstrel shows were not Gary's first. In 1907 the University Club staged its first show, a tradition continued until at least 1916. See *Gary Daily Tribune*, May 19, 1916. For the lesson in race relations, see Mary Walton's Notebook, First Presbyterian Church Records.

39. "Brief History," 5.

40. Session Minutes, Meetings of May 10, 1916, January 28, 1934, February 9, 1915; entry for March 31, 1919, in "Church Register 1908–1918"; Cannon, Loring, Robb, *Lake and Calumet Region*, 2:287.

41. For a description and critique of the new urban history, see Monkonnen, *America Becomes Urban*, 24–30. On the importance of religious leadership, see,

for example, Max Weber, *On Charisma and Institution Building,* selected papers ed. and intro. by S. N. Eisenstadt (Chicago: Univ. of Chicago Press, 1968), 253–67; Joachim Wach, *Sociology of Religion* (Chicago: Univ. of Chicago Press, 1944; Phoenix edition reprint, 1962), 331–74; and Michael Hill, *A Sociology of Religion* (New York: Basic Books, 1973), 140–82.

42. Interview with Lillian Call, Gary, Ind., June 22, 1984; "Handwritten Historical Sketch"; Joder, "Lights and Shadows," 16.

43. Backemeyer, "In Loving Remembrance," 13.

44. Frederick Walton, "Report of the Session to the Congregation, 1922," a handwritten manuscript in notebook entitled "Records," First Presbyterian Church Records.

45. Session Minutes, Meetings of April 1909, March 1911, November 1917, and April 1922; Backemeyer, "In Loving Remembrance," 16; William Clark to James Lewis, November 12, 1984.

46. Foster, *Christ Church,* 5; Walton to Knox, January 22, 1909; Joder, "Lights and Shadows," 15. On the red carpet, see John Vanatta to E. E. Geisel (a trustee of the church), March 27, 1909; E. Thomas (also a trustee) to John Vanatta, April 28, 1909; E. E. Geisel to John Vanatta, March 29, 1909; Grace and Paul West to First Presbyterian Church, September 25, 1965; Joder, "Lights and Shadows," 16.

47. Joder, "Lights and Shadows," 17–19; Session Minutes, Meetings of February 28, 1912, September 191, September 15, 1919; "Brief History," 2–4.

48. Session Minutes, Meetings of September 15 and 18, 1915, September 24, 1916, May 11, 1919, April 25, 1919. See Session Minutes, Meeting of September 9, 1915.

49. Session Minutes, Meetings of November 1917, April 3, 1918, July 10, 1918, and April 29, 1920. For the Interchurch World Movement, see Ernst, *Moment of Truth For Protestant America.* For the New Era Movement, see John E. Lankford, "The Impact of the New Era Movement on the Presbyterian Church in the United States of America, 1918–1925," *Journal of Presbyterian History* 40 (1962):213–24.

50. Call Interview; Program for Dedication Service of Assyrian Presbyterian Church, June 26, 1927, in "Churches-Protestant" folder, Gary Public Library; Joder, "Lights and Shadows," 18; Session Minutes, Meetings of November 23, 1917, and April 6, 1920; *Gary Post-Tribune,* June 22, 1946, and *Golden Jubilee Edition,* 240; letter from Assyrian Presbyterian Church to First Presbyterian Church, June 5, 1926, filed with Session Minutes, First Presbyterian Church Records.

51. George Knox to John Vanatta, January 11, 1909. See also clipping from *Gary Evening Post,* November 16, 1912, attached to a three-page typewritten history of Neighborhood House in First Presbyterian Church Records. The definitive discussion of Neighborhood House is Crocker's "Sympathy and Science,"

321–57, which emphasizes the important role Neighborhood House played in the lives of Gary's immigrant women.

52. Lane, "*City of the Century,*" 56; *Gary Evening Post,* November 16, 1912; Joder, "Lights and Shadows," 25; "Secretary's Report of Ladies Aid Society for 1925–26," First Presbyterian Church Records.

53. Lane, "*City of the Century,*" 58; Session Minutes, Meeting of June 30, 1919; Backemeyer, "In Loving Remembrance," 15; Frohman, "Pastoral Hospitality," 4; Crocker, "Sympathy and Science," 431–32.

54. Joder, "Lights and Shadows," 16; Backemeyer, "In Loving Remembrance," 14–15.

55. *Gary Post-Tribune,* January 2, 1925; Joder, Lights and Shadows," 20; Backemeyer, "In Loving Remembrance," 17. For a recent discussion of the significance of the decline of Sabbath observance among Presbyterians, including Sunday baseball, see Benton Johnson, "On Dropping the Subject: Presbyterians and Sabbath Observance in the Twentieth Century," in *The Presbyterian Predicament,* ed. Coalter, Mulder, and Weeks, 90–108.

56. *Gary Daily Tribune,* June 17, 1918.

57. *Gary Post-Tribune,* January 2, 1925. The front-page headline that day read: "Rev. F. E. Walton Answers the Call of His Master." Religion was still news in Gary.

58. Program for Backemeyer's Installation Service, December 16, 1925, First Presbyterian Church Records.

59. Call Interview; Backemeyer, "In Loving Remembrance," 14.

60. Clark to Lewis, November 12, 1984; Joder, "Lights and Shadows," 21–22.

61. Session Minutes, Meetings of August 28, 1933, and September 24, 1934; letter from Dirk Lay (at the Presbyterian Indian Mission in Sacaton, Arizona) to Howard Schmick (member of the Session), October 26, 1932, First Presbyterian Church Records.

62. Frohman, "Pastoral Hospitality," 5.

63. Letter from Board of Trustees to Members of First Presbyterian Church, April 22, 1925; Quillen, "Industrial City," 394.

64. Session Minutes, Meetings of August 29, 1923, August 5, 1925, June 14, 1925, September 23, 1925, November 1, 1925; *Gary Post-Tribune,* November 4, 1950; J. C. Schwarz, ed., *Who's Who in the Clergy,* vol. 1, *1935–1936* (New York: n.p., 1936), 54.

65. As a rule, joining "by transfer of letter" implies prior membership in another congregation, and joining "on confession of faith" implies new converts to Christianity. Interestingly, the figures defy overall trends in Protestant church membership, with the average growth during the Depression years almost equaling that during the five years following World War II. Annual growth increased to 129 in the 1951–53 period. See "Pastor's Register 1929–1934," First Presbyterian Church Records.

66. Bureau of the Census, *Religious Bodies: 1926,* 1:427, and *Religious Bodies: 1936,* 1:527; Session Records; "Pastor's Register 1929–1934," First Presbyterian Church Records.

67. Letter from Frederick W. Backemeyer to Board of Trustees of First Presbyterian Church, March 23, 1933.

68. "Brief History," 4.

69. Session Minutes, Meetings of November 22, 1927, September 20, 1931, April 14, 1929, September 11, 1933, November 4, 1934, October 2, 1938, September 13, 1943.

70. First Presbyterian Church, Fiftieth Anniversary Booklet, 5; Joder, "Lights and Shadows," 22–23.

71. Undated Four-Page Historical Outline, First Presbyterian Church Records. (The first three pages, ending with 1933, were probably prepared for the church's twenty-fifth anniversary that year. The fourth page lists eight events from 1933– 41.) Session Minutes, Meetings of September 13, 1943, and September 15, 1938.

72. Walton, "Report of the Session to the Congregation, 1922"; Session Minutes, Meetings of May 28, 1928, September 15, 1938, September 13, 1943, February 7, 1944; First Presbyterian Church, Fiftieth Anniversary Booklet.

73. Golden Jubilee Pageant, 5; Frohman, "Pastoral Hospitality," 5; "Book of Elders," First Presbyterian Church Records; Lake County Historical Society, "Personal Records," 1923, s.v. "Seabright," Gary Public Library; Citizens Historical Association, "Biographical Sketches of Gary, Indiana Residents, 1943," Typescript, s.v. "Goris" and "Seyl"; *Gary Post-Tribune,* August 12, 1948 (on Kennedy).

74. Board of Trustees of First Presbyterian Church to C. R. Cox (president of Carnegie-Illinois Steel Corporation), September 12, 1949.

75. *Gary Post-Tribune,* November 18, 1926, and February 13, 1939; Joder, "Lights and Shadows," 23; Session Minutes, meetings of February 7, April 4, and May 23, 1938; August 1 and September 13, 1943; April 9, 1947.

76. First Presbyterian Church, Fiftieth Anniversary Booklet, pp. 4, 6.

77. *Gary Post-Tribune,* October 7, 1947. See also Lillian Call Interview; she lived across the street from the church.

78. Golden Jubilee Pageant, p. 7.

79. C. J. Kennedy, chief engineer at American Bridge Company, was chairman of the Building Committee. *Gary Post-Tribune,* October 8, 1947, and August 11, 1948; Trustee Minutes, Meeting of January 18, 1949; Session Minutes, Meeting of January 19, 1949; First Presbyterian Church, Fiftieth Anniversary Booklet.

80. Frohman, "Pastoral Hospitality," 13.

81. The divided chancel separated the pulpit and lectern at the front of the sanctuary. The Perpetual Lamp, an extremely uncommon phenomenon in Protestant church buildings, hangs from the ceiling of the chancel area. First Presbyterian Church, Fiftieth Anniversary Booklet, 6; Backemeyer, "Symbols in First Pres-

byterian Church." Written after the rebuilding to explain the symbols in the church building, Backemeyer's booklet was reissued on the church's sixtieth anniversary in 1968.

82. Session Minutes, Meeting of November 23, 1917.

83. Dean Peerman, "Forward on Many Fronts: The Century 1923–1929," *The Christian Century* 101 (June 6, 1984):600.

84. Session Minutes, Meeting of October 7, 1940.

85. *Gary Post-Tribune*, November 3, 1941; Session Minutes, Meeting of December 1, 1941.

86. Session Minutes, Meeting of March 9, 1942; First Presbyterian Church, Fiftieth Anniversary Booklet, 6.

87. *Gary Post-Tribune*, March 9, 1951.

88. Session Minutes, Meetings of June 5 and 11 and September 5, 1967; September 21 and December 21, 1970.

89. *Gary Post-Tribune*, April 8, 1932.

90. Joder, "Lights and Shadows," 22; *Gary Post-Tribune*, March 10 and April 8, 1932. August Interview.

91. *Gary Post-Tribune*, April 8, 1932.

92. Thomas Stebbins Pierce, "The Curious Individual and the Churches." See August Interview.

93. August's best friend in Gary was James Foster of Christ Episcopal Church, who "crystallizes for me my ideal of what a minister should be in a man, thoughtful, kindly, reserved and one who steadfastly shuns publicity." *Gary Post-Tribune*, April 3 and April 7, 1932; August Interview.

94. *Gary Post-Tribune*, April 8, 1932.

95. Frohman, "Pastoral Hospitality," 7; Lane, "*City of the Century,*" 173.

96. Lane, "*City of the Century,*" 191, 241; Frohman, "Pastoral Hospitality," 7; *Gary Post-Tribune*, September 26 and October 17, 1938, and May 4, 1941.

97. *Presbyterian Life*, October 15, 1949; *Gary Post-Tribune*, March 7, 1949.

98. *Presbyterian Life*, October 15, 1949; Lane, "*City of the Century,*" 248–49.

99. First Presbyterian Church, Bulletin, November 5, 1950, First Presbyterian Church Records.

100. Lane, "*City of the Century,*" 251. Backemeyer excepted from his indictment former Mayor Floyd Williams, a member of First Presbyterian Church who had run with Ku Klux Klan support in 1925. At Williams's funeral in 1951 Backemeyer wished that "all holders of public office were as upright, as honest, as sincere, as unselfish and as free from any form of corruption as Floyd Williams has been." See *Gary Post-Tribune*, January 15, 1951, and May 24 and July 3, 1954.

101. *Gary Post-Tribune*, November 17, 1926, and February 7, 1927; Backemeyer, "In Loving Remembrance," 16.

102. *Gary Post-Tribune*, January 10, 1935.

103. See First Presbyterian Church, Pastor's Reports to Annual Meeting for 1955, 1956, 1957, 1958, First Presbyterian Church Records, and table 3.

104. First Presbyterian Church, Fiftieth Anniversary Booklet; Call Interview.

105. Pastor's Report to Annual Meeting, January 18, 1956; "Report of the Planning Committee, First Presbyterian Church, Gary, Indiana," December 6, 1956, 1, 4–6, First Presbyterian Church Records.

106. *Gary Post-Tribune*, October 11, 1958; First Presbyterian Church, Fiftieth Anniversary Booklet, 2; Pastor's Report to Annual Meeting, January 20, 1959, and January 26, 1960. After 1959, membership figures were omitted from the pastor's annual report.

107. Frohman, "Pastoral Hospitality," 8–9; Session Minutes, Meetings of October 5, 1959, January 4, 1960, and March 7, 1960; Pastor's Report to Annual Meeting, January 24, 1961.

108. Pastor's Report to Annual Meeting, January 23, 1963; "Report of the Long Range Planning Committee to the Congregation of the First Presbyterian Church, January 22, 1963," First Presbyterian Church Records. See also table 3 above.

109. Long Range Planning Committee Minutes, Meetings of May 17, 1962, and February 13, March 13, and April 10, 1963.

110. Pastor's Report to Annual Meeting, January 23, 1962, January 23, 1963, January 21, 1964; Session Minutes, Meeting of September 8, 1964. Haines, educated at Waynesburg College and Pittsburgh Theological Seminary, came from First Presbyterian Church in East McKeesport, Pennsylvania. *Gary Post-Tribune*, September 27, 1969.

111. First Presbyterian Church, Pastor's Report to Annual Meeting, January 17, 1967, January 23, 1968; Session Minutes, Meeting of October 13, 1969; Frohman, "Pastoral Hospitality," 9. *Gary Post-Tribune*, September 27, 1969.

112. Frohman, "Pastoral Hospitality," 7; Session Minutes, Meeting of October 13, 1969; Pastoral Nominating Committee of First Presbyterian Church, "The Present Church—Gary First Presbyterian, January 1970," First Presbyterian Church Records.

113. Session Minutes, Meetings of November 7, 1960, and December 5, 1960; Pastor's Report to Annual Meeting, January 23, 1962.

114. Minutes of Long Range Planning Committee, Meeting of October 11, 1961.

115. Session Minutes, Meeting of October 13, 1969; Len Coventry, "Data Relating to Communicant Membership of U[nited] P[resbyterian] Churches in the Calumet Cluster, Years 1960 Through 1968" (chart prepared for a meeting of Calumet Cluster of Churches of Presbytery, January 18, 1970 and a meeting of Session of First Presbyterian Church on February 2, 1970); Report of Pastoral Nominating Committee to Session, December 1, 1969, First Presbyterian Church Records.

116. Session Minutes, Meeting of October 13, 1969.

117. Kelley and Greene, "Reconnaissance Study," 34, 26; Pastoral Nominating Committee, "The Present Church," January 1970, a report prepared for the congregation and filed with the Session Minutes; Session Minutes, Meeting of October 13, 1969. The conclusion concerning Hispanics, however, cannot be confirmed by the census, which reported only fifty-four Mexicans and no Puerto Ricans. But the census identified 523 residents as "all others and not reported," and it is conceivable that many of them were Hispanic. The black population of the census tract increased to 1,007 out of 3,974 (25.3 percent) by 1970 and to 2,105 out of 2,999 (70.2 percent) by 1980. The figures for the neighboring census tract containing City Methodist Church were very similar. See Bureau of the Census, *U.S. Census of Population and Housing: 1960,* PHC (1)-54, p. 16; Bureau of the Census, *1970 Census of Population and Housing: Census Tracts,* PHC (1)-79, p. 3; Bureau of the Census, *1980 Census of Population and Housing: Census Tracts,* PHC 80-2-169.

118. See Session Minutes, March 5, 1956; Call Interview.

119. Don Snead, "White Racism in Indiana," prepared for Staff of Synod of Indiana, July 1969, First Presbyterian Church Records; Session Minutes, Meeting of October 13, 1969; Pastor's Report to Annual Meeting, January 19, 1965.

120. Long Range Planning Committee Minutes, Meeting of April 8, 1964; Trustee Records for 1969; Session Minutes, Meetings of June 29, 1969. The Black Manifesto demanded reparations payments from white churches for past oppression of black people. See "Black Manifesto," *Time* 93, May 16, 1969, 94.

121. Session Minutes, Meetings of March 10, 1963; January 21, 1964; January 17, April 3, and May 1, 1967; May 1, 1968; June 2, July 30, and November 21, 1969; September 21 and October 19, 1970; Frohman, "Pastoral Hospitality," 10. See Pastor's Report to Annual Meeting (given by Clerk of the Session), January 27, 1970.

122. Session Minutes, Meeting of September 24, 1969; Pastor's Report to Annual Meeting (given by Clerk of the Session), January 27, 1970; Report of Pastoral Nominating Committee to Session, November 3, 1969.

123. Report of Pastoral Nominating Committee to Session, December 1, 1969, and January 2, 1970.

124. Report of Pastoral Nominating Committee to Session, December 1, 1969; Pastoral Nominating Committee, "The Future of Our Church," report prepared for the congregation and filed with Session Minutes, Meeting of December 1, 1969; Session Minutes, Meetings of November 7, 1960, and April 19, 1970. Educated at the University of California in Berkeley and the San Francisco Theological Seminary, Valentine had been active in urban issues while serving as an assistant pastor in San Francisco. *Gary Post-Tribune,* June 60, 1970.

125. Session Minutes, Meetings of April 19, May 18, and December 3, 1970.

126. Session Minutes, Meeting of December, 1, 1969.

127. Session Minutes, Meetings of January 5, January 16, February 2, and March 2, 1970.

128. Frohman, "Pastoral Hospitality," 12; Session Minutes, Meetings of December 8, 1969, and October 5, 1959.

129. Report of Pastoral Nominating Committee to Session, December 1, 1969; Session Minutes, Meetings of December 1, 1969, November 6, 1970, December 21, 1970; "Report of Joint Strategy Committee of Gary Churches, Urban Committee of National Mission, Presbytery of Logansport," November 23, 1970, First Presbyterian Church Records.

130. Herbert Valentine, "Which Way First," December 1971, First Presbyterian Church Records; "Covenant for a Multi-church" in "Conference Charge" folder, Document Case 58, and Task Force Considering Relationship(s) between City United Methodist Church and First Presbyterian Church, "Synopsis of Meeting Held Thursday, April 6, 1972, at City United Methodist Church," in "House of Worship" folder, Document Case 115, both in DePauw University Archives; First Presbyterian Church, "Report of Mission Strategy Committee of First Presbyterian Church to the Task Force Considering Merger," May 4, 1972, First Presbyterian Church Records; City Methodist Church, Administrative Board Minutes, Meeting of May 21, 1972, Document Case 58, DePauw University Archives.

131. See map attached to Coventry, "Data Relating to Communicant Membership," in First Presbyterian Church, Session Records for 1970. In late 1970, for example, the Session approved a proposal to provide some ministerial assistance to other Presbyterian churches where the situation was "deteriorating," especially Brunswick and East Side, and First Presbyterian Church participated in a Thanksgiving Service with East Side that year. It was reported in 1970 that Brunswick's membership had declined during the 1960s from 425 to 145, and it had been without a minister for eighteen months. Its 1970 expected income was approximately $15,000. See Session Minutes, Meetings of May 18, September 21, and October 19, 1970. Frohman, "Pastoral Hospitality," 11; interview with Roderic Frohman, Gary, Indiana, February 17, 1984.

132. East Side joined the merged congregation on July 1, 1975. Frohman, "Pastoral Hospitality," 11; First Presbyterian Church, "Operating Assumptions for Merger," statement attached to merger covenant statement ratified December 9, 1973, First Presbyterian Church Records.

133. Valentine took over a church of 869 members in 1970 and left one of 302 in 1977. Under Frohman, the church was almost equally divided between white and black members. See Frohman, "Pastoral Hospitality," 11, 12, 14.

CHAPTER 7

1. William F. Switzer, "Notes for Gary First Methodist Church History," [1934], 1, Document Case 116, and Beatrice Lewis, "Methodism in Gary," 1956,

1, both in DePauw University Archives; C. O. Holmes, "First Blast Furnace at Lake's Edge, Holmes Says," clipping from *Gary Post-Tribune*, [1931], in *Biographical Sketches of Gary and Lake County Resident*, s.v. "Holmes," Gary Public Library.

2. Switzer, "Notes," 1; "First Methodist Church," *Gary Tribune*, June 11, 1909.

3. *Northern Indianan*, January 24, 1908; Switzer, "Notes," 1; C. O. Holmes, "First Blast Furnace"; *Gary Post-Tribune*, June 3, 1954; Lake County Historical Society, *Personal Records* (Gary, Indiana: Gary Public Library, 1923), Gary Public Library; Meister, "History of Gary," 16.

4. Switzer, "Notes," 1; George E. Deuel, "Lives in Abandoned Factory; Organizes Methodist Church," clipping from *Gary Post-Tribune*, [1931], in DePauw University Archives. The issue of primacy among Gary's churches is a complicated one. Although Deuel claimed he was the first pastor in Gary, Ora Wildermuth claimed both that A. J. Sullens came to Gary as the Congregationalist minister in early 1907, several months before the formal organization of that church, and that "we are the oldest church in the city." See Wildermuth, "Early Days in Gary," 8. In addition, Quillen reported that Father Thomas Jansen organized a Roman Catholic congregation in Gary as early as May 1906. See Quillen, "Industrial City," 172.

5. Northwest Indiana Conference, Methodist Episcopal Church, *Minutes of Annual Conference* (Crawfordsville, Ind.: Review Press, 1907), 258 hereafter cited as "Northwest Indiana Conference, *Minutes*." The exact title of the Annual Conference *Minutes* varied as denominational mergers occurred and as conference boundaries changed. The denomination's names during the period were: "Methodist Episcopal Church" through 1938, "Methodist Church" from 1939 to 1967, and "United Methodist Church" since 1968. Gary was part of the Northwest Indiana Conference from 1906 to 1967 and part of the North Indiana Conference after 1967. See also Lewis, "Methodism," 5.

6. "First Methodist Church," *Gary Tribune*, June 11, 1909; Lane, "*City of the Century*", 13; Deuel, "Lives in Abandoned Factory"; Rae K. Pritchard, "Visit by Methodist Elder," clipping from *Gary Post-Tribune*, [1931] in "City Methodist Church" folder, DePauw University Archives.

7. Switzer, "Notes," 2; Lane, "*City of the Century*," 44; Lewis, "Methodism," 3.

8. Lewis, "Methodism," 2; First Methodist Church, *Church Promoter* 4 (July 1915):1, DePauw University Archives; Northwest Indiana Conference, *Minutes*, 1908, 1909. The *Church Promoter* was a newsletter published during the pastorate of Joseph Avann. The Presbyterians reported 35 and 84 members in those two years; see table 3 in ch. 6.

9. Contrary to some reports, Judge Gary did not donate the lots; he did, however, contribute 60 percent of the purchase price, and the Gary Land Company waived the remainder. See Lewis, "Methodism," 3; Northwest Indiana Conference, *Minutes*, 1909, 164; Switzer, "Notes," 2.

10. Switzer, "Notes," 2; First Methodist Church, Gary, Indiana, Minutes of Quarterly Conference Meetings, Meeting of May 13, 1911, DePauw University

Archives (hereafter cited as "Quarterly Conference Minutes"); Northwest Indiana Conference, *Minutes,* 1911, 433.

11. First Methodist Church, Gary, Indiana, Minutes of Official Board Meetings, Meeting of May 20, 1912, Document Case 115, DePauw University Archives (hereafter cited as "Official Board Minutes"); Northwest Indiana Conference, *Minutes,* 1911, 433.

12. Switzer, "Notes," 2; Lewis, "Methodism," 4; "First Methodist Church," *Gary Tribune,* June 11, 1909. The early Gary press noted that the Protestant churches were building with the future in mind. See *Gary Daily Tribune,* December 7, 1908.

13. Northwest Indiana Conference, *Minutes,* 1910; Quarterly Conference Minutes, Meeting of October 12, 1909; *Gary Tribune,* September 23, 1910; Lewis, "Methodism," 4.

14. *Gary Tribune,* June 5, 1916; *Church Promoter* 4 (October 1915), City Church Box, Calumet Regional Archives.

15. Northwest Indiana Conference, *Minutes,* 1907, 1908, 1909, 1910, 1911.

16. *Church Promoter* 1 (January 1912), Document Case 116, DePauw University Archives.

17. *Church Promoter* 1 (February 1912), Document Case 116, DePauw University Archives.

18. *Church Promoter* 4 (July 1915) and 4(October 1915); Quarterly Conference Minutes, Meeting of November 15, 1911; Lewis, "Methodism," 5; Official Board Minutes, Meetings of October 14, 1912, November 3, 1913, December 1, 1913.

19. See *Church Promoter* 4 (July 1915), City Church Box, Calumet Regional Archives.

20. Northwest Indiana Conference, *Minutes,* 1912, 1915; Lewis, "Methodism," 5; *Church Promoter* 4 (October 1915), City Church Box, Calumet Regional Archives.

21. *Church Promoter* 4 (October 1915), City Church Box, Calumet Regional Archives; Northwest Indiana Conference, *Minutes,* 1912, 1913, 1914, 1915.

22. Official Board Minutes, Meeting of October 12, 1914; *Church Promoter* 4 July 1915). By late 1915, the steel mills were again becoming active, and "the outlook is full of promise." See *Church Promoter* 4 (October 1915), City Church Box, Calumet Regional Archives.

23. Quarterly Conference Minutes, Meetings of November 15, 1911, and February 14, 1912; Official Board Minutes, Meetings of March 3, 1912, and September 7, 1914; *Church Promoter* 1 (July 1912), Document Case 116, DePauw University Archives.

24. See, for example, Quarterly Conference Minutes, Meeting of March 30, 1914, and Official Board Minutes, Meeting of October 30, 1912. Because of the

early mobility of the population, people were often reluctant to pledge. Consequently pledges for the new building were "for thirty-six months or as long as they remained in Gary if they moved sooner." See *Church Promoter* 4 (October 1915), City Church Box, Calumet Regional Archives. The pledges for the new building varied widely. By October 1912, C. O. Holmes had pledged $1,010, William Wirt $250 and T. E. Knotts $100. See *Church Promoter* 1 (October 1912), Document Case 116, DePauw University Archives.

25. Official Board Minutes, Meetings of April 4, 1912; February 10, 1913; December 7, 1914; March 1, 1915; June 7, 1915; November 1, 1915; December 12, 1915.

26. Quarterly Conference Minutes, Meeting of June 30, 1913; Official Board Minutes, Meetings of October 25, 1911, and September 9, 1912.

27. *Church Promoter* 3 (March 1914) and 4 (July 1915); Quarterly Conference Minutes, meeting of March 30, 1914; Official Board Minutes, meetings of October 16, 1913; November 3, 1913; and January 12, 1914; June 7, 1915 and March 6, 1916; *Church Promoter* 4 (October 1915), City Church Box, Calumet Regional Archives.

28. Official Board Minutes, Meetings of October 14, 1912; November 3, 1913; January 12, 1914.

29. *Gary Tribune,* June 6, 1916.

30. *Church Promoter* 1 (December 1911), City Church Box, Calumet Regional Archives; *Church Promoter* 1 (January 1912), Document Case 116, DePauw University Archives.

31. The W.H.M.S. had been organized in 1884 to support work in urban centers; see Jack J. Detzler, *The History of the Northwest Indiana Conference of the Methodist Church 1852–1951* (Nashville: Parthenon Press, 1953), 85. Switzer, "Notes," 16; *Gary Post-Tribune,* October 7, 1926; *Church Promoter* 2 (March 1913), City Church Box, Calumet Regional Archives.

32. *Gary Tribune,* September 23, 1910; Switzer, "Notes," 6, 20; Quillen, "Industrial City," 143–44.

33. Quarterly Conference Minutes, Meeting of June 30, 1913; Switzer, "Notes," 20, 21; Crocker, "Sympathy and Science," p. 301.

34. Detzler, *Northwest Indiana Conference,* 123. Detzler states that Methodists were leaders in the movement throughout Indiana. *Church Promoter* 4 (October 1915), City Church Box, Calumet Regional Archives.

35. Quarterly Conference Minutes, Meeting of November 15, 1911; William Grant Seaman, typewritten historical sketch, [1925], 3, DePauw University Archives (hereafter cited as Seaman, "Historical Sketch").

36. The church appointed a Methodist minister, H. W. Farrington, as its superintendent of religious education for the first year of the weekday church schools in 1914–15, and he reported regularly to the Official Board on their progress. See Official Board Minutes, Meetings of November 3, 1913, September 7,

1914, November 2, 1914, December 7, 1914, June 7, 1915; *Church Promoter* 4 (July and October 1915), City Church Box, Calumet Regional Archives.

37. *Gary Tribune*, June 5 and June 6, 1916; Seaman, "Historical Sketch," 3; *Gary Post-Tribune*, October 7, 1926.

38. Switzer, "Notes," 4; *Gary Post-Tribune*, October 7, 1926; J. D. Schwarz, ed., *Who's Who in the Clergy*, 2 vols. (New York: n.p., 1936, 1942) 1:1013; Seaman Interview; William R. Seaman to James Lewis, January 31, 1983; *Comprehensive Dissertation Index, 1861–1972* (Ann Arbor: Xerox Univ Microfilms, 1973), 37:2; *Gary Post-Tribune*, October 1 and 7, 1926; Lane, "*City of the Century*," 112.

39. In 1907 he had married Laura Rice. Throughout his career in Gary she remained an important ally and coworker. Seaman Interview; Switzer, "Notes," 5; Quillen, "Industrial City," 451; Lane, "*City of the Century*," 112; Lewis, "Methodism," 5–6; *Gary Post-Tribune*, October 7, 1926.

40. Lane suggests that Seaman's departure in 1929 reflected some sentiment that the congregation needed "an efficient man, not a liberal visionary," and Richard Meister, in recounting the difficulties of the church during the Depression, said the building "stood as a brutal reminder of the dreams of the prosperous twenties." See James B. Lane, "City Church Needed a Miracle," *Gary Post-Tribune*, September 15, 1974; Meister, "History of Gary," 94.

41. Davis Interview; William Clark to James Lewis, December 17, 1984; City Methodist Church, Twenty-Fifth Anniversary Program, 1951, in "Protestant Organizations" folder, Gary Public Library.

42. Except for a few articles on weekday religious education, he wrote little for general publication. To my knowledge, he did not publish his sermons, and no manuscript collection of them has survived. One of his sons claimed that Seaman neither wrote out his sermons nor used notes in the pulpit. See Charles F. Seaman to James Lewis, February, 13, 1983.

43. This Methodist turn toward social concerns in the first two or three decades of the twentieth century was illustrated, for example, by Frank Mason North, who was one of the principal drafters of the Methodist Social Creed, a forerunner of the Social Creed of the Churches adopted by the Federal Council of Churches in 1908. See Detzler, *Northwest Indiana Conference*, 124, 126; *Encyclopedia of World Methodism*, s.v. "North, Frank Mason" by Creighton Lacy.

44. Switzer, "Notes," 4.

45. See, for example, William McKinney, David A. Roozen, Jackson W. Carroll, *Religion's Public Presence: Community Leaders Assess the Contribution of Churches and Synagogues* (Washington, D.C. Alban Institute, 1982), and Coalter, Mulder, and Weeks, eds., *The Presbyterian Predicament*, 10.

46. *City Church Items*, March 9, 1927; William Grant Seaman (compiler), "The Calumet Region," Gary, Indiana, 1921, 8 (typewritten Report "presented to

Dr. M. P. Burns, and to the District Superintendents of the Northwest Indiana Conference, at a special Committee Meeting held in Gary, Indiana, July 6, 1921"), Document Case 116, "Trustee Material 1925–69" folder, DePauw University Archives; William Grant Seaman, "Cultivating the Religious Life of Public School Children," *Homiletic Review* 89 (January 1925):53; Seaman and Abernethy, *Community Schools,* 3; William Grant Seaman, "The City System of Week-Day Schools," *Religious Education* 17 (June 1922):212.

47. William Grant Seaman to H. S. Norton, February 6, 1920, and [William Grant Seaman], "Program of the Methodist Episcopal Church, Gary, Indiana," c. 1920, both in Document Case 60, DePauw University Archives. A copy of the letter to Norton is also in the City Church Box at the Calumet Regional Archives. Many documents in DePauw's City Methodist Collection, although not attributed specifically to Seaman, were evidently written by him, as indicated by writing style, word choice, and so forth. I indicate my assumption of Seaman's authorship by the use of square brackets around his name in note citations of these works.

48. Official Board Minutes, meeting of September 23, 1920; William Grant Seaman to D. D. Forsyth, December 1916, DePauw University Archives; Seaman, "City System of Week-Day Schools," 213; Seaman to Norton, February 6, 1920.

49. City Methodist Church, Souvenir Booklet, October 3–10, 1926; Lewis, "Methodism," 22. To a four-page outline of the "Types of Ministry" to be rendered by City Church, Seaman appended a list of thirty-three ministries taken from H. Paul Douglass, *1000 City Churches: Phases of Adaptation to Urban Environment* (New York: George H. Doran Co., 1926). See [William Grant Seaman], "Types of Ministry," n.d., Document Case 116, DePauw University Archives.

50. See Vidich and Lyman, *American Sociology,* 1, 3–5, 112; Lees, *Cities Perceived,* 219, 254–55.

51. Seaman, "Historical Sketch," 4; Seaman, "Calumet Region," 7–8.

52. Seaman, "Calumet Region," 3–5; Louis Wirth, "Urbanism as a Way of Life, 150, 156, 159, 161, 162; [William Grant Seaman], "Askings for the Building Program," 1920, Document Case 60, DePauw University Archives; [Seaman], "Program of the Methodist Episcopal Church."

53. William Clark to James Lewis, December 17, 1984.

54. William Grant Seaman to H. S. Norton, July 6, 1920, Document Case 115, DePauw University Archives; King, "Emergence of Social Gospel Radicalism," 443; Genevieve B. Rice to James Lewis, April 9, 1983; Lane, "*City of the Century,*" 112. See, for example, the resolution on "industrial conditions," produced by a four-member committee on which Seaman served, presented to the Northwest Indiana Conference. Noting that "long hours of continuous employment in industry tends to the destruction of those sentiments, attitudes, and relations which constitute a really human life," the resolution praised U.S. Steel for adopting the eight-hour day and saluted developments in industry which led to "securing to

employees a voice in the management, profit-sharing, security of position, continuous employment, retiring pensions, and other co-operative plans." See Northwest Indiana Conference, *Minutes,* 1923. Detzler reports (*History of Northwest Indiana Conference,* 126) that during the first quarter of the century the Northwest Indiana Conference supported moderate labor demands for wages, working conditions, and so forth, but deplored attacks on private property. For a good example of this position, see Northwest Indiana Conference, *Minutes,* 1919, 444.

55. First Methodist Church, Untitled Historical Sketch of Music Program, City Methodist Box, Calumet Regional Archives; Shumway, "Gary: Shrine of the Steel God," 29; Switzer, "Notes," 16, 18; Lewis, "Methodism," 13, 14; "Romance of City Church Architecture," DePauw University Archives.

56. Seaman, "Historical Sketch," 3; [William Grant Seaman], "First Methodist Episcopal Church, Gary, Indiana," [1923], Document Case 60; [William Grant Seaman], "What the Centenary Has Done to Meet the Home Missionary Challenge in Gary, Indiana," [1924 or 1925], all in DePauw University Archives; Seaman, "Cultivating the Religious Life of Public School Children," 51, 53, 54. A *Post-Tribune* headline in 1926, for example, proclaimed of City Church: "Efficient Personnel in Charge of Church Program." See *Gary Post-Tribune,* October 7, 1926.

57. Seaman, "Historical Sketch," 3; Lewis, "Methodism," 6; Seaman to Forsyth, December 1916; *Gary Post-Tribune,* October 7, 1926.

58. Squires, *Gary Plan of Church Schools,* 10; *Gary Post-Tribune,* May 11, 1921, and November 30, 1926; Seaman and Abernethy, *Community Schools,* 4–6; Seaman, "Historical Sketch," 5; Soares, "Status of Week-Day Religious School," 135–36.

59. [Seaman], "What the Centenary Has Done," 6; Seaman, "Calumet Region," 7; Seaman, "Cultivating Religious Life of Public School Children," 51; Seaman and Abernethy, *Community Schools,* 3; *Gary Post-Tribune,* October 7, 1926; Seaman, "Historical Sketch," 5.

60. H. R. DeBra, who remained an important figure in local Methodist circles for the next two decades, served as its secretary, and C. O. Holmes of First Methodist Church as its president. See Seaman, "Historical Sketch," 3; *Gary Post-Tribune,* November 19, 1937, and July 14, 1939; Northwest Indiana Conference, *Minutes,* 1917, 165.

61. Seaman, "Historical Sketch," 3; *Encyclopedia of World Methodism,* 1974 ed., s.v. "Centenary Fund," by Elmer T. Clark; First Methodist Church, Souvenir Booklet, 1926; Detzler, *Northwest Indiana Conference,* 124, 141; Lewis, "Methodism," 8.

62. H. R. DeBra, "Report of the Executive Secretary of the Calumet Missionary Society to the Northwest Indiana Conference," Mimeograph, 1923, DePauw University Archives.

63. Lewis, "Methodism," 8; [Seaman], "What the Centenary Has Done," 3, 4;

Gary Post-Tribune, October 4, 1926; Seaman, "Historical Sketch," 3, 4; Seaman, "Calumet Region," 7.

64. *Gary Post-Tribune,* October 7, 1926; Seaman, "Historical Sketch," 4–5.

65. [Seaman], "What the Centenary Has Done," 5; Seaman "Historical Sketch," 4; *Gary Post-Tribune,* September 16, 1929; Seaman, "Calumet Region," 2, 7–8.

66. Seaman to Forsyth, December 1916; Seaman, "The Calumet Region."

67. *Gary Post-Tribune,* October 7, 1926; Switzer, "Notes," 23–24; Lewis, "Methodism," 8; Schwarz, *Who's Who in the Clergy;* Lane, "*City of the Century,*" 113; [Seaman], "What the Centenary Has Done," 4.

68. Seaman, "Historical Sketch," 4.

69. Mohl and Betten, however, describe Seaman as an unrelenting racist, basing their conclusion heavily on the 1920 letter from Seaman to H. S. Norton, discussed below. See their *Steel City,* 64. I contend that Seaman's relationship with black people was far more complex than they suggest, with racism only one factor.

70. Frank S. Delaney, "History of Trinity Methodist Episcopal Church and the John Stewart Memorial Settlement House," Mimeograph, [1935], 1, and Arthur W. Davis, "History, John Stewart Settlement House," Mimeograph, n.d., 2, both in Gary Area Churches Box, Calumet Regional Archives.

71. Delaney, "History of Trinity," 3.

72. According to Crocker, the black subdivision was probably intended to reduce turnover among U.S. Steel's black employees. Although criticized by several blacks, it was praised by the white Calumet Church Federation. See Crocker, "Sympathy and Sciences," 433–34.

73. Gary's black population had increased, in part due to U.S. Steel recruitment practices during World War I and the 1919 steel strike. See Seaman to Norton, July 6, 1920, William Grant Seaman to Elbert Gary, July 1, 1920, both letters in Document Case 115, "Official Board" folder, DePauw University Archives; [Seaman], "Program of the Methodist Episcopal Church," 14.

74. Seaman to Norton, July 6, 1920.

75. Two women in particular, Mrs. J. H. Eppler and Mrs. H. J. Snyder, were concerned about the plight of black former service men who found themselves jobless in the depression of 1921 and asked Trinity to begin a ministry to them. See Delaney, "History of Trinity," 3; Seaman, "Calumet Region," 8.

76. Delaney, "History of Trinity," 3–5; Davis, "History, Stewart Settlement House," 1; "Statement of Significance," Stewart House Folder in Gary Area Churches Box, Calumet Regional Archives. In addition to the site for Stewart House, U.S. Steel provided $25,000. The Methodist Board of Home Missions and Church extension gave another $18,000. Seaman's letter to Norton, however, had requested $150,000. See Seaman to Norton, July 6, 1920, and "Statement of Significance," 3. According to Crocker ("Sympathy and Science," 445–46), U.S.

Steel also paid off the remaining $60,000 debt of Stewart House in 1923, an action criticized in the black press.

77. Crocker, "Sympathy and Science," 432, 428, 447.

78. Mohl and Betten, *Steel City,* 64; Seaman to Norton, July 6, 1920. See also Crocker's discussion of the letter in "Sympathy and Science," 440–41.

79. Seaman to Norton, July 6, 1920; Seaman, "Calumet Region," 4; [Seaman], "What Centenary Has Done," 5.

80. W. R. Seaman to James Lewis, January 31, 1983; Lane, *"City of the Century,"* 114–15.

81. The Commission on Race Relations of the Federal Council of Churches began Race Relations Sundays in 1923; see David W. Wills, "An Enduring Distance: Black Americans and the Establishment, in *Between the Times,* ed. Hutchison, 178. In this respect, Gary was in tune with wider Protestant practices. *City Church Items,* February 7, 1928; *Gary Post-Tribune,* February 14, 1927; [Seaman], "Types of Ministry," 3; Camden H. West, "Will Preach First Serman There Sunday," *Gary Post-Tribune,* September 11, 1929.

82. Seaman, "Historical Sketch," 7; Lewis, "Methodism," 12.

83. Interview with Elbert Cole, Chicago, Ill., May 31, 1985.

84. Seaman to Forsyth, December 1916. Seaman's public writings and extant correspondence on his vision for City Church date from as early as 1916 and extend through the completion of the building in October 1926.

85. [Seaman], "Program of Methodist Episcopal Church," 4, 8, 16; [Seaman], "First Methodist Episcopal Church . . . Types of Ministry," 9.

86. [Seaman], "Program of Methodist Episcopal Church," 4, 9–10. See also [Seaman], "First Methodist Episcopal Church," 11, 13, 14.

87. Goldfield and Brownell, *Urban America,* 292–93; [Seaman], "First Methodist Episcopal Church," 2; [Seaman], "What the Centenary Has Done," 3. In his 1920 report as Corresponding Secretary of the Calumet Missionary Society, H. R. DeBra noted of Seaman's proposed downtown church that "its ministry will not be so directly devoted to the alien peoples, but to the ethical and social well-being of the whole community, in which the aliens will share." See Northwest Indiana Conference, *Minutes,* 1920, 63.

88. An earlier, blander, version of the motto referred to "making the Christ to walk, a Living Presence, through its streets," indicating how much power was lost when the metaphor of the heart was omitted. See City Methodist Church Bulletin, October 10, 1926, and "The City Church," (a fund-raising brochure), 2, both in Document Case 60, DePauw University Archives; *Gary Post-Tribune,* October 15, 1926; [Seaman], "What the Centenary Has Done," 7.

89. [Seaman], "Program of Methodist Episcopal Church," 4; [Seaman], "Askings for the Building Program," 3; [Seaman], "First Methodist Episcopal Church," 2.

90. "The City Church"; [Seaman], "Askings for the Building Program," 3;

[Seaman], "Program of Methodist Episcopal Church," 6; Seaman to Norton, February 6, 1920.

91. *Gary Post-Tribune,* October 15, 1926. See also First Methodist Church, Souvenir Booklet from the Opening and Dedication of City Church, October 3–10, 1926, and "The City Church," both in Document Case, 60, DePauw University Archives.

92. [Seaman], "First Methodist Episcopal Church," 3; [Seaman], "First Methodist Episcopal Church . . . Types of Ministry," 6; *Gary Post-Tribune,* October 5, 1926; "Statements Bearing on Construction of . . . a Downtown Church," 10, Document Case 60, DePauw University Archives.

93. [Seaman], "First Methodist Episcopal Church," 3; [Seaman], "First Methodist Episcopal Church . . . Types of Ministry," 8; "Floor Plans, City Methodist Church," in "Building Fund 1933–1945" folder, Document Case 58, DePauw University Archives. On the roof garden fiasco, see *Epworth Herald,* February 19, 1927, and Lane, "*City of the Century,*" 116.

94. Seaman to Forsyth, December 1916; [Seaman], "The Proposed New First Church, Gary," Document Case 60, DePauw University Archives; [Seaman], "Program of First Methodist Episcopal Church," 9; Seaman, "Calumet Region," 5, 6; "Statements Bearing on Construction of . . . a Downtown Church."

95. *Gary Post-Tribune,* October 15, 1926; First Methodist Church, Souvenir Booklet; [Seaman], "First Methodist Episcopal Church," 3; "The City Church."

96. [Seaman], "What the Centenary Has Done," 1; [Seaman], "First Methodist Episcopal Church . . . Types of Ministry," 2; [Seaman], "Askings for Building Program," 4; [Seaman], "Program of Methodist Episcopal Church," 1.

97. [Seaman], "First Methodist Episcopal Church . . . Types of Ministry," 4; [Seaman], "Program of Methodist Episcopal Church," 5.

98. Seaman, "City System of Weekday Schools," 212, 213; [Seaman], "Program of Methodist Episcopal Church," 7; [Seaman], "First Methodist Episcopal Church . . . Types of Ministry," 2, 3.

99. "The City Church"; [Seaman], "First Methodist Episcopal Church . . . Types of Ministry," 3; [Seaman], "Program of Methodist Episcopal Church," 6. Whether they collaborated or not, Seaman's ideas on recreation were remarkably similar to those of his parishioner, William Wirt. See Wirt, "The Great Lockout."

100. *Gary Post-Tribune,* October 8 and 15, 1926; Clark to Lewis, December 17, 1984.

101. Seaman, "Calumet Region," 4; [Seaman], "Askings for the Building Program," 4; "The City Church."

102. *Gary Post-Tribune,* October 4 and 15, 1926; "The City Church"; Seaman, "Romance of City Church Architecture," Document Case 60, DePauw University Archives.

103. Seaman, "Romance of City Church Architecture"; "The City Church";

Gary Post-Tribune, October 8, 1926; [Seaman], "Program of Methodist Episcopal Church," 4.

104. [Seaman], "Askings for Building Program," 4; Seaman to Norton, February 6, 1920.

105. Lewis, "Methodism," 6.

106. *Gary Post-Tribune,* July 14, 1939; Seaman, "Historical Sketch," 3; Lewis, "Methodism," 8; [Seaman], "Program of Methodist Episcopal Church," 13; Northwest Indiana Conference, *Minutes,* 1917, 165, and *Minutes,* 1919, 457.

107. Seaman to Forsyth, December 1916, and Seaman to Norton, February 6, 1920; [Seaman], "Proposed New First Church, Gary," 1.

108. Seaman, "Historical Sketch," 5.

109. Seaman to Norton, February 6, 1920.

110. [Seaman], "Proposed New First Church, Gary."

111. First Methodist Church, Souvenir Booklet; *Gary Post-Tribune,* October 7, 1926; Seaman, "Historical Sketch," 6.

112. See Davis Interview; Lane, *"City of the Century,"* 115.

113. William Grant Seaman to Elbert Gary, July 1, 1920, Document Case 115, DePauw University Archives.

114. [Seaman], "Proposed New First Church, Gary," 1; Quarterly Conference Minutes, Meeting of July 11, 1920.

115. Official Board Minutes, Meeting of September 23, 1920.

116. Official Board Minutes, Meeting of September 26, 1920.

117. *Gary Post-Tribune,* October 7, 1926; Seaman, "Historical Sketch," 6; Seaman to W. J. Elliott (treasurer, Board of Home Missions and Church Extension), December 16, 1924, DePauw University Archives.

118. Official Board Minutes, Meeting of April 18, 1921; [Seaman], "Proposed New First Church, Gary," 2. The secretary of the YMCA and the superintendent of schools made one of the trips and participated in the study of downtown churches in order to avoid a duplication of services.

119. For a detailed account of this struggle, see Lewis, "At Home in the City," 314–22.

120. See "Program for the Opening and Dedication of the City Church, First Methodist Episcopal, Gary, Indiana," October 3–10, 1926, Document Case 60, DePauw University Archives; *Gary Post-Tribune,* October 4, 8, and 11, 1926; Switzer, "Notes," 9; Beatrice Lewis, "Methodism," 13; First Methodist Church, Bulletin, October 3, 1926.

121. *Gary Post-Tribune,* October 4, 1926.

122. Ibid., November 17 and 18, 1926; *City Church Items,* June 8, 1927.

123. *Gary Post-Tribune,* November 29, 1926, and February 14, 1927; *City Church Items,* April 26 and May 19, 1927, February 7 and 22, 1928.

124. *Gary Post-Tribune,* January 21 and February 7, 1927; Clark to Lewis, December 17, 1984; *City Church Items,* May 19, 1927.

125. First Methodist Church, Historical Sketch of Music Program; *City Church Items,* March 9, 1927. Several years later, Switzer observed that "no satisfactory method or practical program has yet been found for the larger use of the facilities in Seaman Hall that were meant to and could render a much greater service here in Gary." Elbert Cole had a similar judgment during his pastorate in Gary in the 1950s. See Switzer, "Notes," 13–15; Cole Interview.

126. *City Church Items,* April 26, 1927; Switzer, "Notes," 10; First Methodist Church, "Proposed Budget 1927," and William Grant Seaman, "Endowment," Document Case 116, DePauw University Archives. Northwest Indiana Annual Conference, *Minutes,* 1927.

127. Lewis, "Methodism," 14.

128. West, "Will Preach First Sermon There Sunday."

129. Interview with William R. Seaman, Cincinnati, Ohio, November 23, 1983; Clark to Lewis, November 12 and December 10 and 20, 1984; Lane, "City Church Needed a Miracle," *Gary Post-Tribune,* September 15, 1974.

130. *Gary Post-Tribune,* September 14, 16, and 19, 1929.

131. West, "Will Preach First Sermon There Sunday"; Seaman letter to *Gary Post-Tribune,* February 2, 1932; Clark to Lewis, November 12 and December 20, 1984; *Gary Post-Tribune,* April 10, 1942.

132. Quillen, "Industrial City," 456–57; Meister, "History of Gary," 40, 94, 95; Lane, *"City of the Century,"* 116–17; Lane, "City Church Needed a Miracle," *Gary Post-Tribune,* September 15, 1974.

133. Clark to Lewis, December 17, 1984.

134. Ibid.

135. See, for example, the description of Seaman's vision in First Methodist Church, Twenty-Fifth Anniversary Program in 1951, which concluded: "The vision of Dr. Seaman is still true—'that Christ may dwell a living presence at the city's heart.'" Seaman's continuing influence was also confirmed in Clark to Lewis, December 17, 1984, and Cole Interview. See also James P. Wind and James W. Lewis, "Memory, Amnesia, and History," in *Carriers of the Faith: Lessons from Congregational Studies,* ed. Carl S. Dudley, Jackson W. Carroll, and James P. Wind (Louisville: Westminster/John Knox Press, 1991.)

136. In fairness to Millard, he and the Depression arrived simultaneously, and as his successor, William Clark, noted, "like many in that time he failed to trim the sails in time." See Lewis, "Methodism," 15; Lane, "City Church Needed a Miracle," *Gary Post-Tribune,* September 15, 1974; First Methodist Bulletins for November 2, 1930, and November 22, 1931, Document Case 115, DePauw University Archives; Clark to Lewis, November 12, 1984.

137. *Gary Post-Tribune,* March 9, 1946; interview with Herschel B. Davis, Greenwood, Ind., October 11, 1984; Clark to Lewis, December 20, 1984; Lewis, "Methodism," 15.

138. Clark to Lewis, December 20, 1984. See J. J. Booth of City Methodist

Church to F. W. Mueller, September 28, 1934, and correspondence in May 1932 with the Receiver of National Bank of America, both in Document Case 60, De-Pauw University Archives.

139. Seaman returned in October 1940, his first visit to Gary in eleven years, to help Clark in his fund-raising efforts. Clark to Lewis, December 20, 1984. See document concerning mortgage burning in December 1945 and undated 1940 article from *Gary Post-Tribune* concerning Seaman's visit, both in City Church Box, Calumet Regional Archives. H. C. Leonard of Church Extension Department to William Clark, May 8, 1946, DePauw University Archives.

140. Clark to Lewis, December 20, 1984. A "City Church Business Directory" ("Church Organizations-Protestant" folder, Gary Public Library), apparently published during the Depression, listed the professions/businesses of forty-two members, including attorney, carpenter, dentist, printer, and violin maker and repairman.

141. Clark to Lewis, December 10, 1984; Thomas F. Chilcote, Jr., "At the Heart of the Steel City," *Christian Advocate* (August 31, 1944):1079; Clark to Lewis, December 20, 1984.

142. Clark to Lewis, December 20, 1984; *Gary Post-Tribune*, June 13, 1946; pamphlet on Stewart House, March 1935, City Church Box, Calumet Regional Archives; Clark to Lewis, November 12, 1984; Chilcote, "At the Heart of the Steel City," 1079.

143. Clark to Lewis, November 12, 1984, and December 20, 1984; *Gary Post-Tribune*, November 27, 1942, and January 5, 1935; "Programs Held in City Church" folder, Document Case 115, DePauw University Archives.

144. Clark to Lewis, December 10, 1984, and December 20, 1984; *Gary Post-Tribune*, February 5, 1935; clipping from *Gary Post-Tribune*, July 1946, City Church Box, Calumet Regional Archives.

145. Floyd E. Blake, "Where Do We Go From Here?", report presented to Administrative Board, City United Methodist Church, Gary, Indiana, February 4, 1973, DePauw University Archives.

146. Davis Interview; Clark to Lewis, December 20, 1984.

147. Undated clipping from *Gary Post-Tribune*, [1946], in City Methodist Box, Calumet Regional Archives.

148. See *Gary Post-Tribune*, October 20, 21, and 25, 1947; Lewis, "Methodism," 16. See also Murray H. Leifer, "Methodism in Gary and Vicinity," Mimeograph, (Evanston: Bureau of Social and Religious Research, Garrett Biblical Institute, 1957), 29.

149. Davis Interview; Cole Interview.

150. Blake, "Where Do We Go From Here?"

151. See First Methodist Church, "Tower Talk," February 18, 1970, Document Case 115, DePauw University Archives; *Chicago Maroon*, April 30, 1985.

152. The church booklet for 1957–58 emphasized the wide variety of activities

provided for the church family, including the "City Club," an organization for "the young person working in Gary and away from home," led by the Coles themselves. In addition to reversing the membership decline, he stabilized a financial crisis caused by the removal of the Indiana University–Gary campus from the church's commercial wing. See First Methodist Church, "Tower Talk," October 10, 1956, First Presbyterian Church Records; City Methodist Church Annual Booklet for 1957–1958, Document Case 60, DePauw University Archives; Cole Interview; Elbert Cole, "The Church's Ministry to Industrial Areas," September 1958, Mimeograph, Document Case 115, DePauw University Archives; *Gary Post-Tribune,* April 20, 1956.

153. Cole Interview.

154. Cole persuaded the church to open its doors, literally, for meditation during the weekday despite some misgivings about transients taking advantage of the open building. See ibid. See also Davis Interview.

155. The bishop pulled Cole out of Gary and appointed him to a prominent church in Indianapolis in order to heal a major schism in the congregation there. According to Cole, he left with great reluctance, and in 1984 he expressed the wish that he had been allowed to remain in Gary. See Cole Interview, and Davis Interview.

156. The candidate for prosecutor, David P. Stanton, had held the office briefly in the early 1950s, thanks to the help of the Women's Citizens Committee. See *Gary Post-Tribune,* October 22 and 23, 1962.

157. Since the decline in attendance since 1950 was much less than the decline in membership, Kelley and Greene concluded that a considerable amount of City Church's membership loss was the result of inflated 1950 church membership figures. Whereas membership had declined, for example, 33 percent between 1953 and 1963, church attendance had declined only 10 percent. Moreover giving had more than doubled, going from $38,577 in 1950 to $92,941 in 1963. See Kelley and Greene, "Reconnaissance Study of the Inner City, Gary, Indiana," 41, 42, 50, 51. See also Leifer, "Methodism in Gary and Vicinity," 20.

158. See *U.S. Census of Population and Housing: 1960,* PHC 1-54, p. 16; *1970 Census of Population and Housing: Census Tracts,* PHC 1-79, p. 3; *1980 Census of Population and Housing: Census Tracts,* PHC 80-2-169.

159. S. Walton Cole and Elbert Cole were not related. *Gary Post-Tribune,* May 22, 1970. See Blake, "Where Do We Go From Here?"; First Methodist Church, Administrative Board Minutes, Meetings of December 14, 1969, and February 8, 1970; "Church Attendance" folder; all in Document Case 58, DePauw University Archives.

160. *Gary Post-Tribune,* June 27, 1970; First Methodist Church, Minutes of Annual Charge Conference, November 21, 1971, Document Case 58, DePauw University Archives; Administrative Board Minutes, Meeting of January 17, 1971.

161. Minutes of Annual Charge Conference, November 21, 1971; Admin-

istrative Board Minutes, Meetings of January 9 and February 20, 1972; various documents concerning the merger talks are filed in "Our House of Worship" folder, Document Case 115, DePauw University Archives.

162. Administrative Board Minutes, Meetings of January 9, April 16, and May 7, 1972.

163. Ibid., Meetings of May 21 and August 20, 1972; Blake, "Where Do We Go From Here?", 1.

164. Blake, "Where Do We Go From Here?", 2, 4, 5, 7.

165. Ibid., 7; Administrative Board Minutes, Meetings of February 4 and April 17, 1973; First Methodist Church, "Tower Talk," March 18, 1973, Document Case 115, DePauw University Archives.

166. Task Force on the Future of City Church, "Possibilities for City Church," February 11, 1974, and Minutes of Charge Conference, December 8, 1974, both in Document Case 58, DePauw University Archives.

167. A Committee of Nine was appointed to oversee the disposition of the building and its contents. The committee began meeting three weeks later and in January recommended a closing date of October 5, 1975, a date approved by the church on January 19. In subsequent meetings they set guidelines for the disposition of the contents of the building and for the building's lease to the city for $1.00 a year for school purposes. Later the building was sold to a black Baptist congregation. The committee also arranged for the transfer of Seaman's ashes from the chancel. See Committee of Nine Minutes (Meetings of December 29, 1974, and January 5, September 11, and September 22, 1975) and "Resolution," in "Closing of City Church" folder, both in Document Case 58, DePauw University Archives.

168. "Church Attendance" folder, Document Case 115, DePauw University Archives: Switzer, "Notes," 1.

EPILOGUE

1. Lest the contrast be drawn too sharply between the International Institute and the church settlement houses, it should be noted that a prominent board member of the International Institute for many years was Herschel Davis, one of the leading laymen at City Methodist Church. See Davis Interview. A plaque given to Davis by the International Institute was still prominently displayed on his wall in 1984.

2. Roof and McKinney, *American Mainline Religion*, 36–39; Will Herberg, *Protestant, Catholic, Jew: An Essay in American Religious Sociology* (Garden City, N.Y.: Anchor Books, 1960); Hutchison, *Between the Times*, vii–viii.

3. See *The Chicago Reporter* 13 (November 1984) for a study of this phenomenon in Chicago, including Roman Catholics and Jews, as well as Protestants.

Sources Consulted

MANUSCRIPT COLLECTIONS

Calumet Regional Archives. Indiana University Northwest. Gary, Ind.
City Methodist Church Collection. Archives of DePauw University and Indiana United Methodism. DePauw University. Greencastle, Ind.
First Presbyterian Church Records. Gary, Ind.
Indiana Room. Gary Public Library. Gary, Ind.

INTERVIEWS AND PERSONAL CORRESPONDENCE

August, Garry. Interview, March 8, 1984. Gary, Ind.
Call, Lillian. Interview, June 22, 1984. Gary, Ind.
Clark, William E., to James Lewis. November 12, December 10, 17, and 24, 1984.
Cole, Elbert. Interview, May 31, 1985. Chicago, Ill.
Davis, Herschel B. Interview, October 11, 1984. Greenwood, Ind.
Frohman, Roderic. Interview, February 17, 1984. Gary, Ind.
Rice, Genevieve B., to James Lewis. April 9, 1983.
Schuster, Monroe G., to James Lewis. March 3, 1984.
Seaman, Charles F., to James Lewis. February 13, 1983.
Seaman, William R., to James Lewis. January 31, 1983.
Seaman, William R. Interview, November 23, 1983. Cincinnati, Ohio.

NEWSPAPERS AND PAMPHLETS

Anselm Forum. "Anselm Forum. First Decade." Gary, Ind., 1943. Mimeograph.
———. "First Fifteen Years, 1932–1947." Gary, Ind., 1947. Mimeograph.

————. "The Story of Anselm Forum." Gary, Ind., 1947. Mimeograph.

Backemeyer, Frederick. *In Loving Remembrance: Memorial and Founders' Day Services of First Presbyterian Church, Gary, Indiana.* Gary, Ind.: n.p., 1930.

Central Christian Church. *Community Vespers 1959.* Gary, Ind.: n.p., 1959.

————. *A Decennial of Central Christian Church in Christian Fellowship and Enterprise.* Gary, Ind.: n.p., 1938.

Chamber of Commerce. *Gary At a Glance.* Gary, Ind.: n.p., [1928].

————. *Gary Forges Prosperity: A Survey of the City of Gary, Indiana.* Gary, Ind.: Chamber of Commerce, 1924.

————. *Gary Welcomes You.* Gary, Ind.: Chamber of Commerce, 1928.

City Church, Gary, Indiana. Gary, Ind.: n.p., 1926.

Commercial Club. *Gary, Indiana, the Coming Steel and Iron Manufacturing Center of the World.* Gary, Ind.: n.p., n.d.

Delaney, Frank S. "History of Trinity Methodist Episcopal Church and the John Stewart Memorial Settlement House by Rev. F. S. Delaney." Gary, Ind., 1935. Typescript.

First Congregational Church. "Vesper Service, Congregational Church, Gary, Indiana." Gary, Ind., 1927. Typescript.

Foster, James E. *Christ Church, Gary, Indiana: A Sketch Book of Parish History.* Gary, Ind.: n.p., 1940.

Gary, Indiana: America's Magic City, 1906–1912. Gary, Ind.: n.p., n.d.

Gary: "The Magic City". Gary, Ind.: Gary Land Company, n.d.

Gary Daily Tribune, December 11, 1908; September 23, 1910; June 17, 1918; October 7, 1918; September 8–11, 1919; September 27–October 7, 1919; June 29, 1920; August 3, 1920.

Gary Evening Post, May 21, 1914; September 22, 1914; September 29–30, 1919.

Gary Post-Tribune, September 1–17, 1922; January 2, 1925; March 3–6, 1925; March 12, 1926; May 10, 1926; October 1–December 31, 1926; January 3–March 31, 1927; September 1–30, 1927; November 15, 1927; May 13, 1929; October 3, 1929; December 11, 1929; October 1–December 31, 1934; January 1–March 30, 1935; April 26, September 26, October 4, 10, and 17, 1930; February 13, 1939; May 20, 27, June 3, 10, 1956; September 12, 1985.

Gary Public Library. Gary School Scrapbook, 1914–24; 1924–34.

Kemp, Mrs. Frank. *From Sand to Service: The First Thirty-Five Years of Central Christian Church, Gary, Indiana.* Gary, Ind.: n.p., 1943.

Leiffer, Murray H. "Methodism in Gary and Vicinity." Evanston, Ill.: Bureau of Social and Religious Research, Garrett Biblical Institute, 1957.

Lewis, Beatrice. "Methodism in Gary." Gary, Ind., 1956. Typescript.

Seaman, William Grant. Untitled Historical Sketch of City Church. Gary, Ind., 1925. Typescript.

Seaman, William Grant (compiler). "The Calumet Region." Gary, Ind., 1921. Mimeo.

Seaman, William Grant, and Abernethy, Mary Elizabeth. *Community Schools for Week-Day Religious Instruction, Gary, Indiana.* Gary, Ind.: Board of Religious Education, 1921.

Squires, Walter A. *The Gary Plan of Church Schools.* Philadelphia: Presbyterian Board of Publication and Sabbath School Work, 1919.

Tomes, George K. "Central Christian—An Historical Note." Gary, Ind., 1976. Typescript.

Wirt, William. *The Great Lockout in America's Citizenship Plants.* Gary, Ind.: Horace Mann School, 1937.

REFERENCE WORKS AND PUBLIC DOCUMENTS

Brauer, Jerald C., ed. *The Westminster Dictionary of Church History.* Philadelphia: Westminster Press, 1971.

Citizens Historical Association, Indianapolis, Indiana. "Biographical Sketches of Gary, Indiana Residents, 1943." Indianapolis, 1943. Typescript.

Gary Public Library. *Biographical Sketches of Gary and Lake County Residents.* 11 vols. Gary, Ind., 1950. Scrapbook.

Harmon, Nolan B., ed. *The Encyclopedia of World Methodism.* 2 vols. Nashville: United Methodist Publishing House, 1974.

Lake County Historical Society. *Personal Records.* Gary, Ind., 1923. Typescript and handwritten.

Methodist Episcopal Church. *Minutes, Northwest Indiana Conference, Methodist Episcopal Church.* Crawfordsville, Ind.: Review Press, 1906–29.

National Cyclopaedia of American Biography. New York: James T. White & Company, 1931.

Polk's Gary City Directory. Indianapolis: R. L. Polk & Co., 1927, 1935.

Schwarz, J. C., ed. *Who's Who in the Clergy.* Vol 1. (New York: n.p., 1936).

U.S. Department of Commerce, Bureau of the Census. *Thirteenth Census of the United States, 1910: Population.* Vol. 2: *Reports by States, with Statistics for Counties, Cities, and Other Civil Divisions.*

———. *Fourteenth Census of the United States, 1920: Population.* Vol. 3: *Composition and Characteristics of the Population by States.*

———. *Fifteenth Census of the United States, 1930: Population.* Vol. 3, pt. 1: *Reports by States, Showing the Composition and Characteristics of the Population for Counties, Cities, and Townships or Other Minor Civil Divisions.*

———. *Sixteenth Census of the United States: 1940, Population.* Vol. 2: *Characteristics of the Population.*

———. *Census of Population: 1950.* Vol. 2: *Characteristics of the Population.*

———. *Census of Population: 1960.* Vol. 1: *Characteristics of the Population.*

———. *U.S. Census of Population and Housing: 1960.*

————. *1970 Census of Population.* Vol. 1: *Characteristics of the Population.*

————. *1970 Census of Population and Housing: Census Tracts.*

————. *1980 Census of Population.* Vol. 1: *Characteristics of the Population,* Chapter B, *General Population Characteristics.*

————. *1980 Census of Population and Housing: Census Tracts.*

————. *Religious Bodies: 1926.* Vol. 1: *Summary and Detailed Tables.*

————. *Religious Bodies: 1936.* Vol. 1: *Summary and Detailed Tables.*

Who Was Who in America. Vol. 1: *1897–1942.* Chicago: A. N. Marquis Co., 1942.

BOOKS, ARTICLES, AND DISSERTATIONS

Abell, Aaron I. *The Urban Impact on American Protestantism 1865–1900.* Cambridge: Harvard University Press, 1943.

Ahlstrom, Sydney E. *A Religious History of the American People.* New Haven: Yale University Press, 1972.

Albanese, Catherine L. *America, Religions and Religion.* Belmont, Calif.: Wadsworth Publishing Co., 1981.

Ammerman, Nancy Tatom. *Bible Believers: Fundamentalism in the Modern World.* New Brunswick, N.J.: Rutgers University Press, 1987.

Anderson, William H. "The Local Congregation as a Subculture." *Social Compass* 18 (1971):287–91.

Balanoff, Elizabeth. "A History of the Black Community of Gary, Indiana, 1906–1940." Ph.D. diss., University of Chicago, 1974.

Banner, Lois W. "Religious Benevolence as Social Control: A Critique of an Interpretation." *Journal of American History* 60 (June 1973):23–41.

Bender, Thomas. *Community and Social Change in America.* New Brunswick, N.J.: Rutgers University Press, 1978; reprint ed., Baltimore: Johns Hopkins University Press, 1982.

————. *Toward An Urban Vision: Ideas and Institutions in Nineteenth Century America.* Lexington, Ky.: University Press of Kentucky, 1975; reprint ed., Baltimore: Johns Hopkins University Press, 1982.

Berger, Peter L. *The Sacred Canopy: Elements of a Sociological Theory of Religion.* Garden City, N.Y.: Doubleday and Co., 1967.

Betten, Neil, and Mohl, Raymond A. "The Evolution of Racism in an Industrial City, 1906–1940: A Case Study of Gary, Indiana." *Journal of Negro History* 59 (January 1974):51–64.

————. "From Discrimination to Repatriation: Mexican Life in Gary, Indiana, during the Great Depression." *Pacific Historical Review* 42 (August 1973):370–88.

_____. "Nativism and the Klan in Town and City: Valparaiso and Gary, Indiana." *Studies in History and Society* 4 (Spring 1973):3–16.

Blumin, Stuart. "Church and Community: A Case Study of Lay Leadership in Nineteenth Century America." *New York History* 56 (1975):393–408.

_____. *The Urban Threshold: Growth and Change in a Nineteenth-Century American Community.* Chicago: University of Chicago Press, 1976.

Boles, Donald E. *The Bible, Religion, and the Public Schools.* Ames: Iowa State University Press, 1965.

_____. *The Two Swords: Commentaries and Cases in Religion and Education.* Ames: Iowa State University Press, 1967.

Bower, William Clayton and Hayward, Percy Roy. *Protestantism Faces its Educational Task Together.* Appleton, Wisc.: C. C. Nelson Publishing Co., 1949.

Boyer, Paul. *Urban Masses and Moral Order in America, 1820–1920.* Cambridge: Harvard University Press, 1978.

Brody, David. *Labor in Crisis: The Steel Strike of 1919.* Philadelphia: Lippincott, 1965.

_____. *Steelworkers in America: the Non-Union Era.* Cambridge: Harvard University Press, 1960.

Brook, Anthony. "Gary, Indiana: Steel Town Extraordinary." *Journal of American Studies* 9 (April 1975):35–53.

Brown, Arlo A. "The Week-Day Church Schools of Gary, Indiana." *Religious Education* 11 (February 1916):5–27.

Brownell, Blaine A. *The Urban Ethos in the South, 1920–1930.* Baton Rouge: Louisiana State University Press, 1975.

Brunner, Edmund de S. "Harlan Paul Douglass: Pioneer Researcher in Sociology of Religion." *Review of Religious Research* 1 (1959–60):3–24, 64–75.

Buffington, Eugene J. "Making Cities for Workmen." *Harper's Weekly* 53 (May 8, 1909):15–17.

Burton, Charles P. "Gary—A Creation." *The Independent* 70 (February 1911): 337–45.

Calumet Regional Archives. *Steelmaker-Steeltown: Building Gary, 1906–1930, A Photographic Exhibit.* Gary: Calumet Regional Archives, Indiana University Northwest, 1990.

Cannon, Thomas H.; Loring, Hannibal H.; and Robb, Charles J.; eds. *History of the Lake and Calumet Region of Indiana Embracing the Counties of Lake, Porter and LaPorte.* 2 vols. Indianapolis: Historians' Association, 1927.

Carlson, Martin E. "A Study of the Eastern Orthodox Churches in Gary, Indiana." M.A. thesis, University of Chicago, 1942.

Carter, Paul A. *The Decline and Revival of the Social Gospel: Social and Political Liberalism in American Protestant Churches, 1920–1940.* Ithaca, N.Y.: Cornell University Press, 1956.

Chapin, F. Stuart. "The Protestant Church in an Urban Environment." In *Cities and Society,* edited by Paul K. Hatt and Albert J. Reiss, Jr., 505–15. New York: Free Press of Glencoe, 1951. (Originally published in *Contemporary American Institutions* [New York: Harper and Bros., 1935.])

Cheadle, Queen. "Gary—A Planned City." M.A. thesis, University of Chicago, 1938.

Chilcote, Thomas F., Jr. "At the Heart of the Steel City." *The Christian Advocate* (August 31, 1944):6–7.

Christiano, Kevin J. *Religious Diversity and Social Change: American Cities, 1890–1906.* Cambridge: Cambridge University Press, 1987.

Coalter, Milton J; Mulder, John M.; and Weeks, Louis B., eds. *The Presbyterian Predicament: Six Perspectives.* Louisville: Westminster/John Knox Press, 1990.

Cohen, Ronald D. *Children of the Mill: Schooling and Society in Gary, Indiana, 1906–1960.* Bloomington: Indiana University Press, 1990.

Cohen, Ronald D. and Lane, James B. *Gary, Indiana: A Pictorial History.* Norfolk, Va.: Donning Co., 1983.

Cohen, Ronald D., and Mohl, Raymond A. *The Paradox of Progressive Education: the Gary Plan and Urban Schooling.* Port Washington, N.Y.: Kennikat Press, 1979.

Cotter, Arundel. *The Gary I Knew.* Boston: Stratford Co., 1928.

Crocker, Ruth Catherine Hutchinson. "Sympathy and Science: The Settlement Movement in Gary and Indianapolis, to 1930." Ph.D. diss., Purdue University, 1982.

Cross, Robert D. "The Changing Image of the City Among American Catholics." *Catholic Historical Review* 48 (April 1962):33–52.

————., ed. *The Church and the City 1865–1910.* New York: Bobbs-Merrill Co., 1967.

Cully, Kendig B., and Harper, F. Nile, eds. *Will the Church Lose the City?* New York: World Publishing Co., 1969.

Detzler, Jack J. *The History of the Northwest Indiana Conference of the Methodist Church 1852–1951.* Nashville: Parthenon Press, 1953.

Dickerson, Dennis C. "The Black Church in Industrializing Western Pennsylvania, 1870–1950," *Western Pennsylvania Historical Magazine* 64 (October 1981): 329–44.

Dorn, Jacob H. "Religion and the City." In *The Urban Experience: Themes in American History,* edited by James F. Richardson and Raymond A. Mohl, 144–63. Belmont, Calif.: Wadsworth Publishing Co., 1973.

Dorson, Richard M. *Land of the Millrats: Urban Folklore in Indiana's Calumet Region.* Cambridge: Harvard University Press, 1981.

Douglass, Harlan Paul. *The Church in the Changing City.* New York: George H. Doran Co., 1927.

_____. *The City's Church*. New York: Friendship Press, 1929.

_____. *1000 City Churches*. New York: George H. Doran Co., 1926.

_____. "The Present Position of American Churches." *Current History* 33 (January 1931):553–56.

_____. "Religion—The Protestant Faiths." In *America Now: An Inquiry into Civilization in the United States*, edited by Harold E. Stearns, 505–27. New York: Charles Scribner's Sons, 1938.

Ernst, Eldon G. *Moment of Truth For Protestant America: Interchurch Campaigns Following World War I*. Missoula, Mont.: Scholars Press, 1974.

Fischer, Claude S. "The Public and Private Worlds of City Life." *American Sociological Review* 46 (1981):306–16.

_____. "Toward a Subcultural Theory of Urbanism." *American Journal of Sociology* 80 (1975):1319–41.

Fisher, William Dale. "Steel City's Culture: An Interpretation of the History of Gary, Indiana." B. A. thesis, Yale University, 1941.

Frady, Marshall. "Gary, Indiana." *Harper's* 239 (August 1969):35–45.

Frakes, Margaret. "They Put Meaning into Brotherhood." *The Christian Century* 66 (February 16, 1949):204–206.

Frisch, Michael H. *Town Into City: Springfield, Massachusetts, and the Meaning of Community, 1840–1880*. Cambridge: Harvard University Press, 1972.

Frohman, Roderic Paul. "Pastoral Hospitality with Worship Visitors in a Multi-Racial Setting." D.Mn. thesis, Princeton Theological Seminary, 1983.

Fuller, Henry B. "An Industrial Utopia: Building Gary, Indiana, to Order." *Harper's Weekly* 51 (October 12, 1907):1482–83, 1495.

Gans, Herbert J. "Urbanism and Suburbanism as Ways of Life: A Re-evaluation of Definitions." In *The American City: Historical Studies*, edited by James F. Richardson, 389–407. Waltham, Mass.: Xerox College Publishing, 1972.

"The Gary Strike." *The Christian Century* 44 (October 13, 1927):1192–93.

Glaab, Charles N. "The Historian and the American City: A Bibliographic Survey." In *The Study of Urbanization*, edited by Philip M. Hauser and Leo F. Schnore, 53–80. New York: John Wiley and Sons, 1965.

Glaab, Charles N., and Brown, A. Theodore. *A History of Urban America*. New York: Macmillan, 1967.

Goheen, Peter G. "Industrialization and the Growth of Cities in Nineteenth-Century America." *American Studies* 14 (1973):49–65.

Goldfield, David R., and Brownell, Blaine A. *Urban America: From Downtown to No Town*. Boston: Houghton Mifflin Co., 1979.

Green, Constance McLaughlin. *The Rise of Urban America*. New York: Harper and Row, 1965.

Greer, Edward. *Big Steel: Black Politics and Corporate Power in Gary, Indiana*. New York: Monthly Review Press, 1979.

Gunderson, Joan R. *"Before the World Confessed": All Saints Parish, Northfield, and the Community 1858–1985*. Northfield, Minn.: Northfield Historical Society, 1987.

Gusfield, Joseph R. "Tradition and Modernity: Misplaced Polarities in the Study of Social Change." *American Journal of Sociology* 72 (January 1967):351–62.

Gutman, Herbert G. *Work, Culture and Society in Industrializing America*. New York: Random House, 1977.

Hadden, Jeffrey K. "H. Paul Douglass: His Perspective and His Work." *Review of Religious Research* 22 (September 1980):66–88.

Handy, Robert T. "The American Religious Depression, 1925–1935." *Church History* 29 (March 1960):3–16.

―――――. *A History of the Churches in the United States and Canada*. New York: Oxford University Press, 1977.

Harvey, Charles E. "John D. Rockefeller, Jr., and the Interchurch World Movement of 1919–1920: A Different Angle on the Ecumenical Movement." *Church History* 15 (June 1982):198–209.

Hersh, Blanche. "School Crisis in Gary, 1927." Chicago: University of Illinois at Chicago Circle, 1969. (In Indiana Room, Gary Public Library, Gary, Indiana.)

Hill, Michael. *A Sociology of Religion*. New York: Basic Books, 1973.

Hofstadter, Richard. *The Age of Reform: From Bryan to F. D. R.* New York: Random House, Vintage Books, 1955.

Holifield, E. Brooks. "The Historian and the Congregation." In *Beyond Clericalism: The Congregation as a Focus for Theological Education,* edited by Joseph C. Hough, Jr., and Barbara G. Wheeler, 89–101. Atlanta: Scholars Press, 1988.

Hopewell, James F. *Congregation: Stories and Structures.* Edited by Barbara G. Wheeler. Philadelphia: Fortress Press, 1987.

Hopkins, Charles Howard. *The Rise of the Social Gospel in American Protestantism, 1865–1915.* New Haven: Yale University Press, 1940; reprint ed., New York: AMS Press, n.d.

Hough, Joseph C., Jr., and Wheeler, Barbara G., eds. *Beyond Clericalism: The Congregation as a Focus for Theological Education.* Atlanta: Scholars Press, 1988.

Howat, William F., ed. *A Standard History of Lake County, Indiana and the Calumet Region.* 2 vols. Chicago: Lewis Publishing Co., 1915.

Hutchison, William R., ed. *Between the Times: The Travail of the Protestant Establishment in America, 1900–1960.* Cambridge: Cambridge University Press, 1989.

―――――. "Past Imperfect: History and the Prospect for Liberalism." *The Christian Century* 103 (1986):11–15,42–46.

Jacobs, Stanley S. "Brotherhood Solves Gary's Problems." *Coronet* 27 (November 1949):80–84.

Janis, Ralph. "The Brave New World That Failed: Patterns of Parish Social Structure in Detroit, 1880–1940." Ph.D. diss., University of Michigan, 1972.

Johnson, Benton. "On Dropping the Subject: Presbyterians and Sabbath Observance in the Twentieth Century." In *The Presbyterian Predicament: Six Perspectives,* edited by Milton J Coalter, John Mulder, and Louis B. Weeks, 90–108. Louisville: Westminster/John Knox Press, 1990.

Kelley, Arleen, and Greene, Wilma. *Reconnaissance Study of the Inner City: Gary, Indiana.* Indianapolis: Indiana Council of Churches, 1964.

King, William McGuire. "The Emergence of Social Gospel Radicalism: the Methodist Case." *Church History* 50 (December 1981):436–49.

Korros, Alexandra Shecket, and Sarna, Jonathan D. *American Synagogue History: A Bibliography and State-of-the-Field Survey.* New York: Markus Wiener Publishing, 1988.

Lampard, Eric E. "American Historians and the Study of Urbanization." *American Historical Review* 67 (October 1961):49–61.

———. "The Dimensions of Urban History: A Footnote to the 'Urban Crisis'." *Pacific Historical Review* 39 (August 1970):261–78.

Lane, James B. *"City of the Century": A History of Gary, Indiana.* Bloomington: Indiana University Press, 1978.

Lankford, John E. "The Impact of the New Era Movement on the Presbyterian Church in the United States of America, 1918–1925." *Journal of Presbyterian History* 40 (1962):213–24.

Lee, Robert, ed. *Cities and Churches: Readings on the Urban Church.* Philadelphia: Westminster Press, 1962.

Lees, Andrew. *Cities Perceived: Urban Society in European and American Thought, 1820–1940.* New York: Columbia University Press, 1985.

Lenski, Gerhard. *The Religious Factor: A Sociological Study of Religion's Impact on Politics, Economics, and Family Life.* Garden City, N.Y.: Doubleday and Co., 1961.

Lewis, James W. "At Home in the City: Mainstream Protestantism in Gary, Indiana, 1906–1983." Ph.D. diss., University of Chicago, 1987.

Loomis, Samuel Lane. *Modern Cities and Their Religious Problems.* New York: Baker and Taylor Co., 1887.

Lubove, Roy. "The Urbanization Process: An Approach to Historical Research." *Journal of the American Institute of Planners* 33 (January 1967):33–39.

Lynd, Robert S., and Lynd, Helen Merrell. *Middletown: A Study in Contemporary Culture.* New York: Harcourt, Brace and Co., 1929.

McKinney, William; Roozen, David A.; and Carroll, Jackson W. *Religion's Public*

Presence: Community Leaders Assess the Contribution of Churches and Synagogues. Washington, D.C.: The Alban Institute, 1982.

McLeod, Hugh. "Religion in the City." *Urban History Yearbook 1978*:7–22.

McTighe, Michael. "Embattled Establishment: Protestants and Power in Cleveland, 1836–1860." Ph.D. diss., University of Chicago, 1983.

Maloney, James H. "To Strike at Steel: Gary, Indiana and the Great Steel Strike of 1919." B.A. thesis, Harvard University, 1972.

Marsden, George M. *Fundamentalism and American Culture: The Shaping of Twentieth-Century Evangelicalism: 1870–1925.* New York: Oxford University Press, 1980.

――――. *Reforming Fundamentalism: Fuller Seminary and the New Evangelicalism.* Grand Rapids: William B. Eerdman's Publishing Co., 1987.

Martin, David. *A General Theory of Secularization.* New York: Harper, 1978.

Marty, Martin E. "In Praise of the Civil Congregation." *Currents in Theology and Mission* 15 (December 1988):541–46.

――――. *Modern American Religion.* Vol. 1: *The Irony of it All, 1893–1919.* Chicago: University of Chicago Press, 1986.

――――. *Pilgrims in their Own Land: 500 Years of Religion in America.* Boston: Little, Brown and Co., 1984.

――――. *The Public Church: Mainline-Evangelical-Catholic.* New York: Crossroad Publishing Co., 1981.

――――. "Public and Private: The Congregation as a Meeting Place." Written for Congregational History Project at University of Chicago, 1991.

May, Henry F. *The End of American Innocence: the First Years of our Own Time, 1912–1917.* New York: Oxford University Press, 1959.

――――. *Protestant Churches and Industrial America.* 2nd ed. New York: Farrar, Straus and Giroux, 1977.

――――. "Shifting Perspectives on the 1920s." *Mississippi Valley Historical Review* 43 (1956):405–27.

Meister, Richard Julius. "A History of Gary, Indiana, 1930–1940." Ph.D. diss., University of Notre Dame, 1967.

Mohl, Raymond A., and Betten, Neil. "Ethnic Adjustment in the Industrial City: The International Institute of Gary, 1919–1940." *International Migration Review* 6 (Winter 1972):361–76.

――――. "The Failure of Industrial City Planning: Gary, Indiana, 1906–1910." *Journal of the American Institute of Planners* 38 (July 1972):202–15.

――――. "The Immigrant Church in Gary, Indiana: Religious Adjustment and Cultural Defense." *Ethnicity* 8 (March 1981):1–17.

――――. "Paternalism and Pluralism: Immigrants and Social Welfare in Gary, Indiana, 1906–1940." *American Studies* 15 (Spring 1974):5–30.

_____. *Steel City: Urban and Ethnic Patterns in Gary, Indiana, 1906–1950.* New York: Holmes and Meier, 1986.

Monkonnen, Eric H. *American Becomes Urban: The Development of U.S. Cities and Towns 1780–1980.* Berkeley: University of California Press, 1988.

Moore, Powell A. *The Calumet Region: Indiana's Last Frontier.* Indianapolis: Indiana Historical Bureau, 1959.

Mumford, John Kimberly. "This Land of Opportunity: Gary, the City that Rose from a Sandy Waste." *Harper's Weekly* 52 (July 4, 1908):22–23, 29.

Peachey, Paul. *The Church in the City.* Newton, Kansas: Faith and Life Press, 1963.

Peerman, Dean. "Forward on Many Fronts: The Century 1923–1929." *The Christian Century* 101 (June 6, 1984):595–600.

Perrett, Geoffrey. *America in the Twenties.* New York: Simon and Schuster, 1982; Touchstone Edition, 1983.

Petersen, William. "The Protestant Ethos and the Anti-Urban Animus." In *The Church and the Exploding Metropolis,* edited by Robert Lee, 61–75. Richmond, Va.: John Knox Press, 1965.

Pierce, Thomas Stebbins. "The Curious Individual and the Churches." Newspaper clipping (probably from *Gary Post-Tribune* in 1930s), gift of Rabbi Garry August to the author.

Pope, Liston. *Millhands and Preachers.* New Haven: Yale University Press, 1942.

Quandt, Jean B. *From the Small Town to the Great Community: The Social Thought of Progressive Intellectuals.* New Brunswick, N.J.: Rutgers University Press, 1970.

Quillen, Isaac J. "Industrial City: A Study of Gary, Indiana, to 1929." Ph.D. diss., Yale University, 1942.

Raab, Theodore K., and Rotberg, Robert I., eds. *Industrialization and Urbanization: Studies in Interdisciplinary History.* Princeton: Princeton University Press, 1981.

Rodgers, Daniel T. "Tradition, Modernity, and the American Industrial Worker: Reflections and Critique." *Journal of Interdisciplinary History* 7 (1977):655–81.

Roof, Wade Clark. "America's Voluntary Establishment: Mainline Religion in Transition." *Daedalus* 111 (Winter 1982):165–84.

Roof, Wade Clark, and McKinney, William. *American Mainline Religion: Its Changing Shape and Future.* New Brunswick, N.J.: Rutgers University Press, 1987.

Sandeen, Ernest. "Congregational Histories as History." In *The Church and History: A Guide for Archivists and Historians,* edited by Glenn W. Offerman, 2–13. St. Paul: Concordia College, 1981.

Schlesinger, Arthur Meier. *The Rise of the City: 1878–1898.* New York: Macmillan Co., 1933; reprint ed., Chicago: Quadrangle Books, 1971.

Schmidt, Harold E. "Democracy at the Fireside." *The Christian Century* 57 (May 29, 1940):701–703.

Seaman, William Grant. "The City System of Week-Day Schools." *Religious Education* 17 (June 1922):212–13.

———. "Cultivating the Religious Life of Public School Children." *The Homiletic Review* 89 (January 1925):51–54.

Sennett, Richard, ed. *Classic Essays on the Culture of Cities*. New York: Appleton-Century-Crofts, 1969.

Shaver, Erwin L. "A Survey of Week-day Religious Education." *Religious Education* 17 (April 1922):83–142.

Shippey, Frederick A. "The Variety of City Churches." *Review of Religious Research* 2 (Summer 1960):8–19.

Shumway, Arthur. "Gary, Shrine of the Steel God: The City That Has Everything, and at the Same Time Has Nothing." *The American Parade* 3 (January 1929):23–32. (The copy in Gary Public Library is bound with a two-part reply by Rabbi Garry August from the *Gary Post-Tribune*, January 29 and February 6, 1929.)

Singleton, Gregory H. "Religion in the City of the Angels: American Protestant Culture and Urbanization: Los Angeles, 1850–1930." Ph.D. diss., University of California at Los Angeles, 1976.

Soares, Theodore G. "The Status of the Week-Day Religious School." *The Homiletic Review* 89 (February 1925):135–38.

Stelzle, Charles. *Christianity's Storm Centre: A Study of the Modern City*. New York: Fleming H. Revell, 1907.

———. "Decline of American Protestantism." *Current History* 33 (October 1930):23–28.

Stout, Harry S. "Soundings from New England." *Reformed Journal* 37 (August 1987):7–12.

Strauss, Anselm L. *Images of the American City*. New York: Free Press of Glencoe, 1961; reprint ed., New Brunswick, N.J.: Transaction Books, 1976.

Strayer, Paul Moore. *The Reconstruction of the Church With Regard To Its Message and Program*. New York: Macmillan, 1915.

Strong, Josiah. *The Challenge of the City*. New York: Young People's Missionary Movement, 1907.

———. *Our Country: Its Possible Future and its Present Crisis*. Revised ed., New York: Baker and Taylor Co., 1891; reprint ed., Cambridge: Harvard University Press, 1963.

Susman, Warren I. *Culture as History: The Transformation of American Society in the Twentieth Century*. New York: Random House, Pantheon Books, 1973, 1984.

Tarbell, Ida. *The Life of Elbert H. Gary: the Story of Steel*. New York: Appleton, 1925.

Taylor, Graham. "At Gary: Some Impressions and Interviews." *Survey* 43 (November 8, 1919):65–66.

———. *Religion in Social Action*. New York: Dodd, Mead and Co., 1913.

Taylor, Graham Romeyn. *Satellite Cities: A Study of Industrial Suburbs*. New York: D. Appleton and Co., 1915.

Teaford, Jon C. *The Unheralded Triumph: City Government in America, 1870–1900*. Baltimore: The Johns Hopkins University Press, 1984.

Thelen, David. "Memory and American History." *Journal of American History* 75 (March 1989):1117–29.

Thernstrom, Stephan. *Poverty and Progress: Social Mobility in a Nineteenth Century City*. Cambridge: Harvard University Press, 1964; reprint ed., New York: Atheneum, 1975.

———. "Reflections on the New Urban History." *Daedalus* 100 (Spring 1971):359–75.

Tisdale, Hope. "The Process of Urbanization." *Social Forces* 20 (March 1942):311–16.

Trachtenberg, Alan. *The Incorporation of America: Culture and Society in the Gilded Age*. New York: Hill and Wang, 1982.

Turner, Michael A. "Gary, Indiana: the Establishment and Early Development of an Industrial Community, 1906–1930." B.A. Thesis, University of Keele (Eng.), 1971.

Vidich, Arthur J., and Lyman, Stanford M. *American Sociology: Worldly Rejections of Religion and Their Directions*. New Haven: Yale University Press, 1985.

Vidich, Arthur J., and Bensman, Joseph. *Small Town in Mass Society: Class, Power and Religion in a Rural Community*. Revised ed., Princeton: Princeton University Press, 1968.

Wade, Louise. *Graham Taylor: Pioneer for Social Justice, 1851–1938*. Chicago: University of Chicago Press, 1964.

Ward, David. *Cities and Immigrants: A Geography of Change in Nineteenth-Century America*. New York: Oxford University Press, 1971.

Warner, Sam Bass, Jr. *Private City: Philadelphia in Three Periods of its Growth*. Philadelphia: University of Pennsylvania Press, 1968.

———. *Streetcar Suburbs: The Process of Growth in Boston 1870–1900*. Cambridge: Harvard University Press and MIT Press, 1962; reprint ed., New York: Atheneum, 1976.

———. *The Urban Wilderness: A History of the American City*. New York: Harper and Row, 1972.

Weeks, Louis. "The Incorporation of American Religion: The Case of the Presbyterians." *Religion and American Culture: A Journal of Interpretation* 1 (Winter 1991):101–18.

Weinstein, James. *The Corporate Ideal in the Liberal State: 1900–1918*. Boston: Beacon Press, 1968.

Wheeler, Barbara G. "Uncharted Territory: Congregational Identity and Mainline Protestantism." In *The Presbyterian Predicament: Six Perspectives,* edited by Milton J Coalter, John M. Mulder, and Louis B. Weeks, 67–89. Louisville: Westminster/John Knox Press, 1990.

White, Morton and White, Lucia. *The Intellectual Versus the City: From Thomas Jefferson to Frank Lloyd Wright.* Cambridge: Harvard University Press, 1962; reprint ed. with new foreword by authors, New York: Oxford University Press, 1977.

Wiebe, Robert H. *Businessmen and Reform: A Study of the Progressive Movement.* Cambridge: Harvard University Press, 1962.

———. *The Search for Order: 1877–1920.* New York: Hill and Wang, 1967.

Williams, Raymond Brady. *Religions of Immigrants from India and Pakistan: New Threads in the Tapestry.* Cambridge: Cambridge University Press, 1988.

Wilson, Bryan R. *Religion in Secular Society: A Sociological Comment.* Hammondsworth, Eng: Penguin Books, 1966.

Wind, James P. *Places of Worship: Exploring Their History.* Nashville: American Association for State and Local History, 1990.

Wirt, William. "The Gary Public Schools and the Churches." *Religious Education* 11 (June 1916):221–26.

Wirth, Louis. "Urbanism As a Way of Life." In *Classic Essays on the Culture of Cities,* edited by Richard Sennett, 143–64. New York: Appleton-Century-Crofts, 1969. (Essay originally published in 1938.)

Writers' Program of the Works Progress Administration. *The Calumet Region Historical Guide.* East Chicago, Ind: Garman Printing Co., 1939.

Wuthnow, Robert. *Restructuring American Religion: Society and Faith Since World War II.* Princeton: Princeton University Press, 1988.

Index